# STRAWBERRIES IN
# THE WINTERTIME

# STRAWBERRIES IN THE WINTERTIME

## THE SPORTING WORLD
## OF

# RED SMITH

Quadrangle/The New York Times Book Co.

Library of Congress Catalog Card Number: 73-90170

International Standard Book Number: 0-8129-0422-2

Second printing October 1974

Design: Betty Binns

Grateful acknowledgment is made to *Sports Afield* magazine for permission to reprint two articles: "A Fling on the Flats" (pp. 104-110), from the September 1972 *Sports Afield*, copyright © 1972 by the Hearst Corporation; and "Money Game" (pp. 111-117), from the March 1973 *Sports Afield*, copyright © 1973 by the Hearst Corporation.

# Contents

# Foreword

THE question of what to do with old newspaper columns isn't quite the same as how to dispose of used razor blades, but the difference is negligible. The axiom that today's news wraps tomorrow's mackerel applies equally to today's column, no matter how stirring the action, how accomplished the performers or how controversial the issues may have been at the time of writing. This is especially so in a field like sports where today's defeat makes yesterday's victory meaningless and the scenes, the action and the characters constantly change.

Then why preserve dead columns for public display, as the remains of Vladimir Ilyich Lenin are displayed half a century after his death? The answer, if there is one, is: Because everything written is part of the record of its time. Everyone who writes reflects the age in which he lives, and this is not less true of the sports reporter than of the dramatist, poet, novelist, essayist or historian. Games and the people who play them have had a place in every culture; of the ancient Roman monuments that still stand, the most impressive is the Colosseum.

It seems to me that in recent times spectator sports have become almost a national obsession in the United States. The President habitually speaks in sports idiom with frequent references to team players and game plans. His former Attorney General reminds subordinates that "when the going gets tough, the tough get going." The Vice President postures on golf course and tennis court. Kipling could deride "the flanneled fools at the wicket and the muddied oafs in the goal," but the head of his state (Queen Victoria) wasn't crouched in front of a television screen waiting for the coach to send in the flanker reverse she recommended.

This book is offered as a partial record of what has gone on around the playing fields in the last several years. Most of the pieces appeared in *The New York Times* between November of 1971 and September, 1973, but some were written earlier than that for syndication over the copyright of Field Enterprises, Inc. One about fishing in the Florida Keys and another describing a bass tournament in Oklahoma originally appeared in the magazine, *Sports Afield*. Outside of those two, everything was done under pressure of a newspaper deadline.

That doesn't mean everything is reproduced exactly as it ran in the paper. Where there were several columns dealing with the same subject matter, an attempt has been made to combine them. The original typographical errors have been corrected whenever detected, there have been some deletions, and here and there a "which" was changed to "that." I have tried to truss up gerunds and participles inadvertently left dangling at edition time.

Finding a title for such a mixed bag can be a problem. *Strawberries in the Wintertime* happens to be the title of a piece about Willie Mays and it captures, I think, some of the flavor of the sportswriter's existence, which is what the late Bill Corum was talking about when he said, "I don't want to be a millionaire, I just want to live like one." I considered using a catchier title like *War and Peace, Wuthering Heights* or *The Holy Bible* but they struck me as dated. That is something I have tried to avoid. Wherever practicable, specific dates have been eliminated but not in an effort to give these pieces a spurious quality of timeliness. Encountering Joe Frazier as heavyweight champion or finding Oakland and Cincinnati in the World Series, the knowledgeable reader will date the piece for himself.

I have no illusions about the perishable nature of this work nor any apologies for its shortcomings. However many and grievous the faults may be, the reader should know that they would be worse if it were not for the firm editorial hand of Phyllis W. Smith. Make that read mailed editorial fist.

R. S.

October, 1973

# STRAWBERRIES IN THE WINTERTIME

# HITS, RUNS, ERRORS

*The reason why the American League has taken the bat away from the pitcher is that the owners have no faith in baseball as entertainment. They haven't been selling tickets and they think the fault must lie with the game, for they know themselves to be sagacious, enterprising, farsighted, shrewd, dynamic, well-dressed and charming. If there was anything wrong with their merchandising methods, a smart cookie like Alexander Cartwright, or anyway Al G. Spalding, would have pointed it out before now.*

*The thing to do, therefore, was to offer the customers a different game that they would like better. Then what, they asked themselves—for they are logical men who could pursue a syllogism through the Great Dismal Swamp without dropping a minor premise—then what would the customers like better than the game they have loved for a century? More hitting and scoring, they answered themselves. (They had to answer themselves because nobody else did.) Well, if they put up a pinch-batter when it was the pitcher's turn to hit, would there then be more hitting and scoring and cash customers? Nobody could answer that, either, so they said, "Let's do it."*

# ONE OF A KIND

GRANTLAND RICE, the prince of sportswriters, used to do a weekly radio interview with some sporting figure. Frequently, in the interest of spontaneity, he would type out questions and answers in advance. One night his guest was Babe Ruth.

"Well, you know, Granny," the Babe read in response to a question, "Duke Ellington said the Battle of Waterloo was won on the playing fields of Elkton."

"Babe," Granny said after the show, "Duke Ellington for the Duke of Wellington I can understand. But how did you ever read Eton as Elkton? That's in Maryland, isn't it?"

"I married my first wife there," Babe said, "and I always hated the gawdam place." He was cheerily unruffled. In the uncomplicated world of George Herman Ruth, errors were part of the game.

Babe Ruth died 25 years ago but his ample ghost has been with us all summer and he seems to grow more insistently alive every time Henry Aaron hits a baseball over a fence. What, people under 50 keep asking, what was this creature of myth and legend like in real life? If he were around today, how would he react when Aaron at last broke his hallowed record of 714 home runs? The first question may be impossible to answer fully; the second is easy.

"Well, what d'you know!" he would have said when the record got away. "Baby loses another! Come on, have another beer."

To paraphrase Abraham Lincoln's remark about another deity, Ruth must have admired records because he created so many of them. Yet he was sublimely aware that he transcended records and his place in the American scene was no mere matter of statistics. It wasn't just that he hit more home runs than anybody else, he hit them better, higher, farther, with more theatrical timing and a more flamboyant flourish. Nobody could strike out like Babe Ruth. Nobody circled the bases with the same pigeon-toed, mincing majesty.

"He was one of a kind," says Waite Hoyt, a Yankee pitcher in the years of Ruthian splendor. "If he had never played ball, if you had never heard of him and passed him on Broadway, you'd turn around and look."

Looking, you would have seen a barrel swaddled in a wrap-around camel-hair topcoat with a flat camel-hair cap on the round head. Thus arrayed he was instantly recognizable not only on Broadway in New York but also on the Ginza in Tokyo. "Baby Roos! Baby Roos!" cried excited crowds, following through the streets when he visited Japan with an all-star team in the early nineteen-thirties.

The camel-hair coat and cap are part of my last memory of the man. It must have been in the spring training season of 1948 when the Babe and everybody else knew he was dying of throat cancer. "This is the last time around," he had told Frank Stevens that winter when the head of the H. M. Stevens catering firm visited him in French Hospital on West 30th Street, "but before I go I'm gonna get out of here and have some fun."

He did get out, but touring the Florida training camps surrounded by a gaggle of admen, hustlers and promoters, he didn't look like a man having fun. It was a hot day when he arrived in St. Petersburg but the camel-hair collar was turned up about the wounded throat. By this time, Al Lang Stadium had replaced old Waterfront Park where he had drawn crowds when the Yankees trained in St. Pete.

"What do you remember best about this place?" asked Francis Stann of *The Washington Star*.

Babe gestured toward the West Coast Inn, an old frame building a city block beyond the right-field fence. "The day I hit the adjectival ball against that adjectival hotel." The voice was a hoarse stage whisper; the adjective was one often printed these days, but not here.

"Wow!" Francis Stann said. "Pretty good belt."

"But don't forget," Babe said, "the adjectival park was a block back this way then."

Ruth was not noted for a good memory. In fact, the inability to remember names is part of his legend. Yet he needed no record books to remind him of his own special feats. There was, for example, the time he visited Philadelphia as a "coach" with the Brooklyn Dodgers. (His coachly duties consisted of hitting home runs in batting practice.) This was in the late nineteen-thirties when National League games in Philadelphia were played in Shibe Park, the American League grounds where Babe had performed. I asked him what memories stirred on his return.

"The time I hit one into Opal Street," he said.

Now, a baseball hit over Shibe Park's right-field fence landed in 20th Street. Opal is the next street east, just a wide alley one block long. There may not be 500 Philadelphians who know it by name, but Babe Ruth knew it.

Another time, during a chat in Hollywood, where he was an actor in the film *Pride of the Yankees,* one of us mentioned Rube Walberg, a good left-handed pitcher with the Philadelphia Athletics through the Ruth era. To some left-handed batters there is no dirtier word than the name of a good left-handed pitcher, but the Babe spoke fondly:

"Rube Walberg! What a pigeon! I hit 23 home runs off him." Or whatever the figure was. It isn't in the record book but it was in Ruth's memory.

Obviously it is not true that he couldn't even remember the names of his teammates. It was only that the names he remembered were not always those bestowed at the baptismal font. To him Urban Shocker, a Yankee pitcher, was Rubber Belly. Pat Collins, the catcher, was Horse Nose. All redcaps at railroad stations were Stinkweed, and everybody else was Kid. One day Jim Cahn, covering the Yankees for *The New York Sun,* watched two players board a train with a porter toting the luggage.

"There go Rubber Belly, Horse Nose and Stinkweed," Jim said.

Don Heffner joined the Yankees in 1934, Ruth's last year with the team. Playing second base through spring training, Heffner was stationed directly in the line of vision of Ruth, the right fielder. Breaking camp, the Yankees stopped in Jacksonville on a night when the Baltimore Orioles of the International League were also in town. A young reporter on *The Baltimore Sun* seized the opportunity to interview Ruth.

"How is Heffner looking?" he asked, because the second baseman had been a star with the Orioles in 1933.

"Who the hell is Heffner?" the Babe demanded. The reporter should, of course, have asked about the kid at second.

Jacksonville was the first stop that year on the barnstorming trip that would last two or three weeks and take the team to Yankee Stadium by a meandering route through the American bush. There, as everywhere, Ruth moved among crowds. Whether the Yankees played in Memphis or New Orleans or Selma, Ala., the park was almost always filled, the hotel overrun if the team used a hotel, the railroad depot thronged. In a town of 5,000, perhaps 7,500 would see the game. Mostly the players lived in Pullmans and somehow word always went ahead when the Yankees' train was coming through. At every stop at any hour of the night there would be a cluster of men on the platform, maybe the stationmaster and telegrapher, a section gang and the baggage agent watching the dark sleeping cars for the glimpse of a Yankee, possibly even the Babe.

It was said in those days, probably truly, that receipts from the preseason exhibitions more than paid Ruth's salary for the year, even when he was getting $80,000, which was substantially more than any other player earned, or any manager or baseball executive. It was more than President Herbert Hoover received, but if this was ever pointed out to Ruth he almost surely did not reply, as the story goes: "I had a better year than he did." He would have been correct, but the Babe was not that well informed on national affairs.

Crowds were to Ruth as water to a fish. Probably the only time on record when he sought to avert a mob scene was the day of his second marriage. The ceremony was scheduled for 6 a.m. on the theory that people wouldn't be abroad then, but when he arrived at St. Gregory's in West 90th Street, the church was filled and hundreds were waiting outside.

A reception followed in Babe's apartment on Riverside Drive, where the 18th Amendment did not apply. It was opening day of the baseball season but the weather intervened on behalf of the happy couple. The party went on and on, with entertainment by Peter de Rose, composer-pianist, and May Singhi Breen, who played the ukulele and sang.

Rain abated in time for a game next day. For the first time, Claire Ruth watched from a box near the Yankees' dugout, as she still does on ceremonial occasions. Naturally, the bridegroom hit a home run. Rounding the bases, he halted at second and swept off his cap in a courtly bow to his bride. This was typical of him. There are a hundred stories illustrating his sense of theater—how he opened Yankee Stadium (The House That Ruth Built) with a home run against the Red

Sox, how at the age of 40 he closed out his career as a player by hitting three mighty shots out of spacious Forbes Field in Pittsburgh, stories about the times he promised to hit a home run for some kid in a hospital and made good, and of course the one about calling his shot in a World Series.

That either did or did not happen in Chicago's Wrigley Field on Oct. 1, 1932. I was there but I have never been dead sure of what I saw.

The Yankees had won the first two games and the score of the third was 4-4 when Ruth went to bat in the fifth inning with the bases empty and Charley Root pitching for the Cubs. Ruth had staked the Yankees to a three-run lead in the first inning by hitting Root for a home run with two on base. Now Root threw a strike. Ruth stepped back and lifted a finger. "One." A second strike, a second upraised finger. "Two." Then Ruth made some sort of sign with his bat. Some said, and their version has become gospel, that he aimed it like a rifle at the bleachers in right center field. That's where he hit the next pitch. That made the score 5-4. Lou Gehrig followed with a home run and the Yankees won, 7-5, ending the series the next day.

All the Yankees, and Ruth in particular, had been riding the Cubs unmercifully through every game, deriding them as cheapskates because in cutting up their World Series money the Chicago players had voted only one-fourth of a share to Mark Koenig, the former New York shortstop who had joined them in August and batted .353 in the last month of the pennant race. With all the dialogue and pantomime that went on, there was no telling what Ruth was saying to Root. When the papers reported that he had called his shot, he did not deny it.

He almost never quibbled about anything that was written. During the 1934 World Series between the Cardinals and Detroit Tigers, *The St. Louis Post-Dispatch* assigned its Washington correspondent, Paul Y. Anderson, to write features. His seat in the auxiliary press box was next to Ruth, a member of the sweaty literati whose observations on the games would be converted into suitably wooden prose by a syndicate ghost-writer. Babe was companionable as usual.

"You see the series here in '28?" he asked.

"No," Anderson said, "was it a good one?"

"That was when I hit three outta here in the last game."

"Gee," Anderson said, "a good day for you, eh?"

"Yeah," Babe said, "I had a good day. But don't forget, the fans had a hell of a day, too."

Paul Anderson was at ease with men as dissimilar as Huey Long, John L. Lewis and Franklin D. Roosevelt but he had never encountered anyone quite like this child of nature. He devoted his story to the bumptious bundle of vanity seated beside him. To his discomfort, a press-box neighbor asked Ruth the next day whether he had read the story. Ruth said sure, though he probably hadn't. "What did you think of it?" the other persisted while Anderson squirmed.

"Hell," Babe said, "the newspaper guys always been great to me."

A person familiar with Ruth only through photographs and records could hardly be blamed for assuming that he was a blubbery freak whose ability to hit balls across county lines was all that kept him in the big leagues. The truth is that he was the complete ballplayer, certainly one of the greatest and maybe the one best of all time.

As a left-handed pitcher with the Boston Red Sox, he won 18 games in his rookie season, 23 the next year and 24 the next before Ed Barrow assigned him to the outfield to keep him in the batting order every day. His record of pitching 29⅔ consecutive scoreless innings in World Series stood 43 years before Whitey Ford broke it.

He was an accomplished outfielder with astonishing range for his bulk, a powerful arm and keen baseball sense. It was said that he never made a mental error like throwing to the wrong base.

He recognized his role as public entertainer and understood it. In the 1946 World Series the Cardinals made a radical shift in their defense against Ted Williams, packing the right side of the field and leaving the left virtually unprotected. "They did that to me in the American League one year," Ruth told the columnist, Frank Graham. "I coulda hit .600 that year slicing singles to left."

"Why didn't you?" Frank asked.

"That wasn't what the fans came out to see."

Thirteen years after Ruth's death, when another rightfielder for the Yankees, Roger Maris, was threatening the season record of 60 home runs that Babe had set 34 years earlier, I made a small sentimental pilgrimage in Baltimore where the Yankees happened to be playing. The first stop was the row house where the Babe was born. A gracious woman showed visitors through the small rooms. Next came a drink in the neighborhood saloon Babe's father ran when Babe was a boy. Nobody ever came in who remembered the Ruth family, the bartender said. The tour ended at St. Mary's Industrial School, which the wrecker's big iron ball was knocking down.

St. Mary's was Babe's home through most of his boyhood because his parents weren't interested in rearing him. He left the home on Feb. 27, 1914, three weeks after his 19th birthday, to pitch for the Baltimore Orioles of the International League. Jack Dunn, the owner, paid him $600 and sold him late that summer to the Red Sox for $2,900. He was 6-foot-2 and an athlete, thick-chested but not fat. "A big, lummockin' sort of fella," said a waiter in Toots Shor's who had worked in a restaurant near the Red Sox park where young Ruth got sweet on one of the waitresses.

When his hard-pressed employers sold him to the Yankees, he was still a trim young ballplayer who had hit 29 of the Boston club's 32 home runs that season of 1919. He hit an unthinkable 54 in his first New York summer, 59 in his second, and became a god. His waistline grew with his fame, until the legs that nobody had considered spindly began to look like matchsticks and his feet seemed grotesquely small.

He changed the rules, the equipment and the strategy of baseball. Reasoning that if one Babe Ruth could fill a park, 16 would fill all the parks, the owners instructed the manufacturers to produce a livelier ball that would make every man a home-run king. As a further aid to batters, trick pitching deliveries like the spitball, the emery ball, the shine ball and the mud ball were forbidden.

The home run, an occasional phenomenon when a team hit a total of 20 in a season, came to be regarded as the ultimate offensive weapon. Shortstops inclined to swoon at the sight of blood had their bats made with all the wood up in the big end, gripped the slender handle at the very hilt and swung from the heels.

None of these devices produced another Ruth, of course, because Ruth was one of a kind. He recognized this as the simple truth and conducted himself accordingly. Even before they were married and Claire began to accompany him on the road, he always occupied the drawing room on the team's Pullman; he seldom shared his revels after dark with other players, although one year he did take a fancy to a worshipful rookie named Jimmy Reese and made him a companion until management intervened; if friends were not on hand with transportation, he usually took a taxi by himself to hotel or ball park or railroad station. Unlike other players, Ruth was never seen in the hotel dining room or sitting in the lobby waiting for some passerby to discard a newspaper.

St. Louis was one town where he was always met. When the team left

St. Louis, his friends would deliver him to the station along with a laundry basket full of barbecued ribs and tubs of home brew. Then anybody—player, coach or press—was welcome in the drawing room to munch ribs, swill the yeasty beer and laugh at the Babe's favorite record on the Babe's portable phonograph. He would play Moran & Mack's talking record, "Two Black Crows," a hundred times and howl at the hundredth repetition: "How come the black horses ate more'n the white horses?" "Search me, 'cept we had more black horses than white horses."

Roistering was a way of life, yet Ruth was no boozer. Three drinks of hard liquor left him fuzzy. He could consume great quantities of beer, was a prodigious eater and his prowess with women was legendary. Sleep was something he got when other appetites were sated. He arose when he chose and almost invariably was the last to arrive in the clubhouse, where Doc Woods, the Yankees' trainer, always had bicarbonate of soda ready. Before changing clothes, the Babe would measure out a mound of bicarb smaller than the Pyramid of Cheops, mix and gulp it down.

"Then," Jim Cahn says, "he would belch. And all the loose water in the showers would fall down."

The man was a boy, simple, artless, genuine and unabashed. This explains his rapport with children, whom he met as intellectual equals. Probably his natural liking for people communicated itself to the public to help make him an idol.

He was buried on a sweltering day in August, 1948. In the pallbearers' pew, Waite Hoyt sat beside Joe Dugan, the third baseman. "I'd give a hundred dollars for a cold beer," Dugan whispered. "So would the Babe," Hoyt said.

In packed St. Patrick's Cathedral, Francis Cardinal Spellman celebrated requiem mass and out in Fifth Avenue thousands and thousands waited to say good-by to the waif from Baltimore whose parents didn't want him.

"Some 20 years ago," says Tommy Holmes, the great baseball writer, "I stopped talking about the Babe for the simple reason that I realized that those who had never seen him didn't believe me."

# HOUSE THAT RUTH, AND OTHERS, BUILT

THE 51st baseball season in Yankee Stadium was launched Monday on a flood of literature that left the interesting impression that the team that opened the big playpen on April 18, 1923, was composed of two men named Babe Ruth and Lou Gehrig. This was not exactly the case, as witnesses of next Sunday's game with the Red Sox will discover. That afternoon has been chosen for the park's golden anniversary celebration, presumably because it is three days short of the anniversary, and each customer will receive a copy of the "souvenir programme" sold on the original opening day.

Between gaudy orange covers bearing photographs of Col. Jacob Ruppert and Col. Tillinghast L'Hommedieu Huston, the owners, appears an old-fashioned nine-man batting order, not the 10-man lineup we are familiar with today. All the names, not just two, stir memories.

Leading off and playing center field was Whitey Witt, who had been involved in a disturbing incident the previous September. Racing the Browns for the 1922 pennant, the Yankees had taken a half-game lead into St. Louis. In the first game of the series, which New York won, 2-1, a pop bottle hurled from the bleachers bounced off Witt's skull as he chased a fly ball. Whitey was knocked senseless and carried off with blood pouring from a two-inch cut.

Great with righteous indignation, Ban Johnson, president of the American League, posted a $100 reward for identification of the culprit. It was claimed by—and paid to—a fan who reported soberly that the bottle had been tossed onto the field earlier and that Witt had beaned himself by stepping on the neck, causing the bottle to fly up and crown him.

11

If Johnson was satisfied by the explanation, it did not placate Buck O'Neill of the New York press. "When you throw a pop bottle at Whitey Witt's head," Buck thundered in his column, "you are throwing a pop bottle at the foundation stone of the national game!"

Joe Dugan, the third baseman, batted second. There had been hell to pay in 1922 when the Red Sox traded Dugan to New York. With Home Run Baker slowing down—he had been the regular third baseman since 1916—the Yankees had gone to Boston for help on July 23, raising furious charges that they were trying to "buy a pennant." The deal brought about a rule setting June 1 as the deadline for trades.

Ruth batted third, of course, and Wally Pipp, the first baseman, was the clean-up hitter. Gehrig signed a contract in the spring of 1923 but secretly, because he was still playing for Columbia. He didn't join the Yankees until the college season ended in June, and didn't become a regular until June 2, 1925. He replaced Pipp that day because Wally had a headache.

Batting fifth was Bob Meusel, the left fielder with the Springfield Model arm. He was a scowling, uncommunicative sort, sometimes downright unfriendly until his waning days with the Yankees, when he mellowed noticeably. "He is learning to say hello," Frank Graham wrote then, "when it's time to say good-by."

Sixth in the batting order was Wally Schang, one of the many reasons why Jake Ruppert never regretted hiring the Red Sox manager, Ed Barrow, to be his business manager. One of Barrow's first moves in New York in the winter of 1920 was to skin his former employer in a deal that brought Schang, Waite Hoyt and others to the Yankees. Schang not only handled the bulk of chores behind the plate for the next five years; in his first New York summer he became a member of the original Murderers' Row—Pipp, Ruth, Meusel, Baker and Schang.

Next came Aaron Ward, a slender young man from Arkansas who had come out of the Army after World War I and helped out at first, second and third base, shortstop and the outfield before settling down at second. In 1923 he hit .284 and knocked in 82 runs. Today he would be batting third. He hit seventh, with Deacon Scott, the shortstop, eighth.

Scott was to cause a sensation that season. He would be called to home plate on May 2 to receive a gold medal from Secretary of the Navy Edwin Denby for having played in 1,000 consecutive games. It was agreed that although records were made to be broken, this was an exception. Ballplayers were growing soft; never again would there be one tough enough to survive 1,000 games without interruption. Up on Morningside Heights, Lou Gehrig read the sports pages and was impressed. It did not cross his mind that anyone would ever play in 2,130 consecutive games.

In the dark ages of 1923, pitchers in the American League took their regular turns at bat. Usually they were ninth in the lineup, as Bob Shawkey was that opening day. He had been chosen to pitch because he was dean of the staff and a great favorite of Colonel Ruppert's.

"What's the matter with you, Hoyt?" the colonel demanded one day of the club's youngest starter. "You win all your games 1-0 or 2-1. Pennock, Bush, Shawkey, those fellows—they win 9 or 10 to 1. Why don't you win some like that?"


The "Yankee Stadium Anniversary Hymn" had its world premiere yesterday before an audience of 35,700, perhaps the largest conclave of music lovers ever to hear a composition by John L. Motley, the five-borough Cole Porter. Under Mr. Motley's direction, the New York All-City High School Chorus massed on that part of the infield ordinarily patrolled by Horace Clarke and lifted 250 young voices under a spotless Bronx sky:

> *Hail this day of celebration,*
> *Hail this day of jubilation,*
> *Hail to the 50th birthday of Yankee Stadium,*
> *Hail, hail, hail, happy birthday to you.*

As the kids sang, all scrubbed and tidy in white turtlenecks and black slacks, outriders scurried about marshaling a cast of characters to remind the customers that although the Yankees had lost four matches with the Red Sox this year and dropped five of the seven games they had played, their playground did have a glorious past.

It also has a controversial present and a lavish future calling for the expenditure of the city's millions on a renovation project that has caused butting, gouging and kneeing in the clinches around City Hall. Considering that the stately old pleasure dome has raised more excitement in the last couple of years than its tenants have in almost a decade, it was fitting that the first summery day of the baseball season be devoted to celebrating its golden anniversary.

First of the invited guests to arrive was, appropriately, Ladislaw Waldemar Wittkowski, 77, who was the first Yankee to come to bat in the new park April 18, 1923, when he was a 27-year-old center fielder called Whitey Witt. Ushered to the Yankee clubhouse, he paused at the threshold to ask: "Is that kid still here?"

He meant Pete Sheehy, the maitre de clubhouse, who has ruled the team boudoir for 47 years.

A little later, Witt was led into reminiscence, and went along willingly. Somebody remembered that Howard Ehmke was the Boston pitcher whom he helped to defeat in the stadium's first game ever, and that later that season Whitey spoiled a no-hitter for Ehmke, with an assist from Fred Lieb, the official scorer. Ehmke had pitched a no-hit game against Philadelphia in 1923 and this would have been his second of the year except for Witt's hotly disputed single.

"It was a hard shot," Whitey said, "that got to the third baseman on one hop. It bounced off Howard Shanks's chest and caromed over to the third-base coach. Later Fred Lieb asked me about it. 'It was a hit,' I told him, 'but if it means that much to Ehmke, call it an error. I get plenty of other hits.'

" 'I'm calling it a single,' he said.

" 'Well,' I said, 'that's what it was.'

"Years later, while Ehmke was still alive, I heard him interviewed on television. 'It was a weak little grounder the third baseman booted,' he said."

"How were things in Lawrence, Kan., on April 18, 1923?" a man asked Ralph Houk.

"I expect my father was getting ready to plant the corn," said the Yankees' three-decker brain. "I've looked it up and I find I was 3 years old, going on 4 that August." It did not then cross his mind, Houk testified, that 26 years later he would bat .571 in five games as a Yankee catcher.

"Well, I was here when they opened the park," said John Drebinger, whose prose used to brighten *The New York Times*. "It was my first big-league game as a newspaperman. I was on the *New York Globe* where Will Wedge was the baseball writer and I sat out there in the bleachers to do a crowd story. Babe Ruth's home run almost hit me."

By now Mel Allen was at the pitcher's mound introducing guests. The Yankees fired Mel as broadcaster years ago but they keep bringing him back when the script calls for a dash of Auld Lang Syne. He intro-

duced Robert Abrams, the Bronx borough president, who read a proc-
lamation by Mayor John Lindsay, who was booed in absentia. Mel
introduced Walter Smith, whose father, Gov. Alfred E. Smith, threw
out the first ball at the 1923 opening.

Then came the ladies—Mrs. George M. Weiss, widow of the general
manager who built the great Yankee teams of the 1950's; Mrs. Babe
Ruth, Mrs. Houk, and the Babe Ruth of anthem singers, Pearl Bailey.
Finally, Bob Shawkey walked to the mound his spikes had scarred 50
years earlier when he pitched and won the stadium opener.

With Witt in the batter's box on the first-base side, Thurman Munson
crouched behind the plate. Shawkey's first pitch was in the dirt. His
second was a strike. Ken Smith of the Hall of Fame quickly retrieved
the ball which he had brought down from Cooperstown, the same ball
Governor Smith had thrown 50 years earlier.

# BLESSED IS THE PEACEMAKER

Pete REISER, a coach with the Cubs, got knocked out the other day trying to break up a brawl with the San Francisco Giants. He had to be carried from the field on a stretcher—for the 12th time since he burst into baseball. When the Brooklyn Dodgers signed him for a $100 bonus, Pete Reiser had as much natural talent as Willie Mays, Joe DiMaggio, Stan Musial or Mickey Mantle. His weakness was that there never was a ball park large enough to contain his effort.

To him, outfield fences were obstacles unreasonably impeding his pursuit of line drives. To save his life, Branch Rickey had the walls in Ebbets Field padded. Except for Pete, foam rubber might never have been invented.

Only twice during his playing days was he conscious when they carried him off the field. On nine other occasions he woke up in the clubhouse or in a hospital. Once the umpire at second base had to run to the center-field wall, bend over him and pry open his gloved hand to find the ball and call the batter out.

He broke his arm throwing. Sliding into bases, he tore up the cartilage in his left knee, ripped the muscles in a leg and twice broke an ankle. Crashing into fences seven times, he was knocked senseless on five occasions, dislocated a shoulder and broke his collarbone. Twice he was hit in the head by pitched balls.

It wasn't that he was fragile or more prone to injury than the next man, and he resents suggestions that he took unnecessary risks. "Every time I hit a wall," he says defensively, "I was going for a drive that meant the ball game."

Just getting knocked out the other day was nothing, but they took him to a hospital because of his medical history. When he was 39 years old and managing Kokomo, Ind., he suffered a heart spasm. "It was just some muscle or something," he said a few days later. "I can manage again."

In Kokomo he rejoiced in a rookie named Tommy Davis. The next year in Green Bay, Wis., he was enchanted by Frank Howard. Big Frank was the only player to have his own traveling manager. As Howard moved up through the Dodgers' farm system, Reiser always went along to manage the team, and when Howard got to the parent club, Pete went along as coach.

As a rookie in the Dodgers' 1939 training camp, Reiser reached base 12 times in his first 12 times at bat with three home runs, five singles and four walks. The first time at bat against Detroit he hit a home run off Tommy Bridges. First time he saw the Yankees he nailed Lefty Gomez for a home run.

The Yankees offered $100,000 and five players for him. The Dodgers said no. Then one hour before game time on opening day in Brooklyn, Larry MacPhail, the general manager, told Pete to catch a bus for Elmira.

It was there Reiser broke his right arm throwing. That winter he taught himself to throw left-handed. "What the hell's going on?" the Dodger manager, Leo Durocher, demanded in spring training. Pete explained. "I want you right-handed," Durocher said, "so I can use you as an infielder when I want to." Pete tried his right arm and it worked.

Five days after the start of his first full season with Brooklyn, 1941, a pitch by Ike Pearson of the Phillies caught him in the head. When he woke in a hospital the doctor told him he would be in bed five or six days. Pete got up and proved he could walk and the doctor let him out on condition that he would not try to play.

Reiser went to the park, where Durocher saw him sitting behind the dugout and talked him into putting on his uniform—"Not to play, just so the guys can see you're not hurt."

With the score 7-7 in the eighth inning, Pearson relieved the Philadelphia pitcher with the bases full of Dodgers. "Pistol," Durocher said, "get a bat." Pistol Pete hit the first pitch into the center-field seats for an 11-7 victory and just made it trotting around the bases.

Later that summer he was beaned a second time, smashed into the fence lunging for a drive by Enos Slaughter, and hit .343 for the National League batting championship.

The following July Reiser had 19 hits for 21 times at bat in four games in Cincinnati. In Chicago he went 4 for 4 in the first half of a double-header, walked three times and hit safely in his only official time at bat in the second game. Next time around he was batting .381 when he tried to chase another Slaughter drive through the fence. Dr. Robert Hyland told him that would be all for the year. Two days later, Pete was in the stands in Chicago. Once more Durocher talked him into the dugout "for the guys' morale."

The Dodgers got runners on base with the score tied in the 14th inning. Durocher cried aloud that he had no pinch-hitter. Reiser shuffled to the bat rack.

"You got a hitter," he said. He drove a shot over second base for two runs, made it as far as first base and passed out.

"We win!" Durocher told him when he came to. "You're better unconscious than anybody else on their feet."

# FAME ON 60 CENTS A DAY

W EARING a store suit, horn-rimmed glasses and a smile that could light up Yankee Stadium, a sunny gentleman of 64 revisited his past yesterday and recalled what it was like to be the black Lou Gehrig on a food allowance of 60 cents a day. As Buck Leonard views it now from inside baseball's Hall of Fame, it was even better than being an air-brake repair helper in the Atlantic Coast Line shops in Rocky Mount, N.C.

"They say," a man prompted him, "that at $1,000 a month you were one of the three highest-paid players in the Negro National League."

"A thousand a month," Leonard said, "*and* all expenses. I got expenses at home and on the road both. Room rent run about $6 a week and meal money was $2 a day." He interrupted himself with a delighted laugh. "When I started out, meal money was 60 cents a day."

This was at a news conference held to announce that Buck Leonard and the late Josh Gibson, teammates on the old Homestead Grays of Pittsburgh, had been tapped for the Cooperstown shrine. They were voted in by the special committee that selects black men who would have qualified on ability if their color hadn't kept them out of organized ball.

Gibson and Leonard were home run hitters who batted third and fourth in the Grays' lineup as Babe Ruth and Lou Gehrig had done with the Yankees.

"Sometimes if we went in a slump they'd bat me third and Josh fourth," Leonard said. "Then Howard Easterling joined the club and he batted third with me fourth and Gibson fifth.

"The way I got to the Grays, I come to New York in 1933 with the

Baltimore Stars. I was 26 then and just starting out because I had a pretty good job in the railroad shops down home till I got cut off and took to playing ball.

"The Baltimore Stars got stranded in New York and I went with the Brooklyn Royal Giants. Cannonball Dick Redding was the manager. Smokey Joe Williams—he was tending bar on Lenox Avenue—asked me if I'd like to play for a good team. He called up Cum Posey, who had the Homestead Grays. Posey sent travel expenses, but not to me; he sent the money to Williams, who gave me a bus ticket and $5."

"Do you think," Leonard was asked, "that Smokey Joe took a commission?"

Laughter bubbled out of him. "All I know, when I got my first paycheck they held out $50. That bus ticket didn't cost no $45."

Gibson was a month past his 35th birthday when he died in January, 1947, the year Jackie Robinson broke the color line in the majors. Legend says Josh died in anger and frustration because Robinson got the chance, not he.

"I never heard about no frustration," Leonard said. "I went to the funeral. They told me he had some drinks Saturday night and they carried him home. Sunday he had a headache. They thought it was a hangover, but the doctor gave him some pills to make him sleep. Monday morning he still had the headache and they give him more pills. They told me he had a stroke of the brain."

Leonard said today's black player was "smarter than we were, gets better training," but he named Satchel Paige, Cannonball Redding, Slim Jones and Blake ("What's his first name? Big right-hander played with the New York Cubans") among pitchers who were faster than Vida Blue.

The greatest player of all time, in his judgment, was Martin Dihigo, a big Cuban who pitched and played the outfield and occasionally third base.

Questioners kept pressing Leonard about Robinson, implying that he must have envied Jackie his opportunity in organized ball, but Buck said he turned down an invitation from Bill Veeck to join the St. Louis Browns in 1952 because, at 45, he felt too old. He continued playing in Mexico until he was 48. "I told 'em I was 38."

Traveling to Cuba, Puerto Rico and Mexico in the winter, he would play as many as 290 games in a year. "Middle of summer it seemed like 2,000." Often he played three games in a day.

"They say you never had an argument with an umpire," somebody suggested.

"I beat a play at first base and a Cuban umpire called me out," he said. "He couldn't understand English, but from the expression on my face I wasn't saying nothing good. He put me out of the game and next day he fined me $10."

After consulting an interpreter, no doubt.

# NEW BOY ON THE BEAT

**B**Y his own admission, Richard Milhous Nixon has always had a suppressed ambition to be a sportswriter, and now he has had the thrill of seeing his byline over a piece in the sports section. Allowing the cub two or three times as much space as a staff member would get, *The New York Times* published his essay in full, all 2,800 cliché-ridden words. Frankly, the new boy has a long way to go if he's ever going to cut it in this department.

He's got to tighten up his prose, squeeze the wind out, and say in 900 words what took him 2,800. He's got to kick those threadbare platitudes that he uses over and over, like "get the nod." He'll have to bone up on the mother tongue and learn, for instance, not to say "due to the fact" when he means "because" (see *New York Times Style Book* and *American Heritage Dictionary* Usage Panel).

He'll have to get out of the act. Posing as an objective authority, he disqualifies himself when he picks Harmon Killebrew as first baseman merely because Senator Herman Welker of Idaho introduced them when Killebrew was a teen-ager, when he selects Nellie Fox over better second basemen because he knew Fox personally as a coach in Washington, and when he puts Bobo Newson on his pitching staff for similar personal reasons.

Above all, he's got to cover the assignment. He was asked to pick his all-time all-star baseball team and he blew it. He picked four teams, with spares.

Perhaps he should not be blamed for that, however. This is an election year when he could not afford to slight any segment of the electorate. He has, therefore, saluted young and old, white and black, Latin and Nordic, left-hander and right-hander, Catholic and Wasp, Jew and the American Indian (Early Wynn). He has chosen fastball pitchers, curveball pitchers, a master of the knuckleball (Hoyt Wilhelm), and even a specialist in the politically unappetizing spitball (Burleigh Grimes).

To be sure, he is not above demagogy. Among the five starting pitchers on his postwar American League team is Satchel Paige. Beyond doubt, Old Satch could start pitching where most of the others left off, but no conscientious selector could choose him as a star in the American League, where his lifetime record was 28 games won and 31 lost. Paige might be regarded as the Strom Thurmond of 1972, bellwether of the Southern strategy.

As a sportswriter, Richard might do for a weekly like *Sports Illustrated* but he'd have to step up his pace to qualify in the daily press. He started on the assignment Sunday, June 25, and even though he had professional help (David Eisenhower, a son-in-law who worked for the Washington Senators when there was such a team), he missed every edition until Sunday, July 2.

Even after all that time, he discredited himself as an authority. Nobody who saw Hack Wilson play the outfield could pick the fat man over Joe Medwick, not even the year Hack batted in 190 runs. Perhaps Mr. Nixon never heard of Jimmy Wilson, whose wondrous skills as a catcher he ignores in favor of lumbering, lovable old Ernie Lombardi. And as for relegating Frank Frisch to a utility role—well, words fail.

One dislikes to be captious. Branch Rickey, tapped as manager of the National League team, was about as bad as managers get. He got nowhere with the St. Louis Browns in 1914 and 1915 and floundered for six years with the Cardinals, who won the world championship the summer after he was replaced. Still, he was a brilliant man and a holy one from Ohio. More than leadership and inspiration, we need the churchly vote of Middle America.

In the sportswriting fraternity, borrowing from other sportswriters is standard practice, and not everybody is scrupulous about crediting his sources. Thus it is perfectly all right for Mr. Nixon, hailing Lou Gehrig as the bravest of players, to call him "Mr. Profile in Courage." Funny he should think of that title, though.

The man wrote that picking these teams was one of the hardest jobs he ever attempted. Doing a fair critique of his performance is no easier. When you regard him as a sportswriter, you can't help feeling that he really ought to go back to being President of the United States. That's a dreadful, difficult line to write.

# AUTHORS ARE WHERE YOU FIND THEM

**T**HIS is Grand Circuit week in Goshen, N.Y., when the trotters and pacers come back to the peaceful little seat of Orange County and find it much the same as it was when Messenger, the gray progenitor of America's light harness horse, stood at stud there 170-odd years ago, or when Messenger's prepotent descendant, Hambletonian 10, was foaled in 1849.

The years do little to Goshen's tranquil charm or to Historic Track, where the horses have raced for 135 years. Beside the homestretch stands the barn from whose loft Ulysses S. Grant watched the races. The great old tree in the centerfield is the Hambletonian Oak, in whose shade Hambletonian and seven of his most celebrated sons paraded in 1855.

Flora Temple raced there. She was the $13 whirlwind celebrated as the "bobtail mare" in Stephen Foster's "Camptown Races." There the implausible Goldsmith Maid appeared as an 8-year-old maiden off the farm and won a $100 purse for the first of her 322 victories. It was on Historic Track that Greyhound took his world record of 1:59¾. They're all gone now, along with such patron saints as Walter Cox and Bill Cane, Pop Geers and Sep Palin. Yet the flavor lingers. Visitors note that although the new county office building is exuberantly contemporary, its 21st century lines are screened from view by 19th century trees.

Trotting is so much a part of Goshen and Goshen so much a part of trotting that it seems impertinent to mention baseball in connection with the town. However, there is at hand an essay on baseball that richly deserves attention and its author is Paul Dunkelman of Goshen.

Just last Sunday the press made a fuss about the maiden effort of an aspiring baseball writer named Richard Milhous Nixon, who dictated more than 2,800 words into a tape recorder. Mr. Dunkelman dictated his piece to his kindergarten teacher. His 399 words could set an example for other rookies.

"Whitey Ford was one of the greatest pitchers in the world. The Yankees thought it was great that they had him on their team. If they wanted him to strike out anybody he would. At practice he couldn't hit and at the games he couldn't hit, but he could pitch!

"One of his best friends was Babe Ruth and he thought the Yankees would do good when he died. He knew if any other great team came, the Yankees would beat them. He knew when he died Lou Gehrig would take his place.

"Whitey could pitch faster than anything you ever saw. Whitey couldn't hit, but if you wanted to see somebody pitch, just watch Whitey. If Whitey Ford tried to pitch to Babe Ruth he would get a lot of hits but not as much as when other people were pitching to him. If they wanted to try and beat the Red Sox it would be a cinch. They used to call Babe Ruth 'Baby Ruth.' Babe Ruth was one of the champion hitters of all time.

"Whitey Ford was rough and tough and Lou Gehrig's mother didn't know anything about baseball and his father told her about it. He said, 'They run the bases,' and his mother said, 'I run the bases?' and his father said, 'No, *they* run the bases.' And Lou Gehrig flipped over the bats.

"There was a little sick boy in the hospital that Babe Ruth went to see and he asked him if he could hit a home run and the little boy said, 'Could you hit two home runs for me?' And Babe Ruth missed the first two hits and put out one finger and then two fingers. And the last two hits were home runs.

"When Lou Gehrig was up he hit two home runs and all the Yankees jumped up and were glad to have him on their team. Now that Lou Gehrig, Babe Ruth and Whitey Ford aren't playing they thought they would still be a good team without them.

"The little boy that was in the hospital was in jail and when he came out Babe Ruth was walking past and the little boy hollered out, 'Hey, do you remember me?' and Babe Ruth turned around and looked at him and said, 'No, who are you?' and the little boy said he was the little boy in the hospital—'Remember me?' and Babe Ruth said, 'Oh, yea.' "

The work is illustrated by the author in colored crayon.

# UNCONQUERABLE

IN the scene that doesn't fade, the Brooklyn Dodgers are tied with the Phillies in the bottom of the 12th inning. It is 6 p.m. on an October Sunday, but the gloom in Philadelphia's Shibe Park is only partly due to oncoming evening. The Dodgers, champions-elect in August, have frittered away a lead of 13½ games, and there is bitterness in the dusk of this last day of the 1951 baseball season. Two days ago, the New York Giants drew even with Brooklyn in the pennant race. Two hours ago, the numbers went up on the scoreboard: New York 3, Boston 2. The pennant belongs to the Giants unless the Dodgers can snatch it back.

With two out and the bases full of Phillies, Eddie Waitkus smashes a low, malevolent drive toward center field. The ball is a blur passing second base, difficult to follow in the half-light, impossible to catch. Jackie Robinson catches it. He flings himself headlong at right angles to the flight of the ball, for an instant his body is suspended in midair, then somehow the outstretched glove intercepts the ball inches off the ground.

He falls heavily, the crash drives an elbow into his side, he collapses. But the Phillies are out, the score is still tied.

Now it is the 14th inning. It is too dark to play baseball, but the rules forbid turning on lights for a game begun at 2 o'clock. Pee Wee Reese pops up. So does Duke Snider. Robin Roberts throws a ball and a strike to Robinson. Jackie hits the next pitch upstairs in left field for the run that sets up baseball's most memorable playoff.

That was the day that popped into mind when word came yesterday that Jack Roosevelt Robinson had died at 53. Of all the pictures he left upon memory, the one that will always flash back first shows him stretched at full length in the insubstantial twilight, the unconquerable doing the impossible.

The word for Jackie Robinson is "unconquerable." In *The Boys of Summer,* Roger Kahn sums it up: "In two seasons, 1962 and 1965, Maury Wills stole more bases than Robinson did in all of a 10-year career. Ted Williams' lifetime batting average, .344, is two points higher than Robinson's best for any season. Robinson never hit 20 home runs in a year, never batted in 125 runs. Stan Musial consistently scored more often. Having said those things, one has not said much because troops of people who were there believe that in his prime Jackie Robinson was a better ball player than any of the others."

Another picture comes back. Robinson has taken a lead off first base and he crouches, facing the pitcher, feet fairly wide apart, knees bent, hands held well out from his sides to help him balance, teetering on the balls of his feet. Would he be running? His average was 20 stolen bases a year and Bugs Baer wrote that "John McGraw demanded more than that from the baseball writers."

Yet he was the only base-runner of his time who could bring a game to a stop just by getting on base. When he walked to first, all other action ceased. For Robinson, television introduced the split screen so the viewer at home as well as the fan in the park could watch both the runner on first and the pitcher standing irresolute, wishing he didn't have to throw.

Jackie Robinson established the black man's right to play second base. He fought for the black man's right to a place in the white community, and he never lost sight of that goal. After he left baseball, almost everything he did was directed toward that goal. He was involved in foundation of the Freedom National Banks. He tried to get an insurance company started with black capital and when he died he was head of a construction company building housing for blacks. Years ago a friend, talking of the needs of blacks, said "good schooling comes first."

"No," Jackie said, "housing is the first thing. Unless he's got a home he wants to come back to, it doesn't matter what kind of school he goes to."

There was anger in him and when he was a young man he tended to raise his falsetto voice. "But my demands were modest enough," he said, and he spoke the truth. The very last demand he made publicly was delivered in the mildest of terms during the World Series just concluded. There was a ceremony in Cincinnati saluting him for his work in drug addiction and in his response he mentioned a wish that he could look down to third base and see a black manager on the coaching line.

Seeing him in Cincinnati recalled the Dylan Thomas line that Roger Kahn borrowed for a title: "I see the boys of summer in their ruin." At 53 Jackie was sick of body, white of hair. He had survived one heart attack, he had diabetes and high blood-pressure and he was going blind as a result of retinal bleeding in spite of efforts to cauterize the ruptured blood vessels with laser beams. With him were his wife Rachel, their son, David, and daughter, Sharon. Everybody was remembering Jack Jr., an addict who beat the heroin habit and died at 24 in an auto accident.

"I've lost the sight in one eye," Jackie had told Kahn a day or so earlier, "but they think they can save the other. I've got nothing to complain about."

# SUPER STAINLESS CLASSIC

*Detroit*

IN the fourth inning Johnny Bench went to bat for the second time. He had already delivered two runs with a thunderous shot into the upper deck, probably 50 feet above the 415-foot mark in right-center field. He had connected with the second pitch Vida Blue threw him, and his hit was the first ever made by a National League player against Oakland's child prodigy.

Bench has been batting .250 for the Reds this summer, getting his share of hits past the human beings who play third base in his league. Now, though, that monster was out there again, crouched, poised to spring, that fiend he'd been seeing in his dreams ever since **Octob**er.

In John's dreams, the creature was always suspended horizontally in midair, his outstretched glove spearing a line drive that should have been a World Series double or triple.

Bench swung on a pitch by Jim Palmer. The ball was a hummer to the third baseman's left, smoking toward the outfield on one fierce hop. The creature sprang. The ball was already past him, yet the glove seemed to suck it back. Thrown out by 40 feet, Bench flung both hands aloft in surrender.

"Won't you for cryin' out loud gimme a break?" he cried.

Brooks Robinson—for it was indeed he—laughed.

That was the moment of pure beauty in the midsummer exhibition between the pick of the two major leagues. The rest of the time it was the Super Stainless Classic, the sorry exercise in huckstering that baseball has allowed its All-Star Game to become.

Ford Frick was commissioner when the St. Louis beer baron, Gussie Busch, bought the Cardinals and wanted to rename the park Budweiser Stadium. "Knock it off," Frick said. Baseball wasn't holding still for such blatant commercialism.

Today the Gillette Co. runs the election of All-Star players as a gigantic campaign to peddle razor blades and shaving cream. As mementos, the commissioner gives the players Linde Star rings, fake sapphires provided by Union Carbide. The customers—there were 53,559 in Tiger Stadium and some paid scalpers $50 a ticket—are subjected to an unutterably dreary charade by moppets in a "pitch, hit and throw" competition sponsored by Phillips 66.

Then National Broadcasting Co. takes over from Bowie Kuhn and the umpires, and runs the show for the greater glory of the television sponsors.

During the pre-game discussion of ground rules, prop men pick their way over a tangle of TV cables on the playing field and hang lavaliere microphones on the two managers.

In the fifth inning here, Frank Umont, the plate umpire, interrupted the action to order Pete Rose and Ron Santo down off the top step of the Nationals' dugout. "You've gotta be kidding," they said, for a stranger in shirt sleeves was squatting in the playing area at a corner of the Americans' dugout. A TV director. Tardily, Umont waved him away, but the guy was wool-gathering and didn't notice until the Americans' trainer explained that baseball rules older than the commissioner allowed only the manager and trainer on the bench without a uniform.

An inning later, the showman and an accomplice got out of there, but it was later still before another space cadet wearing a headset was ousted from the Nationals' dugout. He finished the game squatting on the playing field beyond the bench, ignored by Umont.

It's an exhibition, a show, an opportunity for the underprivileged clientele in an American League town to enjoy Willie Mays and Hank Aaron. But it isn't baseball because that's not how the game is played.

There was every evidence that Detroit was enjoying all the muscle-bulging that led to the first American League victory in nine years. Vida Blue, the winning pitcher, was 12 years old the last time the Americans made it. Home runs were the agency then, too, but none had the velocity of Reggie Jackson's blast here. It was taking off for Windsor, Ontario, when it smashed against the light tower on the right field roof, approximately 10 stories high.

"Hardest I ever saw," said Al Kaline, who has played here 18 years. "I'm only sorry it hit something."

Starting with Ted Williams in 1939, only eight players have hit fair balls out of this park. Except for the light standard, Reggie would be the first to hit one out of the country.

# WHAT THEY TALK ABOUT

*Pittsburgh*

T HIS is how it is in the ball park after 164 games with the divisional champions holding one victory apiece in the National League pennant playoffs, the 165th game coming up and all the sweat and tears and triumphs and tribulations of six long months simmering down to the last few innings.

"Hi, Rich," a visitor saluted Richie Hebner, third baseman for the Pittsburgh Pirates, "how's it going?"

"Still breathing," Hebner said, "and when I stop, my father'll take care of me." Richie's father is a gravedigger.

Richie's left cheek bulged with enough eating tobacco to fill the $1.85 blue plate special. "How much tobacco does your club eat in one playoff game?" Danny Murtaugh was asked.

"We got some pretty good chewers," said the Pirates' manager, "Richie, me, all the coaches. I don't know how much for a playoff, but in the last game of the 1960 World Series"—when the Pirates beat the Yankees—"I used up four packs, and don't remember spitting."

Somebody mentioned football and Murtaugh asked how Villanova and Delaware had come out Saturday. "Villanova got upset," somebody said. "Good," Murtaugh grunted, and a man who had known him as a rookie infielder out of Chester, Pa., hooted. "Women and quarterbacks never forget," the man said.

Grinning, Murtaugh explained to others: "Villanova was running spring tryouts for high school football players around Philadelphia. I was a quarterback, and the rule was that when the quarterback threw a pass somebody had to put him on his back even if he left the stadium. I took it for a couple days and then went to Harry Stuhldreher, the coach.

" 'You got any scholarships for baseball or basketball?' I asked him. He said no and I said, 'Well, you can take your football scholarships and—' "

Murtaugh broke off as his friend Charles Feeney joined the group. Feeney covers the Pirates for the *Pittsburgh Post-Gazette,* but a strike blacked out the city's newspapers for 129 days during the season. "I really enjoyed the summer," Murtaugh said. "No papers. I gave Feeney 129 stories and he never wrote one."

"You're running second again," Feeney told him. "Ellis has a bigger crowd."

There was a cluster of reporters around Dock Ellis, the Pittsburgh club's ace pitcher and severest critic, who had been calling his employers cheapskates because the bed they provided for him in a San Francisco hotel and the plane they chartered to haul the team East were both too small for his taste. Now Dock was insisting that a man should always speak his mind, right out.

"If you went to a friend's house for dinner and didn't like the food, Dock, would you say so?"

"I certainly would."

"That portrait of you at the Bradenton city limits," a man said to Murtaugh, "is it in the Frick Museum now?" Tourists driving into Bradenton, Fla., last March saw an enormous billboard displaying the manager's flat features in living color to advertise the city as the Pirates' spring training base.

"The Blue Cross made 'em take it down," Murtaugh said. "It was causing too many accidents."

## GOD IN A DILEMMA

*Baltimore*

NINE-THIRTY Mass was about to start in St. Vincent de Paul Church when the pastor, a plump, bald man, spotted Nestor Chylak in an aisle seat. The umpire attends St. Vincent's regularly when he works in Baltimore, and he whiles away evenings playing gin rummy with the priests in the rectory.

"Tough ball game yesterday, Nestor," the pastor said. "Where you working today?"

"Behind the plate," Chylak said.

"Oooh! You're really going to get it!"

Before delivering the homily, the priest told his flock: "I know we should pray for the Orioles, but in Pittsburgh they're praying for the Pirates. So I'll just say this Mass is for the birds."

Put in a dilemma like that, God took the only possible way out. Always a soft touch for the Irish, he let Daniel Edward Murtaugh call the shots in the seventh and final match of the 68th World Series, and that bog-trotter from Chester, Pa., directed a 2-1 rhapsody which enabled the Pirates to dispossess the Orioles as baseball champions of His green footstool.

Steve Blass, the Connecticut Yankee who throws wooden nutmegs, had pitched and won the Pirates' first victory and their fourth.

"The second time you face a club," he was asked before the game, "do you do anything different?"

"I hope not," he said quickly.

This was different, though. When he won the third game in Pittsburgh last Tuesday, he allowed a run and three hits. This time he allowed one run and four hits. Looking on from the upper deck were Steve's wife Karen Louise, his father, his next-door neighbor in Falls Village, Conn., a friend who built Steve a barbecue pit in his backyard, and his high school baseball coach.

"What high school?" a man with a notebook asked.

"Housatonic Valley District High."

The man's pencil never moved. "H-O-U-S-A-T-O-N-I-C," the pitcher spelled it out. "And the fight song is, 'Far Above the Housatonic, Loyal, Brave and True.' That's T-R-U-E."

Blass had slept soundly from 10:30 Saturday night to 8:30 Sunday morning, but once the game started his cool melted. After every turn on the mound from the third inning on, he went alone to the clubhouse to think pure thoughts and lecture himself. Before going out to pitch the ninth, he had to fight back nausea.

His nervousness didn't communicate itself to the customers, though. They sat brooding darkly like the threatening skies above, watching the reign of their Orioles dwindle away. They had whooped it up more than somewhat in the early innings while Mike Cuellar, the Baltimore pitcher, was retiring 11 batters in a row, but then Roberto Clemente came up in the fourth inning.

Roberto was everybody's nominee for the auto which *Sport* magazine gives annually to the individual star of the series. In the first six games he had made 11 hits, including two doubles, one triple and a home run. He had made no mistakes in right field, had run the bases like a hungry cheetah and provided the newspapermen with reams of controversial copy.

A right-handed batter, Roberto hardly ever pulls the ball, but now he came around on Cuellar's first pitch and gave it a 400-foot ride to left center field. Cuellar turned to watch the ball disappear over the fence and regarded Clemente with loathing as he jogged around the bases. No doubt he thought of what Jim Brewer, a pitcher with the Dodgers, once said of Roberto: "One year after he's dead, he'll hit .320."

Cuellar had now yielded one hit and was one run down. It looked as though that situation would prevail all winter. "This thing," a man muttered, "has all the suspense of a presidential election in Vietnam." In the top of the eighth, Pittsburgh's Willie Stargell singled and Jose Pagan doubled him home, making it 2-0. Then and then only did the Orioles get up any sort of a threat. They put runners on second and third with one out but Blass managed to shut them off with only one run.

In the ninth he got three big ones in order—Boog Powell, Frank Robinson and Merv Rettenmund. Blass leaped for joy and the Pirates'

21-year-old pitcher, Bruce Kison, raced gratefully for the clubhouse. He had a date to marry Anne Marie Orlando in Pittsburgh.

As a wedding gift, Bob Prince, who broadcasts the Pirate games, had arranged for a helicopter to be at Memorial Stadium. It was to carry Kison and his best man, Bob Moose, and Mrs. Moose to Friendship Airport where a Pittsburgh steel company had a jet waiting to speed the company to the altar.

Just 34 minutes after the World Series ended, the chopper took off. About the same time, there were phone calls for Murtaugh and Earl Weaver, his rival manager. Camp David, someone said, was on the horn.

# THE BOLL WEEVIL'S FOE

*Oakland, Calif.*

**B**EFORE the third World Series game was rained out a man asked Paul Richards, "Is throwing a bat at a man's head worse than throwing a ball at his head?" The question referred, of course, to the case of Dagoberto Blanco Campaneris, the Oakland shortstop whose misdirected attempt to skull the Detroit pitcher Lerrin LaGrow with a Louisville Slugger recently had caused Joe Cronin, president of the American League, and Bowie Kuhn, the commissioner, to recoil in horror.

Paul Richards was consulted as an authority because as a catcher, as a manager and as a general manager he had dealt with many pitchers who threw baseballs at batters' ears harder and more accurately than anybody could throw a bat, and had never deplored the practice if the pitcher played on his side. In fact, even when he was a sports columnist in Waxahatchie, Tex., Richards wrote with tolerance; editorially, *The Waxahatchie Daily Light* favored an early spring and opposed the boll weevil. It was neutral on the beanball.

"Throwing a ball at a hitter has always been more or less accepted as part of the game," Richards said. "I considered it a compliment when they did it to me."

"Because pitchers seldom felt it necessary to intimidate you, eh? Still, you got your hits now and then. Find a catcher with your batting average today and there'd be 24 clubs bidding for him."

"Ho," Richards said, "with an average like mine, they hold out today. I hit .268 and got traded to the minors."

Wry amusement twisted his gaunt features. "Of course," he said, "Connie Mack and I had a little disagreement. I was catching for the Athletics against Detroit. Charley Gehringer got on base and for some reason Hank Greenberg tried to bunt; Pinky Higgins, our third baseman, was playing him in the left field. Hank tipped it foul but the umpire called it a ball. I turned to argue. The ball was lying there a few feet away, so Gehringer took second. I saw him, but what the hell, you can't advance on a foul ball.

"I turned back to argue some more. Next time I looked, Gehringer was on third. Finally Connie's son, Earle, the first-base coach, came out and picked up the ball."

"And that night you went to Atlanta in the Southern League?"

"Yes, but there's a little-known sidelight. About four years earlier I had a basketball team down in Waxahatchie. There was this big, tall young fellow around there doing nothing much and I wanted him to play center for us. 'I'll play if you'll get me a job pitching,' he told me.

"'You ever do any pitching?' I asked him. He said, 'No, but I can really throw that ball.'

"We went out and warmed up and he really could throw. He didn't know what a pitching mound looked like or how to stand on the rubber or throw a curve, but he could fog it in. I asked around and got him a job with Atlanta. They sent him out to the Piedmont League or somewhere, and the next thing I heard he was winning 17 games for some team.

"By that time Earl Mann had taken over the Atlanta club, and after that business about Greenberg's bunt, Connie traded me to Atlanta for this kid. Almon Williams, his name was."

"I remember Williams," a man said. "The first game he pitched for Philadelphia was one of those Presidential previews opening the season in Washington, and this country guy beat the Senators with F. D. R. and everybody looking on. How was he as a basketball player?"

"Damn good," Richards said. "Carl Hubbell, the Giants' great pitcher, had a basketball team in Meeker, Okla., and they came down to play us. We had a referee around there who was about half blind. 'Now listen, Tom,' I told him, 'don't you favor us. I don't want Hubbell saying he got jobbed in Waxahatchie.'

"Well, it was murder. He must have called about 30 fouls on us and maybe four against Meeker. They beat us a point or two.

"The next spring I met Hubbell in training camp and we got to talking about our basketball game. 'We woulda beat you by 50 points, Hub said, 'if it wasn't for that burglar you had refereeing.'"

·

# KISSES SWEETER THAN WINE

*Cincinnati*

ⒶND so, as Bobby Tolan contemplates a plunge into the turgid Ohio, we tiptoe silently away from Riverfront Stadium and a love scene of almost unbearable tenderness.

The athletes have quit the field following the seventh and last match of the World Series, the Oakland A's to douse one another with champagne in celebration of a 3-2 victory, the Reds to sip a weary beer and lay plans to go kill some quail.

The stage is empty now save for the stars of the piece. Charles O. Finley, proprietor and operator of the baseball champions of creation, leaves his seat behind the Oakland bench and springs to the dugout roof, pulling his wife Shirley up behind him. They clinch.

Helped by a couple of ushers, Dick Williams, the Oakland manager, clambers up beside his bosses and is joined by his wife Norma. They embrace.

Charley kisses Shirley again. Dick busses Norma. Now Dick kisses Shirley. Now Charley smooches Norma.

It is the most poignant display of connubial affection on coast-to-coast television since Tiny Tim got married on the Tonight Show. It cannot go on into prime time, however, for the men are needed in the locker room. Dick goes to tell the press how he brought it off. Charley proceeds to pour champagne over authors whose prose has not pleased him.

It seemed that it would never end, but baseball is through for the year.

The end came at 3:57 p.m. (Eastern daylight time), concluding the longest death scene this side of *La Bohème*. After the regular season closed Oct. 4, five playoff games were required in each league to establish a pennant winner. Starting two days after that, this tournament consumed nine days and covered approximately 4,000 miles.

The Reds, beaten four times in five games by the Yankees of 1961, four of five by the Baltimore Orioles of 1970 and four of seven by Oakland this year, have now lost the world championship three times in 17 games. Yet even with two out in the ninth inning today, they still seemed to have a chance.

Darrel Chaney was on first base, having been struck on the foot by a pitch from Rollie Fingers. Pete Rose aimed a drive at the black wall in left center field. Chaney could have gone home easily with the tying run if the ball had fallen safe, but Joe Rudi made a routine running catch and leaped three times like a jubilant springbok.

That was the cue for Charley and Shirley and Dick and Norma.

By this time, Bobby Tolan was in the Cincinnati clubhouse, his muttonchop sideburns drooping. Nobody has rejoiced more exuberantly than he over the Reds' successes this year, for the whole summer was a triumph for Tolan. He was a major factor in Cincinnati's romp to the pennant two years ago, batting .316 and leading both leagues with 57 stolen bases. Then he underwent surgery twice for a torn Achilles tendon and didn't play an inning last season.

Returning to center field this year, he was one of the big three at the top of the batting order. He reached base 221 times, stole 42 times and his 82 runs-batted-in were exceeded only by Johnny Bench and Tony Perez. In the first six games against the A's, he was Cincinnati's most productive batter and dangerous base runner, with six runs-batted-in and five steals.

The year of his comeback began to ravel in the first inning today, before more witnesses than ever had seen a ball game in Cincinnati. With one out, Oakland's Angel Mangual sent a drive to right center. Tolan broke in on the ball, slammed on his brakes, leaped in a despairing try for a one-handed catch, and the ball skipped off his glove for a three-base error. Mangual scored the first run when a grounder by Gene Tenace found a wrinkle in the infield carpet and hopped over the third baseman's head.

Things got worse for Bobby in the sixth after Tenace doubled home a second run. Chasing a smash to center by Sal Bando, Tolan pulled a hamstring muscle in his left leg. He was sprawled on the Axminster when the winning run scored. A little later he limped from sight.

# PISTOL PACKING PITCHER

WORD that Denny McLain has been carrying a shooting iron should not surprise anybody who has noted the annual sales of toy machine guns, rocket pistols, cannons and pop guns in department stores. Firearms have always had an irresistible attraction for immature males with half-formed minds.

Announcing the latest suspension of Detroit's pistol-packin' pitcher, Bowie Kuhn was, if possible, even more vague and ambiguous than he was when he set McLain down for bankrolling a betting shop. This makes for a sorry situation fraught with peril for baseball's image. Kuhn's cloudy language about "certain new allegations" invites the public to believe the worst—that McLain has been going armed because of the mob entanglements charged last winter by the magazine *Sports Illustrated*; that he wanted to be prepared in case he should meet a *Sports Illustrated* editor or one of his many creditors; that he decided he could handle his press relations more effectively with a roscoe than with a bucket of ice water; that the commissioner, having realized tardily that his lenience in the gambling case was no more than a cop-out, was now grabbing an excuse to get tough.

Perhaps none of these inferences is correct, but in the absence of open disclosures, such inferences are going to be drawn. Bowie Kuhn's biggest mistake as commissioner is his belief that, because he is a well-scrubbed barrister of good repute, commanding presence and urbane manners, he can tell the fans less than the whole truth and they'll be satisfied.

Thus on All Fools' Day when he explained that he was suspending McLain only until July because instead of making book Denny had merely been swindled into thinking he was a bookmaker, this colloquy with the press occurred:

"How do you determine whether he was a partner or not a partner?"

"On the basis of various sources of information available to me."

"But you haven't told us what the evidence is."

"Nor am I going to."

He thinks he can drop it there and everybody should be satisfied. When it was suggested that his evasiveness might be a smokescreen to cover some deeper scandal, he was angered. "Are you questioning my integrity?" he asks at such times. Integrity, no; candor, si.

It would help clear the air if the commissioner could express himself in some language other than lawyer-talk. Instead of using circumlocutions like "certain allegations" and "conduct consistent with his probationary status," he ought to have Joe Reichler of his office write his statements with the simple clarity that used to characterize Joe's baseball coverage for the Associated Press. Joe could write, for example:

"The new suspension has nothing to do with McLain's gambling activities, for which he has already served his suspension. It has nothing to do with his dousing two Detroit sportswriters with ice water, for which the Detroit club suspended him for a week.

"It is (or is not) partly because he has recently disobeyed orders to stop hitting fungoes into the stands, refused to pose for photographs and said mean things for publication about Jim Campbell, the Tigers' general manager.

"He has not denied carrying a gun but it was not for protection against mobsters, etc."

There is a report from Detroit that McLain was not licensed to carry a rod, so it could become a police matter. The cops, though, tend to be tolerant in these affairs.

They raised no great stink back in 1961 when Frank Robinson, then with the Reds, pulled a shooting iron in a Cincinnati restaurant or a little later when the Yankee pitcher Marshall Bridges caught a slug in a joint in Fort Lauderdale, Fla.

More recently a pitcher with the Kansas City Athletics got bombed out of a game one night, retired to his quarters with a couple of six-packs, and proceeded to shoot up the office building across the street. The fuzz held still even for that.

Then there was the time the Cardinals of Pepper Martin, Frank Frisch, Dizzy Dean and the rest got bounced out of a Boston hotel for shooting pigeons in the courtyard. It was a hardship to the newspaper men covering the team; the lobster thermidor in that hotel was sheer music.

# JANUARY CLEARANCE

THE annual list of the world's best-dressed men came out the other day and Mike Burke didn't make it. Masking his disappointment, he stood up to a microphone in the Yankee Stadium Club and announced that he and 11 others were buying the Yankees from Columbia Broadcasting System. In his dark blue double-breasted pinstripes, with a red handkerchief blossoming from the breast pocket, Mike didn't look envious of John Lindsay or David Susskind or Mick Jagger, who did make that list. He looked like ten million dollars—or anyway, like $833,333, the ante required from each of the doughty dozen to make them equal partners.

"Do you feel you got a bargain?" Burke was asked.

"We're delighted with the whole deal," he said, "including the price paid."

"It's the best buy in sports today," said George Steinbrenner 3d, the Cleveland shipping magnate who got the buyers together.

Both understated the case. Three seasons ago, when automobiles and meat cost less than they do today, a Milwaukee group paid $10.5-million for the Seattle Pilots, a bankrupt baseball team with a one-year record of artistic, athletic and financial failure. Since then the buyers have sunk more than $3-million into the club and they are now in the bucket for a shade less than $14-million. They operate in a city of 750,000 with a club that, like the Missouri mule, has neither pride of parentage nor hope of progeny.

For $10-million Mike Burke and friends get a team with a half-century tradition of unmatched success, a territory with 15 million potential customers, and a promise that the city will spend at least $24-million on a playpen for them.

Maybe Peter Minuit found a better buy downtown, but this was a bargain.

Steinbrenner described the new ownership as a limited partnership, which makes the partners eligible for certain tax benefits. When you buy a ball club for $10-million you enter $1-million, say, on your books as the cost of the franchise and perhaps you appraise the office equipment, locks, bats, balls and leftover adhesive tape at $500,000. The remaining $8.5-million is the value of your players.

For tax purposes, you may depreciate the players over five years at $1.7-million a year. That means you can make a $1-million profit in any year and still show a loss of $700,000.

If an individual owns the club, he may deduct this loss, dollar for dollar, on his personal-income-tax return. If the club is a limited partnership or a sub-Chapter S Corporation (no more than 10 investors), the tax deduction may be prorated to each partner up to the limit of his investment.

Thus anybody in the new group putting up his $833,333 can take that much off his tax return in the next five years if the club shows a loss or just breaks even. If it makes money, the depreciation is applied against the profit to reduce the corporate tax.

This is called a tax shelter. It is cozy.

Some listeners were puzzled when Burke said that C.B.S. "substantially broke even." It seemed to them that when you buy merchandise for $13.2-million and sell it for $10-million you've got to do a hell of a volume to break even.

Well, say the players represented $12-million of the C.B.S. investment and they were fully depreciated over five years. The corporate tax runs about 50 cents on the dollar, so this would mean a saving of $6-million, reducing the total price paid for the club to $7.2 million.

Now say the Yankees lost $4-million during the eight years C.B.S. owned them. That would be an actual loss of $2-million after taxes, bringing the C.B.S. investment in the club to $9.2-million. Reckoned that way, $10-million from the Burke-Steinbrenner mob gets C.B.S. out clear.

To be sure Dan Topping, Del Webb and Larry MacPhail did better. When they bought the Yankees in 1945 for $2.8-million they got a team staffed by players named Joe DiMaggio, Charley Keller, Tommy Henrich, Bill Dickey and Phil Rizzuto, they got Yankee Stadium, they got the good Newark and Kansas City clubs complete with ball parks and they got all the other holdings in a far-flung empire.

After buying MacPhail out for $2-million, Topping and Webb had operating profits well above $20-million before taxes, not counting loot from sale of the stadium and the land underneath. Then they sold to C.B.S. for $13.2-million.

To this day, the American League has never told how much Bill Daley, Dewey Soriano and associates profited from the sale to Milwaukee after one disastrous year in Seattle. If they did better than C.B.S., it just shows that in baseball you have to do a really lousy job to make it fast.

# PURELY RELATIVE HUMIDITY

THE girl in the American League office said: "Did you pick up four, Mr. Cronin? Well you're not on. Just a minute."

There was a pause while Joe Cronin walked out of the door marked "President" and into another office. Then his melodious tenor came over the phone sounding remarkably chipper for a man bearing responsibilities that would drive an ordinary mortal into the ground like a peg.

"Have you fined Bill Lee?" he was asked.

He laughed. "I haven't seen today's papers yet, but I imagine the club has told him to shut up. He's a typical left-hander, juicy as they make 'em."

"Did you say 'juicy,' Mr. Cronin?"

"Juicy in more ways than one."

The other day Cronin fined Jim Merritt of the Texas Rangers for saying he had thrown "25 or 30 Gaylord fastballs" in a 9-0 victory over the Cleveland Indians. The losing pitcher was Gaylord Perry, who enjoys an enviable reputation for lubricating the ball with greasy kid stuff without getting caught. Cronin's action loosened Lee's tongue.

"Tell Cronin I threw a spitter in Detroit a while back," the Red Sox pitcher said. "Tony Taylor hit it into the upper deck. . . . Yes, I have a tube of K-Y petroleum in my locker. So do a lot of others who throw it more than I do. . . . Hell, if K-Y jelly went off the market the California Angels' whole staff would be out of baseball or pitching in Pittsfield. . . . So tell Cronin he'd better fine me because I was a bad boy."

"Lee has the kind of color we need," Cronin said. "Left-handed all the way. He ought to direct his messages to Ellie Rodriguez, the catcher, who chased him clear across Puerto Rico in a fight last winter."

Perry is a recent addition to the sweaty literati and in a forthcoming book he tells about throwing juicy pitches until "about five years ago." He worked for the San Francisco Giants until 1972, so the iniquities he is now confessing would not fall within Cronin's jurisdiction. However, the American League is crawling with witnesses eager to testify that Gaylord did not leave either his depravity or his unguents in San Francisco.

"We've undressed Perry all year," Cronin said, "the umpires have. They've searched him and wiped him off and taken the ball away from him and we haven't found anything yet.

"That terminology, the 'Gaylord fastball,' that came from Merritt's manager, Whitey Herzog. Here was this guy Merritt telling everybody he was breaking the rule, so I fined him. I called him and told him his remarks were unwise and foolish."

"You hit plenty of spitballs in your day," Cronin was reminded. As a shortstop on his way to the Hall of Fame, Joe batted .301 over 20 years, facing men who used the spitter legally, like Burleigh Grimes, Clarence Mitchell, Spittin' Bill Doak and Urban Faber, and scores who sneaked it across in moments of need.

"Plenty," Cronin agreed. "And I think the knuckleball is tougher. The American League favored legalizing the spitter when Perry was in the National League. I'd rather have a guy use it legally than have the connotation of 'cheater' pasted on him."

As far as historians could ascertain, no pitcher in the American League had been disciplined for drooling on the ball since Nelson Potter in 1944. That was a heart-rending case, for Nellie Potter was the most amiable of men, he had given devotion, unflagging effort and the cartilages of both knees to the national game, and as a pitcher he needed all the edge he could get. He was pitching the St. Louis Browns to their only pennant when he was evicted from a game for slobbering. His substitute got credit for the victory and this cost him the only 20-game season he would ever have.

The baseball hierarchy views throwing the spitter and sex the same way. Doing it openly is considered indelicate and if a man does it he is not supposed to talk about it, yet the authorities have never made it unpopular.

Not only the rule but also the conventions are often flouted. When Grady Hatton managed Houston, he said freely that he had instructed his pitchers to throw the spitter if they knew how and to learn if they didn't. He said one of his men had obediently sought instructions from Phil Regan, then with the Los Angeles Dodgers, and that Regan had not only obliged but had given the pupil slippery elm to chew from his own supply. Hatton didn't get fined, but like all managers, he eventually got fired.

Of all the pitchers renowned for clandestine driveling, probably the most famous was Lewis Selva Burdette of Nitro, W. Va. When Lew was a 20-game winner for the Milwaukee Braves, papers needed three columns for his pitching record: won, lost and relative humidity. Printers setting his middle name instinctively misspelled it.

# THE MAN WHO SIGNED THE MIDGET

T HE man who signed the midget is about to be stuffed and mounted "for long and meritorious service to baseball." After 26 years, many good deeds and an occasional venial sin as a baseball man, Robert Oscar Fishel, vice president and public relations director of the Yankees, has been tapped by the New York baseball writers for the Bill Slocum Award and will receive same at their annual hog-killing.

If the writers had drawn a seine from Pelham Bay Park to the Battery, they couldn't have caught a happier choice. Nor could they have found a talent scout with a higher batting average. Since he got into the game in 1946, Bob Fishel has signed two individuals to baseball contracts—Eddie Gaedel, the greatest midget ever to play in the major leagues, and Harry Brecheen, a crafty and gifted pitcher who became a brilliant coach of pitchers. Thus the Fishel batting average stands at 1.000.

Fishel is not a tall man, and he specialized in signing players of somewhat less than average stature. When he got Brecheen to put his name on a contract as player-coach with the St. Louis Browns of 1953 —Bob did the business because all other club officials were away in training camp—Harry was a scrawny 158 pounds. Gaedel weighed 65 pounds and stood 3-foot-7.

The Gaedel caper brightened the season of 1951. Since then, a whole hairy generation has learned to read, perhaps without ever hearing how Bill Veeck traduced, debauched and desecrated the national game and increased the Browns' attendance from 247,131 to 518,796—more than they had drawn the year they won their only pennant.

Fishel and Veeck had formed a warm friendship in 1946 when, as account executive for a Cleveland advertising agency, Bob put together a radio network for the Indians, whom Veeck had just bought. When

Veeck, impelled by a death wish, sold the Indians and bought the Browns, Fishel went along.

"Many critics," John Lardner wrote at the time, "were surprised to know that the Browns could be bought, because they didn't know the Browns were owned."

They soon learned. With the unmitigated Veeck calling the shots, bombs burst in air, beer flowed, bands played, and the Browns lost and lost and lost. Veeck dreamed up a special promotion as a birthday celebration for Falstaff Brewery, the team's radio sponsor. "I'll do something so spectacular it'll get you national publicity," he promised the beer people.

He had no idea what he was going to do, but that never deterred William O. Veeck. He asked a booking agent to deliver a midget for the birthday party, a Sunday when the Detroit Tigers would be in St. Louis for a doubleheader.

"The agent kept trying to send us dwarfs," Fishel recalls now, "grotesque gnomes you couldn't present in a baseball uniform. Veeck held out for his midget and we finally got Eddie Gaedel, a nice-looking little guy. The uniform was no problem. The 7-year-old son of Bill DeWitt, our vice president, had one hanging in the clubhouse. We swiped it and had the number ⅛ sewn on the back."

In their first interview, Veeck handed the midget a toy bat and had him crouch low. The strike zone is measured from just above the batter's knees to his armpits "when he assumes his natural stance." Since Gaedel was going to bat only once in his life, his natural stance could be whatever Veeck said it was.

"His strike zone was just visible to the naked eye," Veeck relates in his memoirs. "I picked up a ruler and measured it for posterity. It was 1½ inches."

They hid Eddie out in a hotel a few blocks from the ball park. Fishel drove his old Packard to a nearby street intersection, parked, and the waiting Gaedel climbed in and signed two standard player contracts for $15,400 a season, or $100 a game. One contract was mailed on Friday to the American League office, where it wouldn't be scrutinized until Monday. The other was entrusted to Zack Taylor, the Browns' manager, in case of resistance from the umpire.

By the time the great day arrived, Gaedel had begun to feel like a big league star. Though he had been warned to stay in that crouch and draw a base on balls, he was striding about swinging his toy bat with authority. "We were all terrified," says Fishel, who had smuggled Eddie into the park.

Before the first game, a seven-foot birthday cake was wheeled out, appropriate greetings extended to the sponsor, and the tiny Brownie popped out of the cake. "I should have been fired right then," Fishel remembers. "I was so nervous I forgot to alert the photographers to stay around. By the time the second game started, only the United Press cameraman was still around."

Gaedel led off in the second game as a pinch-batter. "What the hell!" said Ed Hurley, the plate umpire, but Taylor showed him the signed contract and the roster of players.

Bob Swift, the Detroit catcher, got down on his knees to offer Bob Cain, his pitcher, some sort of target. Weak with laughter, Cain couldn't find the strike zone even though Gaedel stood almost erect. The midget walked and gave place to a pinch-runner, who was left on base. The Browns lost, 6-2.

# THE GOVERNOR PACKS IT IN

W ORD comes from Cailfornia that Gov. Garry Schumacher, scholar, raconteur and bon vivant, is retiring as the San Francisco Giants' public relations administrator. This is the right season for it. During his years of service on two coasts, Garry knew the glory that was Mays and the grandeur that was Marichal. Now Willie wears the double-knit regimentals of the Mets, Marichal's won-lost record stands at 2-10 and Candlestick Park is the home of baseball's most accomplished losers.

The origin of Garry's political title is obscure, for he has never held public office. However, when he and the late Fred Weatherly were making the scene together, it was Governor Schumacher and Senator Weatherly. Fred, a sports cartoonist on *The New York Mirror,* shared Garry's enthusiasm for gracious living, though he didn't have Garry's knowledge of food and wines. Trying out a restaurant for the first time, he would leave the ordering to the Governor.

On one such occasion in Manhattan, Garry tasted the first sip of wine, gave a noncommital nod, watched as the sommelier filled both glasses and departed, then studied the label on the bottle.

"They're giving it to us, pally," he told the Senator. "This is from up the coast a little ways."

The diction was redolent of Brooklyn but the palate was continental.

Before Horace Stoneham lured him into the Giants' office around the end of World War II, Garry had been a newspaperman unsurpassed as a baseball reporter. Watching him watch a game, alert to the nuances of every pitch, was a lesson in concentration. There comes to mind a double-header in Washington between the Senators and Detroit Tigers, both pennant contenders. The first game was a lusterless exercise won easily by Detroit without noteworthy incident, a bore to most press-box tenants but not to Garry.

"I think your guy mighta been just a little bit timid," he was overheard telling a Washington writer between games. "There in the sixth when he had the pitcher just about on the ropes, I think if he'd hit away instead of bunting he mighta got a big inning going."

Garry was a meticulous writer who blacksmithed his pieces line by line and would wind up knee deep in crumpled copy paper, but he wasn't struggling for the purple phrase or deft quip. In the end he would deliver a few paragraphs that told more about the game and what it meant in the context of the pennant race than readers could learn from any other source. This priceless economy of words characterizes his speech as well as his writing. Friends rejoice in his gift for boiling a large subject down to a few short phrases; they remember his choice lines and swap them around.

An omniverous reader with a special flair for military history, he might encapsulate a war in a sentence or two of baseball idiom. Thus he summed up the Napoleonic campaigns: "Napoleon coulda took Moscow. Trouble was, the bum had no bench."

Perhaps the subject that attracts him most is the American Civil War. In his admiration for the fighting quality of the Confederate troops, he makes only one reservation: "Real good club. Couldn't win on the road."

He was elated at an opportunity to lunch with the Civil War chronicler Bruce Catton a few years ago, but they hit a snag. Garry wanted to talk about George B. McClellan, and Catton wanted to hear about Mel Ott.

The Mexican leader Santa Anna was another who interested Garry. "So we said to him, 'Hey, pally, how about making peace?'

" 'I got to put up a little more token resistance for my people,' he kept saying. Finally we had to go up the hill to get him, to Chapultepec. And ever since then at West Point they teach 'em: 'You got to go up the hill.' "

In the field of public relations, perhaps the most masterful coup ever brought off was Garry's creation of a living legend named Clint Hartung, who had pitched and played first base and batted .351 for Eau Claire, Wis., away down in the Giant farm system, and then had gone into the Army. A big kid out of Hondo, Tex., he played some ball in the service, and while the Giants awaited his return, Garry regaled the press with tales of his superhuman feats on coral diamonds in the

Pacific. By the time the Hondo Hurricane blew into training camp in Phoenix, Ariz., he dwarfed every immortal in the Hall of Fame.

That was Garry's one mistake—letting him stop over in Phoenix instead of shipping him direct to Cooperstown. The fact that he couldn't play ball very well might never have come out.

# ON FAT PITCHES FOR CHARITY'S SAKE

NOW that Bowie Kuhn and his playmates have had their annual fling at selling razor blades, perhaps they can find time to reexamine the case of the mysterious stranger who loves Bob Robertson enough to buy him a hit for $2,000. As soon as the commissioner heard that Cincinnati's Wayne Simpson had been offered that sum to throw a fat pitch to Pittsburgh's docile window-breaker, he put the office sleuth on the case but was unable to press the investigation himself because he had to go to Atlanta and shill for the sponsors of the All-Star exhibition. If any progress has been made toward clearing up the mystery, Kuhn has been too busy to announce it.

Telling about the anonymous phone call to Simpson before he pitched against the Pirates last Saturday, the news services described it as an attempted bribery but it is improbable that the caller's motives were sinister. One gopher pitch won't necessarily affect the outcome of a game, even if it is hit squarely. Tell a good hitter that the cripple is coming, and like as not he'll pop it up.

That's especially so when the batter is as desperate as Robertson has been this summer. Last year and the year before, he was one of the rowdiest members of Pittsburgh's goon squad but this season he lost his job at first base because, as the saying goes, he couldn't buy a hit. Apparently Simpson's caller was trying to do just that for him. Considering the price the guy was willing to pay, he should be saluted for his godlike charity.

Authenticated cases of pitchers purposely serving soft stuff out of the goodness of their hearts are rare because the normal relationship between healthy, red-blooded American pitchers and batters is a mongoose-cobra sort of thing. Each says of the other, "The son of a bad woman is trying to take the bread and butter out of my mouth."

Catchers, however, do not share the pitcher's instinctive animus and might in special circumstances call for some confection as a favor to a friend. One documented case of a man's better nature taking over involves the former catcher, Birdie Tebbetts.

This notoriously kindly soul was a veteran with Detroit when Dick Wakefield, not yet 20 years old, was signed by the Tigers for a bonus of $52,000 and a new automobile, unimaginable wealth in those days. Wakefield's father had been a professional ballplayer and Dick's mother, aware of the temptations that could beset a lad, wrote to Tebbetts asking him to keep an eye on her son.

Birdie found it easy to comply, for Wakefield was an enormously personable young man. They formed a warm friendship that endured longer than their years as teammates. Eventually Tebbetts moved on to Boston and later to Cleveland.

Wakefield had two outstanding seasons during their time together, went into the service during World War II, and after that he never came close to fulfilling his early promise. When the Tigers turned him loose he wrote for a newspaper a soul searching letter of apology to the Detroit fans and got a tryout with the Yankees but failed to make it.

In the spring of 1952 the Indians took him to training camp in Tucson, Ariz., and for a little while he and Tebbetts were teammates again. Before they broke camp, however, Al Lopez gave Wakefield his release.

"As things stand," the manager said, "you're my sixth outfielder, which means that when we cut the squad you'd be the first outfielder to go. If I waited till the season started and all the other clubs were set, you might not be able to catch on anywhere. So I think your best bet is to start right now looking for another job."

Wakefield went to the Giants' camp at Phoenix and Leo Durocher agreed to take him on for a trial. In those days the Giants and Indians barnstormed together on their way home from camp. In one of their first exhibitions, Wakefield went up as a pinch-hitter with two out in the ninth inning.

The Indians had a one-run lead and there was nobody on base. A rookie was pitching for Cleveland and Tebbetts knew the decision had already been made to send the kid back for another year in the minors.

He called for a fast ball inside, the pitch he thought Wakefield would be most likely to hit well. Dick lined a triple against the wall. The next batter popped up and Cleveland won.

Herman Franks was the Giants' coach at third base.

"You took real good care of your boy," he yelled at Tebbetts.

"Yeah?" Birdie said. "Did the ball have anything on it?"

"Pretty good stuff," Franks conceded.

"What was the next pitch?" Birdie demanded. "The one that was popped up."

"Fast ball like the other one," Franks said.

"So you see?" Tebbetts said. "Now let me tell you something. When I'm calling the pitches, I don't take care of my own mother."

Recalling the incident later, Birdie lowered his voice. "I didn't say anything about Wakefield's mother," he said.

# MEESTER TEACHER

*St. Petersburg, Fla.*

**B**ERNARDINO RIVAS of the Dominican Republic stood beside the blackboard, pointed to the figure of a man and asked the question chalked alongside the drawing: "Is she Meester Jackson?"

"He," said Prof. Al Miner, dean of men in the Payson School of Basic English. "He. Is he Mister Jackson? Repeat."

"He," Rivas said. "Is he Meester Jackson?"

"No," said Angel Contres of Puerto Rico, staring hard at the next line on the blackboard. "He is not Mrs. Jackson."

"Mister," Prof. Miner said. "Mister Jackson."

"No. He ees not Meester Jackson."

"Who is he?" Rivas read.

"He is Meester Gibbs."

"Okay your turn," Miner said. Rivas sat down beside Contres, and Felix Minaya of the Dominican Republic went to the board. "Is he—"

"She."

"Is she Mrs. Roberts?"

"No, she is not Mrs. Roberts," said Francisco Estrada of Mexico.

A trifle short on ivy and decidedly lacking in academic tradition, campus unrest and alumni, Old Payson took her place in the world of education Monday when Prof. Miner conducted the first class of a 25-day crash course for Spanish-speaking ball players in the minor league system of the New York Mets.

Ten students in baseball flannels sat around a table in an office adjoining the locker room of the Payson Field complex where the Mets train their farmhands. Gloves and spiked shoes lay beneath their chairs. Their stockinged feet wriggled on the floor as they concentrated. They giggled, prompted one another, grinned self-consciously, laughed aloud, squirmed like children. They had a good time.

Joe McDonald and Whitey Herzog, the Mets' minor league and personnel directors, got the idea for the course after the club acquired

Estrada, a 23-year-old catcher from the Mexico City Reds, for their farm in Tidewater, Va. Estrada once had a cup of coffee with the Yankees but didn't stick, partly because of a "communication problem," according to the Mets' information.

McDonald discovered that the Mets this year had 17 players in their system—eight from the Dominican Republic, seven from Puerto Rico, one from Mexico and one from the Bronx—who just looked blank if the manager said, "Stick it in his ear."

That did it. Al Miner was imported from the Berlitz School in New York, and Old Payson rose as the Harvard of the Citrus Belt. It is an innovation in baseball, but not quite unique in sports: some years ago an incursion by Latin jockeys drove the New York Racing Association's clerk of scales into a Berlitz Spanish course.

Miner, a New York University graduate who has taught English in Venice, does not speak Spanish. Combining gestures with a few basic words, he manages to communicate with the students and draw responses out of them in English.

"Ask me a question. Who am I? Am I Mr. Pischardo?"

"No, you are no Meester Pischardo."

"Who am I?"

"You are Meester Teacher."

Two daily sessions of an hour and a half each are planned, mornings at Old Payson and evenings in the players' motel. That's for beginners. Half a dozen Latins who already know a little English will get more advanced instruction.

The goal is a vocabulary of 750 to 1,000 words with emphasis on baseball terms and phrases—"throw to the cut-off man," "hit and run," "if you miss the bus it will cost you money," "sirloin medium rare," "I need more money," "so is your sister."

The kid from the Bronx is Arnulfo Espinosa, a pitcher born in Puerto Rico. Soon after the class began, effects of his exposure to Ryer Avenue were evident; he was prompting the others, correcting them, grinning with self-esteem. He'll be in the advanced class soon.

Half a dozen sportswriters audited the course gratefully. Sportswriters need all the English lessons they can get.

"Too bad Bob Fishel never attended a class like this," said Harold Weissman of the Mets. On the Yankees' recent visit to Venezuela, Bob Fishel, their public relations director, couldn't understand when the tax collectors hollered for more money. They wouldn't let him out of the country.

# GIL AND HIS GUYS

IT was opening day of the baseball season, gray at 11 a.m. and as chilly as usual on opening day, though the skies would brighten and temperatures climb later in the day. The New York Mets had expected to be in Pittsburgh playing the world champions with Tom Seaver, naturally, starting against the Pirates. Instead, Seaver and most of the others were in the simple brick church of Our Lady Help of Christians, each in his own way mourning the "quiet giant," as the Rev. Charles E. Curley described Gil Hodges, the manager and friend they lost last Sunday.

Our Lady Help of Christians is at East 28th Street and Avenue M, a neighborhood of small homes, detached and semidetached, in the Flatbush section of Brooklyn. Gil and Joan Hodges raised their four children in the neighborhood but celebrities were never so numerous there as to make the neighbors blasé. Now with a chance for a close-up view of visitors as famous as Yogi Berra and Ralph Houk, the curious were out in force, many housewives and many, many children.

They stood behind police barricades that fenced off the church steps and the street immediately in front, packed in tight ranks from the curbs back onto stoops and shallow lawns. Overhead, higher than the stoops, small boys perched in trees. There was small but ceaseless jostling movement, constant but subdued chattering, small cries of recognition as cars and taxis discharged passengers. Then a black limousine pulled up.

It was a signal for quiet. In silence, the crowd watched Gil's immediate family enter the church, his mother going first. They had hardly disappeared when there was a burst of small cheers and slightly larger boos. Accompanied by Police Commissioner Patrick V. Murphy and Bud Palmer, the municipal handshaker, Mayor John Lindsay emerged from a car and walked swiftly up the steps, looking straight ahead. The voices were mostly treble, though there may have been a few boos of voting age.

Inside, several floral displays flanked the casket below the main altar. Easter lilies still decorated the side altars of the Blessed Virgin and Sacred Heart. The church filled rapidly, baseball people making up somewhat more than half the congregation.

Jackie Robinson was in a pew near the front and near him were other stars of the Brooklyn Dodger teams that Gil Hodges helped toward National League championships—Carl Erskine, Carl Furillo, Joe Black, Don Newcombe, Pee Wee Reese, Sandy Koufax. Reese seems never to age and the immaculate Koufax remains as slim as a boy, but Erskine's silver hair, Robinson's whitening poll and Black's bulk were reminders that this was the 16th opening day since these exceptional athletes last played with Gil in Ebbets Field.

The Yankees had postponed their opening game out of respect for Gil even before they knew their players would still be on strike. Mike Burke, their president, was in the church along with Lee MacPhail, the general manager; Bob Fishel, vice president, and Ralph Houk, the manager. There were others present who might have been otherwise occupied except for the strike, for not all clubs were prepared to show the same decency as the Yankees, especially those with large advance sales.

However, there was no baseball business to prevent attendance by Bowie Kuhn, the commissioner, and Mrs. Kuhn, or Chub Feeney and Joe Cronin, the major league presidents. Mrs. Joan W. Payson, owner of the Mets, was there, of course. So were M. Donald Grant, chairman of the board; G. Herbert Walker Jr., executive vice president; Bob Scheffing, general manager, and the Mets' office staff as well as the players.

Gil's coaches sat near the front—Rube Walker, Joe Pignatano, Eddie Yost and Yogi Berra. Perhaps by then all shared Yogi's knowledge that he had been selected to move into Gil's office.

Bishop Francis J. Mugavero was chief celebrant of the Mass of Resurrection, and the homily by Father Curley, Gil's pastor and friend, was a eulogy. "Gil was an ornament to his parish," the priest said, "and we are justly proud that in death he lies here in our little church."

Describing Gil as "a hero of authentic stamp," Father Curley recalled the occasion when another Brooklyn priest, aware that Gil was in a batting slump, told his congregation: "It's too hot for a sermon. Keep the Commandments and pray for Gil Hodges."

"This morning in a far different setting," Father Curley said, "I repeat that suggestion of long ago: Let's all say a prayer for Gil Hodges."

During mass the crowd outside pushed past the barricades and the church emptied slowly through the congestion. "There's Ken Singleton," said a boy whose windbreaker identified him as a member of the 1969 champions, Gil Hodges Little League. "Ken Singleton," he sang out again, and other voices joined his: "There's Agee, talking to Jackie Robinson." "Tug McGraw and Duffy Dyer." "Yogi Berra . . ."

Little cheers kept going up, unexpected at a funeral, but somehow good to hear.

# LIKE OLD TIMES, SORT OF

T HIS was how it used to be when excitement was New York's daily bread. There was a time when the town wouldn't have seemed the same without the Yankees and Red Sox at the top of the league, going for the jugular.

Ralph Houk would remember Sept. 26, 1949. In Yankee Stadium that day, Johnny Pesky slid home on a squeeze play, Willie Grieve called him safe, and Boston took over first place with one week to go. Houk, the Yankees' catcher, was sure he had tagged Pesky out and he told Grieve so in the cool, measured accents of a homicidal maniac. Frothing delicately at the lips, Casey Stengel, the Yankees' manager, bumped bellies with the umpire. Joe Page, the Yankees' great relief pitcher, hurled his glove away in a fashion tending to incite to riot. Nevertheless, the Red Sox left town that Sunday night with a one-game lead.

They brought it back six days later, needing one victory in their last two games. On Saturday Johnny Lindell's home run won the game and Page's relief pitching kept it won. John Lindell was known to take a drink now and then; Page was known to take two. In the press room below decks, the baseball scholar Garry Schumacher lifted a glass. "What I liked about this game," he said, "the rogues win it."

On Sunday the Yankees' Vic Raschi protected a 1-0 lead for eight innings. In their last turn at bat, the Yankees scored four runs. In theirs, the Red Sox got three. There had been 72 recorded injuries on the Yankee team that year. When Tommy Henrich caught a foul for the seaon's last putout, Bill Dickey, a coach, sprang from the bench and split his head on the dugout roof. No. 73.

It was in Boston that the 1948 Yankees had lost the pennant and their manager, Bucky Harris. They were back in the Bronx for a

double-header on Sept. 28, 1951, with the Yankees two games away
from another championship. With two Red Sox out in the ninth inning
of the first game, Allie Reynolds had an 8-0 lead and his second no-
hitter of the season. But the man at bat was Ted Williams.

Williams hit a towering foul behind the plate. Yogi Berra circled
under the ball, lunged for it, and missed. Yogi wanted to die, but
Reynolds helped him to his feet, patted his bottom and went back to
the mound. Williams hit another foul, a twister toward the first base
side. Chasing it blindly, Berra was a step from the dugout. "Plenty of
room!" Tom Henrich bawled. Yogi clutched the ball and Reynolds
clutched Yogi. While the pitcher savored his second no-hitter, the
Yankees won the second game and the pennant.

That's how it used to be. There was a time when you thought it
would always be that way. Then came a time when it wasn't that way
at all. One year the Red Sox won a pennant but no excitement rubbed
off on the Yankees, who were ninth. For eight years nothing that was
good rubbed off on the Yankees.

Now, at long last, it seemed like old times. The Red Sox were in
town with a half-game lead in the American League East, a half-game
over the Yankees and Baltimore. To be sure, in these days of divisional
play a pennant race is a race for only half a pennant, but such as it is,
this is the only race the Yankees have enjoyed in eight years.

At the end of a showery day, the crowd was under 16,000 but the
Beautiful People were there. Mrs. Charles Shipman Payson, a lifelong
National League fan who married a Red Sox fan before she brought
the New York Mets into the world, sat near the Boston dugout and her
husband wore his old Red Sox cap. In an anguish of divided loyalties,
M. Donald Grant split away from his boss and sat on the Yankees' side
as a proper New Yorker should. Bowie Kuhn, the supreme being of
baseball, sat downstairs robed in majesty. Pete Rozelle, supreme being
of professional football, sat upstairs with Lee MacPhail, the Yankees'
supreme being once removed. In a gathering of such brilliance, only
a great game could have shone.

This one was shiny only in the early stages. Rob Gardner, who
pitched for the Mets one summer but repented, gave the Yankees four
perfect innings, though three of his pitches in the fourth were struck
with cruel ferocity. Tommy Harper hit one into the bleachers but Roy
White flung himself halfway over the wall and picked off the home run.
A line drive by Luis Aparicio was caught on the dead run by Bobby
Murcer. Carl Yastrzemski smashed a putout to deepest left.

Getting nowhere with this heavy artillery, the Sox brought out pop-guns in the fifth. They bunted, they chopped, they poked at the ball, and got four runs with an attack that sent only one hit skipping through the infield. With large Lynn McGlothen throwing hard for Boston, subsequent developments were of no consequence.

In his office, Ralph Houk set fire to a 10-inch cigar. His troops had won four straight games and lost the one that would have put them in first place. The manager was stained, sweaty, and probably tired, but calm. He spoke highly of Gardner and McGlothen. He said he was delighted with the Yankees' position, a game and a half out with the Orioles coming in for three games. Somebody said he seemed oddly cheerful in defeat, and Houk did a double take.

"Should I lie down and cry with Baltimore coming in in two days?" he said. "Because we lost a ball game? I never heard of anybody winning them all. I hope my players don't lie down and cry."

"I don't think they will, Ralph," a man said.

# DUKE OF CARTERET

**T**OOTS SHOR was explaining baseball to Chub Feeney, president of the National League, when a mugger set upon him from behind, clamping a forearm like an iron bar across the Adam's apple. Released before rigor mortis could set in, the victim recognized his assailant as Joseph Michael Medwick, of Carteret, N.J., and the Cooperstown Hall of Fame. This was at the Waldorf-Astoria, where the baseball clan was assembling to hear Brooks Robinson saluted as "the player who best typifies the game on and off the field."

"Creep!" Shor said cordially, and turned back to Feeney. "Around 1938," he said, poking a thumb into Medwick's abdomen, "this bum said he'd give me half his salary if I got the Cardinals to trade him to the Giants. That's how bad he wanted to play opposite Joe DiMaggio. Those days we had to have the best players, because visiting teams always played twice as hard in New York as anywhere else because this is where the publicity was."

"We loved the Polo Grounds," Medwick said, "especially a guy who could hit down the lines. A team came to New York, all the pitchers had sore arms and all the hitters were happy." Something like tenderness came into his voice when he remembered the tall stands less than 260 feet from the plate.

"The way the outfielders played me," he said, "they'd give me the whole of center field, because I made it a rule never to hit to center unless we needed a single to win the game.

"The first time I played in the Polo Grounds Freddie Fitzsimmons was working for the Giants. I hit a knuckler on the handle and it just popped into the seats. I trotted around, a rookie feeling great, and when I got to the plate here's Fitz. 'Listen, bush,' he told me, 'it's all right to hit a home run, but don't be laughing when you run it out.' Next time up, the first pitch put me on my back.

65

"I remember the first time I hit against Burleigh Grimes. I'd just come up from Houston and he was working against us in Chicago— two-three days' beard on his face, showing those yellow teeth of his when he loaded up the spitter. I nailed one that was just barely foul and he really loaded up the next one. Whoeee! My bat flew this way, my cap over here and I was flat on my face.

"Burleigh came walking in and looked down at me, showing those yellow teeth. 'Okay, busher,' he says, 'how many do you think you'll hit from there?'

"I got three hits that day and Burleigh said, 'Say, you're not a bad hitter, but watch out for Charlie Root tomorrow.' I told him, 'I'm not worrying because we'll have Dizzy Dean going for us.'

"On my first time up, Root aimed one right at this ear. Down I went. I got up and he put me down again. When I got back to the bench I said, 'Diz, I can't knock in many runs for you lying flat on my back.' Dizzy got the message.

"In the bottom half Gabby Hartnett led off for the Cubs. Wham! The first pitch was right there. Well, you know Gabby. You coulda fried eggs on that red neck of his. 'What the hell's going on here?' he said, and Diz says, 'Just give your friend Root the message, huh?'

"So the next day we got Guy Bush."

Guy Bush, called the Mississippi Mudcat, ruled as chieftain of the headhunters for 17 years. Frank Frisch, Medwick's teammate and manager on the Cardinals, took it for granted that he'd be in the dirt twice on every turn against Bush.

"Hell," Medwick said, "the Cardinals had a flat rule for the first pitch against Chicago or Pittsburgh. Stick it in his ear or it's a $100 fine."

It challenges belief that in this jungle warfare a man like Medwick could bat .324 over 17 years and even call his shots, employing the bat as a precision instrument to pull a drive down the line in left, slice one to right or line one straight up the middle. "I hate all hitters," Early Wynn once said, "and most of all those that hit back through the box. They're not only taking the bread and butter out of my mouth, they're trying to cut the legs from under me."

Medwick laughed.

"When Warren Spahn came up he was knock-kneed," he said. "Then he had an operation and came out of it bowlegged. 'You crumbum,' I told him, 'if you'd had the operation earlier I'd have 10 more hits on my record.'"

# MAN HERE HATES TO WORK OVERTIME

*Philadelphia*

**T**HE Phillies are running second in the National League East, and while this may not be quite so hard to credit as the performance of the San Diego Padres, it is not the sort of thing that happens every spring. For the benefit of clients who have been living in a cave, it should be mentioned that the Padres, who consolidated their position as the worst team in baseball by losing 309 games in their first three years, have won oftener this season than the Giants, Braves, Cardinals, Cubs, Yankees, Red Sox, Angels, Royals, Rangers or Brewers, and just as often as the Pirates, Orioles or Reds. The big story in this town, though, is the Phillies, and one of the biggest things about them is a young stranger named Greg Luzinski, who hates late hours.

Let the business day run past the prescribed nine innings, and Luzinski takes it upon himself to sweep out, roll down the shutters and lock up.

One day the Pirates scored twice in the top of the ninth and then brought Dave Giusti in to protect a 4-3 lead. Luzinski tied the score with a home run, tripled with two out in the 11th and scored the winning run.

Three days later in San Francisco the score was 4-4 going into the 10th. Luzinski started a two-run rally with a leadoff double. The Giants came back to win that game, 8-6, so the next day, with the score 6-6, Greg homered in the ninth for the winning run. In a 12-inning game with San Diego last week, he came up with two on and two out and broke it up with a single.

He doesn't always insist on playing the curtain scene. When the Phils won a double-header from San Diego April 30, he hit all day, getting five singles and a double. Another time a two-run homer in the eighth stretched Philadelphia's lead over the Cardinals to 6-2, and there was still another two-run shot in the eighth that helped bury the Giants, 8-3.

Is it a delayed-action fuse in his psyche that accounts for those tardy explosions?

"I just hate to work overtime," he said, "I like supper on the table at 6 o'clock."

"And once he starts eating," said his blond wife, "he wants no distractions."

They seem a rather solemn pair, though Luzinski is capable of an occasional deadpanned gag. He was a first baseman until this spring, when the Phillies shifted him to left field. After the opening exhibition, his first day in the outfield in Florida, he was summoned to the office of Frank Lucchesi, the manager. He shaped up wearing a hard hat and carrying a laundry basket.

Luzinski played fullback in high school in Niles, Ill., and he is fast for his size (6 feet 1 inch, 233 pounds). Bombarded with offers of football scholarships, he signed a letter of intent with Kansas, but turned pro instead when the Phillies made him their first choice in the 1968 draft of free agents.

"I don't think it was the money," he said. "I didn't get all that much. I think I got the smallest bonus the Phillies ever gave their No. 1 draft choice. It was just that . . ."

"He just wanted to play ball," his bride said.

They were high school sweethearts, but didn't marry until Greg had served his rookie season in Huron, S.D., and another season in Raleigh-Durham, N.C. They had a season together in Reading, Pa., then moved out of the bus leagues to Eugene, Ore., for 1971.

"I hated Eugene," he said. "All that rain, and it never got hot the way I like it. And it was still a bus league because we'd take the bus four hours to play in Tacoma, or two hours to play in Portland, and if we were playing someplace else we'd still bus to Portland to catch the plane. I didn't like the Carolina League either, playing in Raleigh one day and an hour away in Durham next."

"Did you ever regret going into baseball?"

"I was never that unhappy."

He was always happy at bat—.325 in Reading with 120 runs batted in and 34 home runs, .312 in Eugene with 112 and 36. Though he's still only 21, he isn't eligible for the rookie-of-the-year honor because he had 100 times at bat with the Phillies last September.

"In 1970 they brought me up to pinch-hit a few times and I was scared," he said. "When I came up last September, I didn't expect to play. Then, when Frank told me I was the first baseman for the rest of the season, I thought, well, if I was going to play a month, I'd try to show what I could do. I hit .300."

He's still a .300 hitter, with right-handed power that has produced six home runs.

"If it's Tom Seaver or Bob Gibson pitching, I don't worry about it," he said. "I just try to learn. Like the other night, with Claude Osteen going for the Dodgers. I got a single and double. Then, in the eighth inning, we were losing, 3-1, and I came up with a man on and he struck me out. He'd been pitching me outside all night, but this time he jammed me. There was no way I could of been looking for the inside pitch, but the next time I'll be looking."

# THE BUCK PASSES

$\mathbb{A}$RGUING Curt Flood's suit before the Supreme Court, former Justice Arthur J. Goldberg reviewed the long and seamy history of buck-passing between the Court and Congress, both of whom have stalled for half a century over baseball's privileged position with regard to antitrust law. Borrowing from Harry S. Truman, he told the justices: "The buck stops here."

He was dreaming. The 5-3 vote for the status quo was the most unappetizing cop-out yet. Once again the Court declined to consider either the legal and moral complexion of the reserve system or the merits of Flood's case against that system. Even though the majority opinion delivered by Justice Harry A. Blackmun conceded that baseball's exemption from antitrust regulation was an "aberration" and an "anomaly," the Court once again backed off and invited Congress to correct the situation. The views of the several justices deserve to be set apart and examined individually.

¶Justice Blackmun cited the "positive inaction" of Congress as justification for the Court's refusal to act. In other words, if Congress wanted antitrust law to apply to baseball, Congress would have passed a bill to that effect.

¶Justice William O. Douglas, dissenting, said it was high time to correct an error which he and his fellow justices had compounded in the so-called Toolson case 19 years ago when they took just the attitude Blackmun was expressing now. He said baseball should be subject to antitrust law. In effect he asked how anybody could tell what Congress wanted when Congress had never acted to regulate baseball or to exempt it from regulation.

¶Chief Justice Warren E. Burger, voting with the majority, said the

Court probably booted one in the Toolson case but it was such an old error that Congress, not the Court, should correct the Court's mistake. He agreed that Congressional inaction was no basis for a decision but said dumping it back into the lap of Congress was the "least undesirable course now."

Justice Blackmun suspected that there might be inconsistency or illogic in the opinion he wrote, but he found it old, familiar, comforting inconsistency and illogic. You could even call it ripe, yet it did not offend the nostrils of Bowie Kuhn. The commissioner found the decision "constructive." Now, he said, baseball could reshape the reserve system through "renewed collective bargaining."

"I am confident," he said, "that the players and the clubs . . . will both take a most responsible view of their respective obligations to the public and to the game."

Unhappily, the past performance charts do little to support the commissioner's confidence in this respect. In the spring of 1970, before formal discussion of the reserve system was suspended for the duration of the Flood case, the players' representatives pointed out to the owners that the contract that bound a player for life only bound his employer to give him 30 days' severance pay if he was fired. How about a contract that would bind the player for some period shorter than life?

The owners said no, that would never do, but they wanted to be fair. Let the existing arrangement stand for 1970 and 1971, they suggested, and starting with 1972 they would make it 45 days' severance pay.

This reflected the clubs' view of their obligations, the responsible view Bowie Kuhn foresees in renewed collective bargaining. "Renewed?" says Marvin Miller, executive director of the Players' Association. "It has never begun."

The Court's cop-out is a disappointment for several reasons that have nothing to do with Curt Flood's bid for $3-million in damages. He was a grand little centerfielder, he is an accomplished portrait painter and at last report he was getting by as a sports broadcaster in Majorca, but even so he may not be entitled to $3-million.

It is a disappointment because the highest Court in the land is still averting its gaze from a system in American business that gives the employer outright ownership of his employes.

It is a disappointment because none of the nine justices except William Douglas will admit that the Supreme Court has been in error.

Eight of them duck responsibility and say that if there is an error, Congress should rectify it. But it was not Congress that exempted baseball from antitrust regulation; nothing in the Sherman or Clayton Act says "except professional baseball."

It is a disappointment because this Court appears to set greater store by property rights than by human rights.

# THE COMPANY WAY

W HATEVER gains are achieved, or damage done, in the current
contract dispute between the baseball players and the men who own
them, there has already been at least one result. Any misconceptions
about the role of the commissioner that may have lingered in the minds
of fans have been eliminated. On two or three occasions since the hag-
gling began, Bowie Kuhn has abandoned the pretense of neutrality and
has issued press releases presenting the owners' side to the public. No
longer can there be any illusion that the commissioner's office is a court
of last appeal or its occupant an impartial magistrate or a house dick
riding herd on the bosses to protect the players from exploitation.
From here out everyone must accept Kuhn for what he has been ever
since he was hired—his employers' mouthpiece, a front man, a figure-
head.

During the owners' December convention in Honolulu, Kuhn called
a press conference to publicize modifications the bosses had offered to
make in the reserve system that gives them ownership of their employes. Although he was aware that the players already had rejected
the offer as inadequate, he called it a "spectacular breakthrough,"
"historic."

Marvin Miller, executive director of the Players' Association, was in
the Bahamas at the time and was given 10 minutes' notice of Kuhn's
announcement. When Miller accused Kuhn of violating an agreement
not to argue the dispute in the press, Kuhn replied that the league
presidents, Chub Feeney and Joe Cronin, and John Gaherin, the
owners' representative in labor talks, had assured him there was no
such agreement. He did not say in so many words that Miller and Dick
Moss, the players' counsel, and Tom Seaver and Joe Torre were lying
when they said there was an agreement.

73

More recently, Kuhn took it upon himself to issue another statement accusing Miller of trying to mislead the players, the public and the owners. This time he conceded out loud that he was on the owners' side.

Not that the players needed to hear this admission from him. In 1968, when the owners replaced William D. Eckert with their own lawyer, not one living soul confused the new commissioner with the first commissioner, Kenesaw Mountain Landis. From that day forward, everybody realized, the game would be played the company way. That is why the players fought for and won impartial arbitration of grievances, bypassing the commissioner.

The office of commissioner was created, and Judge Landis lured from the Federal bench to fill it, in order to restore public confidence in baseball after the crooked World Series of 1919. Fifteen of the 16 frightened owners pledged themselves to acknowledge the commissioner's supreme authority without question or complaint. (Only Phil Ball, owner of the St. Louis Browns, refused and fought Landis as long as Ball lived.)

Landis was a tyrant, and the player's best friend. He told the men who paid his salary how they must behave and he threw the book at any who tried to cheat. When he decided a player had been kept down on the farm too long or otherwise treated unfairly, he declared him a free agent entitled to sell his services to the highest bidder. In a single ruling he would free as many as 100 farmhands of the Detroit Tigers or St. Louis Cardinals. Players felt no need of a union or a lawyer or agent because the commissioner's door was always open and they were confident he would give them a square shake.

Happy Chandler, who succeeded Landis, posed as the player's friend, too, but he was a posturing politician who sang in public without due process. Once he was called upon to adjudicate a quarrel between a club owner and a man in uniform. He fearlessly threw the man in uniform out of baseball for a year.

Happy left office for reasons of health; that is, the owners got sick of him and moved up Ford Frick from the presidency of the National League. Ford didn't regard the owners as rascals who had to be watched. As he saw it, they were responsible men with the right to make their own rules and it was his job to enforce the rules. He was capable and honest, and farsighted by comparison with his employers, but there were times when a firmer hand at the top would have benefited baseball.

Spike Eckert, the fourth commissioner, was an invisible presence who barely kept the swivel chair warm. The owners played two dirty tricks on him, in 1965 when they hired him and in 1968 when they fired him.

By this time the owners had a fairly clear idea of what they wanted in a commissioner and were dead sure what they didn't want. What they didn't want most was impartiality, so they chose the lawyer who had acted for them in such matters as the sack of Milwaukee.

They have not been disappointed. There has never been a commissioner who stood more erect, wore better clothes or kept his shoes more meticulously polished than Bowie Kuhn.

# THE SLAVE TRADE

W HEN the Supreme Court turned back Curt Flood's break for freedom, Bowie Kuhn welcomed the decision as "constructive." Now, he
said, baseball could reshape the reserve system for itself through "renewed collective bargaining." "I am confident," he said, "that the
players and the clubs will both take a most responsible view of their
respective obligations to the public and the game."

Now that another round of collective bargaining has been concluded,
one wonders whether the commissioner's confidence remains un-
shaken. Those obligations to the public et cetera have been discharged
by forgetting them for three years. Through the negotiations, the
owners' position on the reserve clause was firm: "Don't mention it before 1976 at the earliest."

Still, the players did gain important ground in the agreement they
have just ratified, and anyway, the chances are the struggle over the
reserve system is one they couldn't win at the negotiating table or even
through a successful strike. Any concessions the owners were forced
to make on paper would probably be nullified by so-called "gentlemen's agreements."

The "gentlemen's agreement," which does not require that par-
ticipants be gentlemen, has been employed by the owners for approximately a century to circumvent their own rules. If, through changes
stuffed down the bosses' throats, a player became free to sell his services to the highest bidder, the chances are there wouldn't be any
bidders.

Wouldn't that be illegal? If a player like Johnny Bench went shop-
ping and couldn't get a single offer from anybody except the Cincinnati
Reds, wouldn't that be a provable violation of the antitrust laws? It
would indeed, but the Supreme Court has ruled that the business of
baseball, unlike other sports and other businesses, is exempt from the
antitrust laws.

There are two possible ways to effect meaningful changes in the system that binds a player throughout his professional life to an employer who may trade him, sell him or discard him like a used car. It could be done through negotiation if the baseball hierarchy were made up of men who would come forward in good faith and work on the problem. To say this could never happen is like saying water can never run uphill.

The other avenue of reform is Congressional action, either to bring baseball within the scope of antitrust law or to deal directly with the reserve system. In the Flood decision, as in a number of cases earlier, the Supreme Court invited Congress to take such action, but up to now the boys on Capitol Hill haven't twitched.

Apparently they fear that if they required baseball to conform to the law, their constituents would regard this as an attack on motherhood, a denunciation of apple pie, a desecration of the flag. It is difficult to believe that American voters favor slavery that ardently, but Congressmen think they do.

So we have owners who will not change their ways even under duress, we have courts that refuse to put a stop to the slave trade and a Congress obviously unwilling to intervene. There is no prospect whatever of baseball players finding a truly competitive market for their services, such as professional basketball and hockey players have with rival leagues. What is left?

Nothing is left except the prospect of improving the players' lot within the system. The new agreement does this. As Marvin Miller, the players' leader, pointed out, there are two great evils in the reserve system: the concept of the player as property and the fact that the employer has always been in a position to dictate terms.

"Salary negotiations" is a euphemism that appears frequently in the press, but as Sandy Koufax observed wryly a few years ago when he and Don Drysdale were holding out on the Los Angeles Dodgers, there is no such thing as negotiating. In the end, the employer sets the figure and the player accepts it or begins a new life driving a truck.

Never again need this be true. Now the player can submit his salary argument to impartial arbitration, binding upon both sides. If the arbitrator, using valid criteria, decides Dick Allen isn't worth $675,000 over three years, Allen doesn't get it. If he decides Mike Kekich is worth $75,000 to the Yankees, Mike does get it. At long last, labor relations in baseball advance into the Pleistocene period.

# THE FORDHAM FLASH

D̲RIVING home from the Polo Grounds, where he was a broadcaster covering the New York Giants, Frank Frisch was weaving through the East Bronx on what he hoped was a shortcut to New Rochelle. He got too close to the curb and the car brushed a fat lady. She was Puerto Rican and excitable, with the pitch of a steam calliope, and her caterwauling drowned out the screech of brakes. She was hitting C over high C and drawing a crowd when she broke off abruptly, peering at the face behind the wheel.

"You Fronkie Freesch?" she asked.

The Dutchman admitted it, but she wasn't altogether convinced.

"Say base on balls," she said.

"Oh," Frank wailed in his reedy soprano, "those base on balls!" The lady wanted to kiss him.

Now that reedy soprano is still. Six weeks after an auto crash, Frank Frisch died yesterday. Never at his peak as a second baseman destined for the Hall of Fame—not even when he was the player-manager leading Dizzy and Paul Dean, Pepper Martin, Joe Medwick, Leo Durocher and the rest of the St. Louis Gas House Gang to the championship of the world—not even then did the old Fordham Flash have so many people rooting so hard for him.

If Frisch wasn't the best second baseman that ever lived, then Eddie Collins or Rogers Hornsby was. A swift and venomous halfback at Fordham who was captain of the football, baseball and basketball teams, Frank had the speed to lead the National League base stealers three different years and the range to set league records for total assists and total chances accepted that still stand after 45 years. He had sure hands and a powerful arm. He batted .316 over 19 years and could hit home runs from either side of the plate, though he seemed to generate the greatest power as a left-hander.

At least, he was swinging from the first base side when he connected for the longest home run ever hit. This happened in the last game of a St. Louis homestand in 1931. Ray Benge of the Phillies had the Cardinals shut out, 1-0, in the bottom of the ninth. The Cardinals were going to win the pennant easily that year but they didn't know it at the time. What they did know was that to lose to the Phillies, 1-0, was a crime against nature.

George Watkins, third man in the batting order, hit a screamer over the one-story pavilion in right, tying the score. Frisch, batting fourth, lifted a fly just inside the foul line. The ball was maybe a half-inch higher than the pavilion when it ticked the edge of the roof 310 feet from the plate, took a feeble little hop, seemed to scrabble for a finger-hold and then drag itself over. Cardinals win, 2-1.

An hour later the players were aboard a train for Boston, then the longest jump in baseball. Their waking hours for the better part of two days would find them at five-cent fantan or replaying the ball game just completed. The Flash replayed the game, hitting that home run over and over again with every click of the wheels all 1,208 miles from Bremen Avenue in St. Louis to Back Bay Station.

Frisch could do everything on the field, and most of all he could compete, he could beat you. The Cardinals and Philadelphia Athletics split the first two games of the 1931 World Series in St. Louis, had a day off for travel, and the next day it rained. When Frisch stepped out of bed on the morning of the third game he fell flat on his face. He dragged himself to the phone and called Dr. Harrison Weaver, the club osteopath, to tape up his back, rendered useless by lumbago.

When your back goes, you just don't operate. That Series went seven games and Frisch played every inning. He made seven hits, stole a base, handled 42 chances in the field and took part in five double plays without an error.

Later when he was a manager, this same fiery combativeness brought countless clashes with his friends the umpires. Yet even while he was tearing a passion to tatters, laughter was never far away. He was managing the Pirates and doubling as coach at first base one day in Philadelphia when a Pittsburgh runner was called out after beating the play by half a step. At the instant the judicial thumb jerked up, Frisch pulled a slapstick swoon. Apparently lifeless, he lay supine while the umpire nudged him with a toe, muttering threats of vengeance, and spectators howled with joy.

Another day when he was managing the Cubs he was genuinely furious with an umpire who tossed him out of a game in the Polo Grounds, where he had broken in as a kid from Fordham 30 years earlier. Blind with anger as he trudged toward the clubhouse in center field, he jerked open a door, stepped through, and found himself locked out on Eighth Avenue.

For a moment he kicked on the door in rage. Then two or three kids came at him for his autograph and as he fended them off he saw the ludicrous quality of the scene—a man in uniform and spiked shoes throwing a tantrum under the elevated tracks of the subway. His anger dissolved in laughter, the laughter his friends will not hear again.

# STRAWBERRIES IN THE WINTERTIME

W HEN Willie Mays was the biggest thing to hit New York since the Great Snow of '47, Charley Einstein ghosted a book for him, one of those slightly autobiographical quickies that publishers are forever throwing onto the market in the hope of capturing the first fine careless rapture of discovery. A day or so after the job was finished, Einstein telephoned his collaborator.

"Hello, Willie? This is Charley."

"Who?"

"Charley. Charley Einstein."

"Charley who?"

"Charley Einstein. The fellow who did the book with you."

"What book?" Willie asked.

The best stickball player in Harlem was like that in those days. He knew people, not names. He was aware of things outside of baseball, like girls and money and clothes and cars, but all that was part of a world he only visited. Baseball was where he lived.

"We got to take care of this kid," said Garry Schumacher of the Giants. "We got to make sure he gets in no trouble because this is the guy—well, I'm not saying he's gonna win pennants by himself, but he's the guy who'll have us all eating strawberries in the wintertime."

Willie was batting .477 for Minneapolis, the Giants' farm in the American Association, when he was called to New York the first time. He was 18 days past his 20th birthday, and scared. In his first 21 turns against big league pitching, he made one hit, which is about the way he was hitting this year prior to his second coming.

Not since Abner Doubleday converted a cow pasture to unnatural uses has baseball witnessed anything like the deal that brings Willie back to the scenes of his youth. It isn't his age alone that makes the case unusual, for others have changed uniforms in the sere, the yellow leaf. Grover Cleveland Alexander was 42 the last time the Cardinals suspended him for getting drunk, yet a year later the Phillies took him in a four-player trade. John Picus Quinn confessed to 47 when he started a two-year hitch with Brooklyn, and Cincinnati took him on after that. As for Satchel Paige, the charitable records make him 42 in his rookie year with Cleveland, 59 in his last time around with Kansas City.

However, no significant investment was involved in those cases. To get title to Willie's 41-year-old torso, the Mets are lifting Horace Stoneham's mortgage and sending the Giants a pitcher who spent all last season on the varsity—allowing two hits in five scoreless innings against San Francisco on one occasion—and assuming Willie's $165,000 salary.

Folk heroes come high, too high for any but the pure of heart.

About a year ago a man made headlines by paying $5,000 for one bottle of Chateau Lafitte Rothschild. There are some pleasures in life whose value can't easily be expressed in monetary terms. For a considerable body of baseball fans in New York, watching Willie Mays play is one of those pleasures. And if the Mets' fans haven't earned such a privilege, no group has.

Willie's time in the Polo Grounds was the golden age of center fielders in New York. Willie and Mickey Mantle arrived in the same season, which was Joe DiMaggio's last. Across the river in Brooklyn Duke Snider was at his peak. Never before did one city enjoy such wealth at one position, and it can never happen again.

Snider, Mantle and Mays—you could get a fat lip in any saloon by starting an argument as to which was best. One point was beyond argument, though: Willie was by all odds the most exciting.

As Roger Kahn phrased it: "He was the ultimate combination of the professional full of talent and the amateur, a word that traces to the Latin 'amator,' lover, and suggests one who brings a passion to what he does."

"How do you feel being the only one left?" Kahn asked Mays a couple of years ago after Snider and Mantle had departed.

"Proud," Willie said. "Proud that I'm still playing."

And now? "I'm with a club that really wants me," Willie said yesterday. "Seems like they're looking for my future more than I'm looking for it. The arrangement is, I'll play as long as I want and after that I'll either be in public relations or coaching, or whatever I want and the Mets think I'll be best."

Chances are Willie is the first player who ever sat in on trade talks that involved him.

"Is 'at the first time it happened?" his voice rose two octaves the way it used to do when he was an excited rookie. "There was just the three of us there, Mr. Stoneham and me and—and, the boss of the Mets."

"Don Grant," he was prompted. He'll remember names more easily when he's been around longer.

# THE
# INCOMPLEAT
# ANGLER

*If some enterprising head-shrinker ever gets around to studying the behavior patterns of sport fishermen, he will find that the three most powerful forces motivating the species are the instinct of self-preservation, the reproductive urge, and the compulsion to try the other side of the lake, or river, or planet. To an angler living beside a New England trout stream, it is a crime against nature to drop a fly on any water closer than Montana.*

# BIG SKY COUNTRY

*Greenough, Mont.*

THE winter was almost snowless on Montana's western slopes and, with hardly any spring runoff to keep them green, the hills are already beige, except where mantled by the dark, dark green of ponderosa pine. In this premature summer, Skipper Lofting said, the salmon fly hatch had already come and gone. The Clearwater was finished for the year and the Blackfoot was lower than he had seen it at this season in 40 summers. Nevertheless, the Lofting Expeditionary Force had assembled two men strong and orders had been issued for a piscicidal offensive against the rainbow, brown and cutthroat trout inhabiting the lovely waters east of Missoula. With only a few days available, there could be no turning back.

Surefooted as a burro, Skipper led the way across the Clearwater at the Schoolhouse Ford. This is a crossing that would daunt the Flying Wallendas and to attempt it on legs accustomed to nothing more strenuous than riding the elevator to the Yankee Stadium pressbox is asking for a bath. Somehow, though, the passage was negotiated, wheezing ascent was made to the railroad embankment and the party went stumbling over the uneven ties past the point where the Clearwater joins the Blackfoot and on down that stream to the log jam.

The log jam isn't there anymore and hasn't been since high water took it out three or four springs ago. It remains a kind of landmark for anglers because a mother bear once treed a fisherman there and he spent hours aloft before she decided he meant no harm to her cub.

"As you remember," Skipper said, "this bank fishes just about all the way up to the pinnacle rock. I'll go down a mile or so and probably catch up to you about lunch-time."

As soon as he was out of sight his follower sat down thinking about Sugar Ray Robinson and the late Lew Burston. When Sugar Ray was middleweight champion of the world he had a howling holiday in Paris, then went to England and lost his title to Randy Turpin. Lew, who had lived in Paris for years, was not surprised. "After a vacation like that," he said, "a fighter trains and thinks he's in shape, but after three or four rounds he's got Montmartre in his legs."

At length a Humpy was set afloat on the riffles. Fished dry, the Humpy is just about as reliable a fly for these waters as anybody has tied since Walton. It is a bristly tuft of deer hair that looks something like a cocklebur with a red belly. To human eyes, that is; to a trout it looks like ambrosia.

It turned out that the Blackfoot trout weren't having ambrosia that morning. Now and then a fish took a perfunctory slap at the lure, but it was like a horse's tail brushing away flies. Naturally, each little rise triggered instant reaction at the butt end of the rod. Yanked violently aloft, the fly would (a) hang high in a tree or (b) break the hook off against a rock or (c) do loops and rolls in the breeze until line and leader were tied in knots that no sailor ever fashioned.

It set a guy wondering: Did Izaak Walton never find a willow tree with his backcast? Did the wind never fashion a running bowline in his leader? Did he never step on a rolling stone and fill his waders? Of all the valued instruction in *The Compleat Angler,* is there one word of advice on how to remove a barbed hook from the seat of the pants? How compleat was that old crock, anyhow?

When Skipper showed up for lunch, a party of strangers with spinning tackle was working the far bank, heaving worms or other comestibles into midstream. Skipper bared his teeth. He is a companionable man who likes almost everybody, provided almost everybody stays away from his river when he is fishing.

He had half a dozen trout in his creel, two or three one-pounders and the others breakfast-size. He said he had seen enough fish to make him think the river was almost ready to come to a boil. He had been kept busy releasing little ones. The fact that he had fish and his companion didn't surprised nobody. There are several reasons why Skipper is a better fisherman than some. One is that he keeps his fly on the water, where the chances of attracting trout are better than in trees.

The pair worked upstream together after lunch, walking around each other to alternate in the pool ahead. In front or in the rear, Skipper raised fish. His companion hooked and released two little ones. Then he saw a promising rise.

The way it says in the book, he floated a fly over the spot and the way the book says, the trout rose. The way it never says, the strike was missed. The fish was covered again, prayerfully. He took. He was on. He jumped six times by honest count. He wasn't a big fish, maybe a pound and a quarter, but the fast water gave him added weight, and he was beautiful.

It was enough for the first day, which was meant for physical culture, anyhow. Limping back to the car with gravel in his wading shoes, a guy remembered a comment offered years earlier by a young lady amused by his heavy breathing during a stroll on the beach.

"With old sports *writers*," she had said, "the legs go first, too, eh?"


Soon after the start of the second day's offensive on the Blackfoot River, a rainbow trout counterattacked. This was in an area that Skipper Lofting calls the Vatican because there used to be a cabin nearby occupied by a cheerful little fat man named John Pope and known, inevitably, as Pope John.

Tumbling down the western slope of the Continental Divide, the Blackfoot rushes through a chute at the foot of Cougar Cliff just above the Vatican, flattens out in a deep, swift run studded with rocks, then takes another dive among great boulders. Skipper had left his companion at the tail of this last stretch while he went up to work the chute. They would meet in neutral water in between.

The fish that opened hostilities was young and green in judgment. He may have mistaken the floating tuft of deer hair for something to eat, or he may have been driven by a death wish. Anyhow, he got a faceful of barbed steel. At this point his captor made a discovery: the landing net had been left in the car. Ah, well, "the sleight is to land him," Mr. Walton said, and if the fisherman had to get down in the fish's element and fight it out hand to fin, the contest would be that much fairer.

Tiring soon, the young trout was eased in until the fly stuck in his jaw could be taken between the fingers and the hook disengaged. He went away mad. This process was repeated seven times on the way up into the quieter water. Some were lovely creatures, bright and fat and sassy, and each went home with a cracked lip no worse than a bad cold.

At one point the angler climbed a tangle of driftwood on the bank about 15 feet above the water. Looking down into the pale green depths, he saw a fish rise straight from the bottom, inspect the fly with interest and dive. On the next float, the trout did the same thing. On the third, he decided to try a snack. He went slashing and swearing around in the rapids where he couldn't have been touched with a 10-foot pole. The angler did a giant slalom to the water's edge to turn him loose.

Skipper came down out of the chute frowning. He had spent the morning fighting off small trout, he said, but this was big-fish water and he had seen no big ones.

"I've caught eight fish," his disciple reported. "I lost two that were hooked and missed a hundred strikes. There's one been feeding just up there. Ooops!"

"That's a nice size for breakfast," Skipper said as the trout made like Dick Fosbury. "Let's keep him." For the first time that day, piscicide was committed.

Minutes later another rainbow was doing cartwheels in the rapids. "He looks old enough to smoke," Skipper said. "I'll net him for you." This was a full-figured beauty. A couple of days hanging head down in the little smokehouse Skipper's son Hugh had built on the E Bar L Ranch would convert this fellow into canapes worthy of the very best whiskey.

In the last pool below the chute lay a trout with a chip on his shoulder. Rising for the fly, he kept right on coming in a headlong leap at the angler, who reared back trying frantically to gather his slack line. Again the creature sprang, creating still more slack. With utter disdain he spat out the hook. "One more jump," Skipper said, "and he would have been all over you like Joe Frazier."

As Skipper led the way back to the car, a sudden snort made him turn in time to see his companion in arching flight. A toe had caught a protruding root in the streamside trail. A graceful half-turn propelled the diver into the river, face first.

"Your form off the board was superb," Skipper told him later, "but entry into the water left something to be desired." The plunge removed several tracts of skin and one submerged wristwatch is still in the repair shop.

In spite of contusions, bruises and abrasions, enough energy remained for a courtesy call on the local aerie that evening. You climb a tall hill above the Clearwater and as you approach a grove of ponderosa pine near the summit you hear the stridulous complaint of a rusty axle over and over again. This is Ma and Pa Eagle warning their offspring to give nothing but name, rank and serial number.

For donkeys' years a pair of bald eagles, presumably the same couple, has set up housekeeping here each summer, made love, hatched and fed and taught aerodynamics to one or two young. About 50 yards down the hill in the top of a dead tree is the untidy tangle of sticks the couple abandoned a few years ago to move up to the high rent district. This summer there are two fledglings in residence, adolescent loafers as big as Christmas turkeys and still sponging on the folks. While we sat watching, a Western tanager blushed in a pine tree. At length an adult eagle soared into view, head and tail pure white in the sunset light. That one sailed away and the other parent showed up, wheeling and swooping.

As the car returned to the ranch, a black-billed magpie sailed past on black and white wings, its long tail streaming behind. A bobolink in white tie and tails made his way across a meadow. A matronly marmot—they're just woodchucks with a highfalutin name—scampered up a grassy knoll with her children following in single file. They looked like a rope of link sausage.

# THE LADY IS A PRO

*Martha's Vineyard*

HERRING gulls screamed strident curses as the *Katama* slid away from her berth in Oak Bluffs Harbor, and a mother duck paddled by casting nervous glances back at the three half-grown offspring in her wake. The sun was a red ball on a hazy horizon.

The *Katama* is an elderly lady with a rakish air, which is a polite way of saying she's an old bat who had her face lifted and turned pro. Her New York owner left her here in charge of Danny Olivara, commercial fisherman and skipper. Danny and his friend Manny Silva did a job on her.

Manuel Silva is a builder by trade and a striker, or harpoonist, by preference. Five days a week he puts up handsome houses; weekends he goes to sea with Danny, aiming to skewer broadbill swordfish for the market. Last June they fixed a 15-foot boom to the *Katama*'s snout with a railed pulpit out on the end, set up a great brute of a mast with a crosspiece for a tower, nailed a carpenter's ladder to the mast, and rigged a block-and-tackle arrangement so the spotter aloft could steer with ropes.

The *Corsair* or the *Flying Cloud* she isn't, but the *Katama* knows her job. On her maiden voyage Manny put the iron into two swordfish.

This day she carried, in addition to Danny and Manny, two young guys—Duane Johnson and Roger Gibson. Roger took her around Cape Poge and south along the beach of Chappaquiddick, heading for "The Hole" about 40 miles at sea.

Manny fitted a lily iron to the shaft of his harpoon and lashed the ten-foot javelin athwart the pulpit. The detachable lily, a wicked arrowhead of bronze, was attached to 100 fathoms (600 feet) of rope three-eighths of an inch thick. The line lay coiled in a bushel basket on deck with the butt end lashed to a metal beer keg painted neon red. If Manny could sink his barb into a broadbill, he would pay out line as the fish ran, then heave the keg overboard and the *Katama* would pursue the float.

Meanwhile, Danny brought out two fishhooks big enough to gaff a nine-foot shark. He was going to troll for tuna—"and I don't fool around with fish," he said, admiring the monstrous hardware.

He knotted a red bandanna to one hook, cut the handkerchief off leaving a three-inch skirt, and slit the skirt into tatters. That was one lure. With his fishknife he cut the top and bottom off a Budweiser can, flattened the tin and sliced it lengthwise, saving a strip half an inch wide. Forcing this strip onto the second hook, he twisted it corkscrew-fashion.

"Like the man says," he announced, "don't make no difference what it is, if you throw it in the wake they'll grab it."

Considering the way Gussie Busch's Cardinals have been playing baseball this summer, it would be a pleasure to report that his beer can was a smash hit among the tuna. Unfortunately, neither the Anheuser-Busch Minnow nor Manny's Skirted Strumpet drew a fishy glance all day.

Still it was hardly a fair test, for this was an empty ocean. Hour after hour the *Katama* coursed like a bird dog, all eyes sweeping the surface. Once in a while a shout from Danny or Duane, who were riding the mast, sent Manny scuttling out to his pulpit to unship his spear and crouch, tense and watchful. Never a swordfish.

There were several big sharks. Danny said he saw a few tuna breaching. Now and then the boat lay to alongside an ocean sunfish, or mola mola, which looks like a prehistoric mistake. It is a huge, flatsided head without a tail, with a flabbily waving fin at top and bottom.

It is the easiest of targets for a harpoon, but getting an iron through its leathery hide is like shooting an elephant with a .22. A monster was wallowing just below the surface, mottled gray on top, shading to dirty white below, with a mouth as red as a chorus girl's, when Roger spoke: "Look, a pilot fish."

Through the clear water could be seen the skinny length of a remora, or sharksucker, stuck to the sunfish's belly by the suction disk on its head. Contrary to popular belief, the remora is not parasitic, unless the young folk who summer on Martha's Vineyard can be called parasites. Like the kids, sharksuckers are hitch-hikers who ride along and share scraps of food.

At last Danny turned for home. Manny was disconsolate. "We went out four times straight without getting skunked," he said. "Now we're paying for it."

"It's all luck," he said. "A fisherman we know was going to Block Island to raise some hell. Wanted us to come along, but we went fishing. We worked all day and got skunked. He picked up three fish on his way."

A crimson stain leaked from the setting sun as the *Katama* rounded Poge. The breeze had freshened to 12 knots or more. Something wet and red rose glistening on a wave, broke clear of the water in a somersaulting leap. It was one of those inflated rubber rafts kids use in swimming. It must have got loose on Edgartown Beach several miles away; now wind and tide were flinging it headlong toward Chatham on Cape Cod.

Danny steered downwind, Manny reached over the side and snatched the raft aboard. It wasn't a great catch, but Manuel Silva does not come home skunked.

# "AND HERE AND THERE A LUSTY TROUT"

HERB SHULTZ's letter bore a caption, "Humpy Report," which may call for explanation. Herb Shultz, husband of Bolly, is a member of a fishing club whose property includes a small mountain lake that is matted with brook trout. The fish don't run big, but they are agreeably gullible, lovely to look upon, and highly palatable. They are all wild homebreds, for no stream gives access to the lake and it has not been stocked in more than 35 years.

Now, the Humpy is a round-shouldered trout fly with a red belly, dark tail and a fright wig of deer hair, highly esteemed by fish and fishermen of the West, particularly on such streams as the Blackfoot, Clearwater, Clark's Fork, and Big Hole on the far slope of the Montana Rockies. The pattern used to be difficult to find in tackle shops; in those days an angler with a good supply could trade off his surplus for rubies, steam yachts or blondes as his preference dictated. In the last few years, however, Humpies have become available in the East.

Recently, as a reward for thinking pure thoughts and doing good deeds, there came an opportunity to visit the Shultzes in their cottage on the lake. It turned out that they were friends of Leonard M. Wright Jr., heretical author of *Fishing the Dry Fly as a Living Insect*. There was some casual discussion of Wright's theory that a dry fly twitched into lifelike motion is more tempting to trout than one floated in a dead drift.

Rain restricted fishing to about two hours between showers. On the first cast with a Black Gnat, a trout was hooked and lost. He was the only fish interested in that fly. A Royal Coachman, dry, and a little black streamer fished wet got less action. On impulse, a Humpy was offered just to see what Eastern trout would make of a Western bug. Left motionless on the surface it drew passing notice from only a few undersized fish, but to move it was to incite a riot. Without benefit of dressing to help it float, that single fly took five breakfast-sized trout up to 11 inches. At least a dozen or 15 strikes were missed and two or three pygmies were released. That Humpy got gummy, tacky, chewed out of shape, frowzy and disheveled, but even under water it was attacked.

In the interest of scientific research, a few Humpies of assorted sizes were left with Herb Shultz. This is his report:

"On the day you left, the weather finally turned clear toward evening and I went down to try out the Humpy after dinner. Bailed out boat at 8 o'clock. Made first cast at 8:10.

"With a little luck and some help from above, I was able to place four sidearm casts in under the trees where we had watched the big trout feeding the morning before. Each time, as soon as the Humpy dropped on the water, I gave it the old Leonard M. Wright Jr. twitch and awaited developments.

"Second cast drew a nice rise. Which I missed clean, in characteristic form.

"A moment after the fourth cast-and-switch there was a gorgeous great splash and chug. My theory is that the fish decided he would hook himself this time, realizing he would get little assistance from me. In any event, he took that Humpy real hard and started pulling off line while the reel sang merrily, just as it does for Old Doc in the *Outdoor Life* fishing stories.

"I didn't have a net and it was 10 minutes before I felt safe landing him by hand beside the boat. He was a beauty, deep orange rim on his belly, 13 inches long, 6¾ around the belly.

"He weighed in at precisely one pound. The way we found this out, lacking regular fish-weighing equipment, was Bolly's idea. She stood on the bathroom scale, carefully balancing the scale arm. I handed her the trout, and she rebalanced the arm. Then came the hard part—the subtraction—but with the help of paper and pencil we calculated that he weighed one pound exactly.

"After that one, I had about 25 minutes of fishing time left. Keeping on the Humpy (which, like yours, was now slightly frayed and draggle-tailed), I had six more nice hits and landed four fish, a couple of very nice size, though nothing like the first.

"That first one was the nicest trout I've seen taken from the lake in several years. A great tribute to the Humpy."

# LEWIS AND CLARK NEVER HAD IT SO GOOD

*Snoqualmie Falls, Wash.*

ROD KVAMME steered the helicopter past the sheer rock face of Mount Si, sailed over Hancock Lake and eased down toward Lake Moolock, which lies in a cleft in the Cascade Range almost 4,000 feet high. Hovering like a big, noisy dragonfly, the eggbeater settled slowly until the plastic tub slung under its belly was about 15 feet from the lake's surface. Then a trap door opened and water poured from the tub, carrying with it some 4,000 rainbow trout fry the size of fat bobbypins.

The chopper climbed on a steep slant and turned back to the Tokul Creek Hatchery for more fish to plant in other lakes. As the whitecaps created by the downdraft subsided, the new tenants must have headed directly for the shallows, for inside an hour a trout about a foot long was seen in rapacious pursuit of minnows near the shore.

Kvamme is one of the pilots employed by the Weyerhaeuser Company to operate the seven helicopters that the forest products firm uses to fight fires, transport seedling firs for replanting, fertilize new trees and haul personnel from here to there. On this particular day, Kvamme was a double agent; before delivering infant fish to Moolock as the stork delivers babies, he had put a party of fish-killers down on the same lake's marshy shore.

Helping the Washington Department of Game restock hard-to-reach fishing waters is one of many services Weyerhaeuser provides to make goody points with sportsmen, environmentalists and the public in general. In the mountains, a chopper can accomplish in minutes jobs that would take days if the fish had to be packed in overland. This day, for example, four remote lakes would be stocked with about 18,000 fry in the time it took the party at Moolock to fail hideously as anglers.

The party that day was led by Jim DeShazo, fisheries biologist with the Game Department, and Norm Nelson of Weyerhaeuser's public affairs section. Norm is an outdoorsman and former newspaper editor dedicated to the proposition that cutting down trees in a nice way is good for forests. Also in the group were Will Yolen, former world champion kiteflyer, and Jack Murphy, the avocado king of Poway, Calif., who moonlights as sports editor and columnist of the *San Diego Union*.

Routed cruelly from sleep at 6 a.m., the anglers had flown east from Tacoma across upsy-downsy fir forests where the changing scene below always embraced at least three lakes. Now and then they looked down briefly on patches of soiled snow that may have survived several summers, for precious little fell last winter even in the high mountains.

The plan had been to fish either Lake Philippa or Isabella, which anglers seldom visit, but neither offered a clear shoreline where the helicopter could land. Coming into Moolock instead, Jim DeShazo said that a few years ago he had taken trout here up to three pounds, but since then a logging road had approached within hiking distance. As a result, he said, the lake was badly in need of restocking. Of course, he added, it was now about 10 o'clock, maybe the worst time possible to start after rainbow or cutthroat.

The man who travels 3,000 miles to go fishing will only make himself miserable if he demands fish. At Moolock, all the ingredients necessary to a happy life were present—fir forests of rich dark green rising abruptly to craggy peaks against a spotless sky, mountain air that nobody else had breathed recently, just enough breeze to ruffle the preposterously blue water and the company of sinless men. Fish would have been a luxury.

Not that there weren't some fish in residence. Within the first half-hour, Will Yolen brought in a rainbow that must have measured a good seven inches. The trout was caught on hardware, a gaudy spinner flung into the depths by a spinning rod. Will Yolen has no shame, but he did have the grace to release his catch.

The others had spinning tackle, too. They had been told the fish were out of flyrod reach. At least, though, their lures were flies, with a plastic bubble for casting weight. For a long time the trout paid no attention to flies, but at length a pattern was found that roused some interest. It was a hair fly with a cerise body—a Royal Wulff, maybe? Many fish slapped at it and a few were hooked.

It was all pleasant, leisurely, educational and beneficial to the moral fiber. Most spiritually rewarding was the sight of Yolen stripped down to his drawers for an attempt to retrieve a spinner hooked among sunken logs. Entering the icy water in a bellyache crouch, he lost his balance and pitched forward slowly like a ship sinking by the head, went down on all fours and continued the act of obeisance like a Moslem facing Mecca. Not until forehead had touched bottom did his mustache reappear, dripping from both ends.

All this was just for openers, a bit of preliminary conditioning like the hour or two of fishing done the evening before on Hancock Lake as guests of Jerry Emerick, retired postmaster at Snoqualmie Falls. No piscicide had been committed there, either, but Jerry had baked apple and blueberry pies, he had laid on steak and corn on the cob in a style that made one fact abundantly clear: the fishing might improve as this expedition proceeded but the cuisine couldn't.

*Kelso, Wash.*

The waitress in the all-night coffee spot surveyed the customers straddling stools at her counter. A pretty kettle of fishermen they were —Norm Nelson, Will Yolen, and Jack Murphy. They had asked the waitress for coffee and her prayers. She consulted a man down at the end of the counter, who may have been the only resident besides herself abroad at that unearthly hour before sunrise. "Think they can catch some steelhead?"

The local authority answered without looking up: "With a du Pont spinner, maybe, or a net." In piscatorial circles in the Pacific Northwest, "du Pont spinner" is a euphemism for dynamite.

The steelhead is a rainbow trout with wanderlust. Probably two years ago, but maybe as many as five, he quit the freshwater stream where he was hatched and went to sea as a seven-inch smolt. He adventured widely, ate hugely, and now is coming home with nothing but love in view. He has silvery sides, a dark back, the grayish head that gives him his name, and a deep-seated animosity toward people.

Night grew pale while Norm Nelson drove north and east into the forest Weyerhaeuser calls its St. Helens Tree Farm. This is a valid designation today, when forest management regards timber as a renewable resource and replants trees as fast as it cuts them down. Timber is a crop like corn, but people who do not object to cutting corn raise hob about harvesting trees because trees are beautiful and leave an ugly scar when they are removed.

The sun was up when the car drew up to the Toutle River, a tributary of the Cowlitz, which is a tributary of the Columbia. The Toutle is a beautiful river of white rapids and pale green depths. Downstream a little way is Hollywood Gorge, so-called because it was the locale for a scene in a movie called *God's Country and the Woman,* starring George Brent. In the film a logging train was derailed on the canyon's lip and the logs plunged into the foaming rapids far below. Every now and then somebody tries to navigate Hollywood Gorge with a rubber raft or a canoe. It isn't a good idea. One who tried it with an inner tube came to the surface four days later in the Cowlitz.

As the party arrived, two fishermen clambered up the stream's steep bank. "Good morning," one of the newcomers said. "Good afternoon," a fisherman said. He said he had started in pitch dark before 4 a.m. He said there were hordes of fishermen downstream, taking nothing. Just then a boy of about 13 climbed the bank.

"The kid caught one yesterday," the man said, and the pride in his voice told whose son the boy was. "I took him home and gave him a licking and broke his pole."

Dried flotsam caught in trees a good 15 feet above the water showed how far the river had dropped after a snowless winter. Still there was water enough in the noisy torrents and deep, swift pools to accommodate every fish in Fulton Street.

Fishermen were spaced about 50 feet apart casting with spinning tackle or picking their way over a desolation of jagged rocks. "I'm 67 years old," one said. "Had a heart attack six years ago and my legs aren't much account." He gazed mournfully at the terrain ahead. "The boardwalk at Atlantic City it is not," another agreed.

One dreamer was using a streamer on a flyrod. The others drifted plastic imitations of steelhead roe along the bottom. Always in view was an angler with a tight line and a bow in his rod, but always it was a rock he was fighting. The banks of the Toutle are littered with tangled monofilament and broken lures. The bottom must bristle with hardware.

A couple came slowly upstream. She wore a blue bandanna around her head and a look of studied nonchalance on her round face. In each hand he carried a steelhead hooked on a forked stick. "She caught 'em," he said.

"How much would you say the bigger one weighed?" he was asked.

"About nine pounds," he said. It looked closer to five or six. Love isn't blind; it just sees double.

An hour or so later another man came by carrying two slightly larger fish, which he estimated at six pounds. He said that as far as he knew, only he and milady of the blue bandanna had scored that morning. More fish had been moving earlier in the week, he said.

"The Russians and Japs got 'em all," a man with a long-billed cap said, speaking around a pipestem. "Those fish factories they've got off the coast, they take hake, bottom fish, salmon, everything. They're even ruining our crabs."

Norm Nelson showed up with sweet rolls and canned tomato juice. Jack Murphy sank the tins in the river to cool the juice, turned back for a bun, and heard a splash behind him as of a fat man dropped from a height. Twenty feet upstream a reel whined and a man came down the bank with his rod bent in a wriggling arc.

"He was sneaking up on you from behind when I hooked him," he told Murphy.

There was a small waterfall just below the fish, then rocky rapids rushing into a pool where submerged logs offered shelter under a huge boulder. "I want to keep him out of there if I can," the fisherman said. "No, he's going. Son of a ———."

He stumbled on down below the falls, worked the fish close to the bank, got his gaff into a gill and flipped him ashore.

The fish was a silvery torpedo of eight pounds or so. His captor was Louis Parchich of Olympia, Wash. He showed the inch-long spoon that had done the deed. "I'd just broke off my regular rig," he said, "and didn't want to tie up another."

He slung the fish over his shoulder and started upstream. "The fella that built this sidewalk," he said happily, "shoulda been fired."

*Ethel, Wash.*

The Cowlitz River is formed by ice water from the Cowlitz Glacier on Mt. Rainier. It flows southwest to the Oregon line, where it joins the Columbia for the last leg of the journey to the sea. Partly because of the generosity of nature, partly because of Tacoma's demand for hydroelectric power and partly because of the biologists and engineers of the Washington Department of Game, it has become the most productive steelhead river in the world. In 1972, anglers took 46,000 of these seagoing rainbow trout from the Cowlitz and in the record month of December, 1971, the catch was 19,000, which is more than the state's number two river, the Skagit, produces in a year.

The spawning run of most steelhead comes in the late fall, but instinct brings some back to fresh water in the summer. By trapping and breeding these nonconformists, the Game Department has greatly increased the summer runs. This work is done at a hatchery the city of Tacoma built here to compensate for the damage its two power dams did to natural spawning waters upstream.

Having met with minimal success on trout lakes in the Cascade Mountains and total failure on the Toutle River south of here, a small but discouraged band of fishermen set sail on the Cowlitz in two boats. Tom Knight and Roger Bogden of the game department took on Will Yolen and Jack Murphy as passengers armed with spinning rods. Dave Gufler, biologist, and Jim Briscoe, engineer, took care of the other visitor, a flyrod man.

Gufler and Briscoe had casting rods and their lures were little wads of wool yarn in two tones of pink. Steelhead go for this concoction, though nobody knows why. They don't feed actively during the spawning run, but they pick up a variety of bright morsels through instinct or curiosity or plain cussedness. Maybe they mistake the lures for fish eggs or perhaps they just remember how good shrimp tasted out in the ocean.

For whatever reason, a steelhead latched onto Gufler's tuft of yarn soon after sunrise. He came out of the water in twisting frenzy like an Atlantic salmon. Gufler was using light tackle and he fought the fish cautiously. Three times Briscoe tried to get a landing net under him and three times the fish took off for other parts. Finally he came into the boat, maybe eight pounds of silvery rage.

"A buck," Dave said, "the female has a shorter, rounder face."

To unpracticed eyes, the river was a tossing torrent impossible to read, but Gufler and Briscoe knew the location of pools. They would anchor at the head of a pool and let the current roll their lures along the rocky bottom. Their supercargo was retrieving line when he saw a small splash where the streamer fly rode the wavelets.

"Probably a jack salmon," Briscoe said. "They're immature king salmon, all males. The river's full of them."

"Immature?" said Gufler, the biologist. "Let's say precocious. They come back to the river ahead of their age group."

Several casts later, a fish took the fly. As king salmon go, he was a mere princeling, but he raised more commotion than the whole royal family. He was the first of three jacks that attacked the fly and lost. Chances are none weighed more than a pound, but they fought like Willie Pep at the top of his game.

A steelhead took Briscoe's lure, leaping again and again. "Mamma," Gufler said. "The females seem to jump oftener than the bucks."

By now the boat was about four miles below the starting point. Briscoe steered back upstream, where it turned out that Yolen had taken a steelhead. "I never saw a fish take a Hot Shot the way this one did," Knight said. "There wasn't half an inch of the plug showing out of his mouth. He had hooks in both jaws, must've drowned on the first run."

The Hot Shot, a comparatively new lure, is the next best thing to dynamite. It is a plastic minnow that comes in iridescent colors, and the village idiot can fish it. You drop it in the current and let the anchor drag so the boat moves more slowly than the water. The Hot Shot dives, wriggles and cries, "Help! Help! I'm a defenseless little minnow and a steelhead's sure to eat me!"

"Will you let me try that flyrod for a while?" Jim Briscoe asked innocently. He handed over his own casting rod, having surreptitiously tied on a green Hot Shot. Pretty soon the passenger had a steelhead on. The fish leaped six times, honest count. "Mamma mia!" Dave Gufler said. The fish was a lady, but she didn't act like one.

On the next drift the same Hot Shot lured another steelhead to her end. She took the lure purposefully, leaped once or twice, and then the line went slack. "She's off," the angler said, "or swimming this way fast." He cranked frantically, the fish reappeared just off the bow and dived clear under the boat. She went once around the outboard, dived again and surfaced off the bow before Briscoe got the net under her.

"That's characteristic of the summer run," Gufler said. "Swimming upstream like that. Winter-run fish hardly ever do."

This fish had been in from the sea long enough to regain some of her rainbow color. The stripe was clearly defined and the points of her gill covers blushed pink. She was as pretty as the Washington scenery, and in Washington, scenery is a drug on the market.

# FUN ON THE FLATS

*Islamorada, Fla.*

POSTED on the restaurant door is an admonition that the management of New York's Cote Basque has not yet deemed necessary: "Shirts, please," but in spite of that formality the interior decor is casual—plaster walls of a slightly seasick green, formica-covered tables with paper napkins. Ushered to a seat, the guest has a minute to admire a hand-painted picture of roseate spoonbills before Ziggy Stocki, his host, arrives. Ziggy wears a short-sleeved white sports shirt and an air of quiet weariness. He stands leaning against the wall, eyes fixed on a point two feet above the horizon.

"We have some items not on the menu," he says. "We have grouper Senegalese, that's grouper in a brown sauce with almonds, shallots, apples, raisins and curry served with chutney and rice on the side . . ."

This is not a commercial, but the place is The Conch (pronounced Konk) and anybody bent on piscicide in the Florida Keys is advised to fortify himself first with dinner there. It stirs the juices, refreshes the spirit, lifts up the heart and braces a man for whatever indignities the bonefish and permit have in store for him.

Having prepared himself thus in the evening, an angler presented himself the following morning to Jack Brothers at the Islamorada Yacht Basin. Jack Brothers began life in Sheepshead Bay, Long Island, wandered south shortly after World War II and eventually set up as a fishing guide, thus saving himself from a career as an architectural draughtsman. His invulnerable amiability is proof even against the sports who employ him, and his ability to see fish is admired by Ted Williams, whose own eye could count the stitches on Bob Feller's fast ball.

Loading a skiff with Brothers was Arnold Sobel of Chicago, still walking several inches off the ground after setting a world record for light tackle by taking a bonefish of 12 pounds two ounces, on six-pound-test line. These two have fished together every year since Brothers started guiding, and they have shared some big days.

"In the Miami Metro tournament four or five years ago," Sobel said as Jack steered away from the dock, "I took a big bone on a fly. We headed for home right away so the fish wouldn't dry out and lose weight. The first weighmaster checked it out at 12 pounds 12 ounces, an all-time record for the tournament.

"That tall man on the dock when we left just now, that's Bart Foth, easily the best man with a fly rod around here. He was leading the tournament with a bone of 12-6 taken on a fly. From his boat he could see us come in and he saw a crowd gathering so he came in to find out what was going on. 'Hey, Bart,' they were calling, 'come take a look at a real fish.'

"We had to wait an hour for the second weighmaster, and the photographers wanted pictures so we let that fish lie in the sun on the concrete. When it was weighed again it had shrunk to 12 pounds 10 ounces. We won the tournament but lost the record."

It was an almost windless day, and the sea was a medley of colors Winslow Homer never dreamed of—turquoise and chartreuse, royal blue, lime green, beige and mauve. Brothers steered through a crooked cut to the Atlantic side.

"This is Tavernier Creek," Arnold Sobel said, "where pirates hid out in the old days."

"And rumrunners later," Jack said.

He shut off the motor in an area called Rodriquez Flats, baited two spinning rods with shrimp and began to pole through the shallows. This is what sets bone fishing apart from most other kinds of angling. Sneaking up on the spooky critters is like stalking game in the woods. There is the same sense of stealth, suspense building like steam in a pressure cooker until the dark underside of every wavelet looks like a fish to the unpracticed eye. It takes a fish hawk like Jack Brothers to spot the pale puffs of mud stirred up by feeding bones, the tail of a bottom feeder breaking water or the shadowy torpedos cruising over coral.

"Fish ahead," Jack said quietly. "No, see that motion? It's a shark. Swishes the tail like a blonde on Fifth Avenue. There's something at 11 o'clock, Arnold. Try it."

Sobel cast a little white jig, his line tightened for an instant, then came in slack. A barracuda had hit the lure, his wicked teeth severing the leader. Twice more Jack saw fish, twice more Arnold cast and two more barracuda had lures for souvenirs.

The other passengers let fly two or three times with one of the rods Brothers had baited. The guide watched with interest as a shrimp shot straight up or splattered into the water a dozen feet away. Quietly he reached for the other rod and set it at his feet.

They moved on to an area called Newport, off Key Largo, and the hunt began again. Jack stiffened. He stopped poling and pointed. Sobel cast straight ahead, dropping his jig with a tiny *plip* in front of a shadow moving from left to right. Then there were two shadows, three, half a dozen. . . .

The other passenger cast, and a shrimp splotched into the water close to the boat. At that moment Arnold struck. He had a fish on, but still the shadows kept coming—a dozen of them, two dozen. Bones came thronging, trooping, traipsing by. Even to the unschooled eye, it was like Times Square at lunch hour.

"Take this," Jack said. He had cast the other shrimp and now he handed the rod over. In a moment a fish was on. "Don't horse him," Arnold said, still playing his own fish cautiously on the six-pound-test line. The bone that had grabbed the shrimp took off like a striped ape. At length he eased to a halt, and with the first turn of the reel the rod straightened. Sharp coral had cut the line.

"Is there any way to prevent that?" Brothers was asked.

"Just hold the rod tip higher," Jack said, "and try to keep pressure on."

With exquisite care, Sobel brought his fish in. "Ten pounds?" Jack guessed. "Where's that Mickey Mouse scale of yours?" The fish went nine pounds.

Holding it just above the tail, Jack lowered it into the water and applied artificial respiration, moving it gently back and forth. Each time he drew the fish backwards its gill covers spread. When he let it go, the fish moved tentatively at first, then swam strongly away.

"It's years since I've seen a school like that," Arnold said. "Must've been a hundred of 'em."

Hour after hour the search-and-destroy mission proceeded—all search and no destruction. Once the sport sitting amidships managed to get a cast out in front of cruising bones. He could see nothing, but Jack said a fish paused over the bait and went on.

"That tackle you're using belongs to Ted Williams," Jack said. "He checks it out for the manufacturer all winter, and when his ball club goes to training camp he leaves it with me. 'See if you can bust it up,' he tells me, 'and let me know how it works.'"

As the afternoon wore on, visibility diminished. A freshening breeze rumpled the surface and the reflection of clouds—"them big white snow sails," Jack said—made it difficult even for him to see fish before they saw the boat.

"We'll still-fish 25 minutes," Jack said. Thrusting his pole into the mud, he snubbed the boat against it and flung handfuls of shrimp downwind. Arnold Sobel, a purist, shipped his tackle without impatience. After half an hour he said, "Five o'clock, Jack."

"Five minutes more," Jack said.

Sobel grinned. "Yesterday," he said, "the wind was blowing like hell and we decided to quit. I said, 'One more cast,' and took a ten-pound redfish."

"So," it was suggested, "the moral is clear: Always take one more cast or fish five more—ooops!"

The rod tip was a quivering bow. Monofilament peeled off the reel and disappeared as a bonefish raced for the Azores. For 38 minutes by Jack's watch, single combat raged. Muscles barely fit to carry a portable typewriter were aching when the fish came in, worn out but quivering with rage.

"Would you believe 13 pounds?" Jack said. Considering that the American record is 15 the answer had to be no. Still Jack and Arnold sang their hosannas of praise, never once hinting that in still-fishing it is not necessary to stalk fish, it is not necessary to present a lure and a retarded chimpanzee can hold a rod.

Back at Islamorada, Mary Frances Dressing weighed the fish officially—12 pounds, five ounces.

"When you see Williams," Jack said, "tell him you caught it on that Mickey Mouse reel of his and then step back and hear him scream. You don't have to tell him how you caught it."

Two hours later Ziggy lounged over and leaned against the wall. "We have some items not on the menu," he said. "We have Oysters Bienville, that's oysters loosened in the shell, wrapped in crab with capers and baked under a blanket of Parmesan cheese with 12 or 14 seasonings. I'm not sure what-all. I've got three chefs, a Bavarian, a French-Canadian and a Dane, and they like to surprise me."

Next morning Jack, who had another commission, introduced his friend Eddie Wightman. By local terminology Eddie doesn't qualify as a conch because he foolishly got himself born in Miami up on the mainland. However, before he was a year old he mended his ways and moved down to the Keys. Those green gobbets of coral and mangrove have been home ever since, but Eddie keeps informed about the outside world and its burning issues, from Indo-China to the forced busing of schoolchildren.

"Would you like to try for permit first?" Eddie asked. In the estimation of Florida guides, the permit, or great pompano, is Stanley Ketchel with fins. He offers a challenge no man of spirit could resist.

"Let's go," said Eddie's new acquaintance.

In a shallow bay within earshot of trucks howling down U.S. Route 1, Eddie shut off the motor and began poling. He said, "A sport I had here asked how a spooky fish like permit could be so close to the highway. I told him the fish were coming through this passage long before there was a road, or men to travel on it."

He had baited a spinning rod with a crab the size of a silver dollar, thrusting the hook through the very edge of the shell so the crab would stay alive. "Want to be strictly on your own or should I back you up?" he asked.

"By all means back me up." He baited a second rod with a crab.

In a little while he saw permit—a school of four or five—or smelled them, for the breeze was fresh and it didn't seem humanly possible to see beneath the ruffled surface. He pointed. The sport took aim. Caught in a crosswind, the little crab sailed wildly. Eddie plucked up the other rod and fired a low line drive. In a moment he spoke in a hoarse stage whisper.

"A big one's looking at it. No, he passed it up. Must've weighed 40 pounds." The great permit hunt was over.

Eddie started the motor and headed into Florida Bay, the shallow sea between the Florida peninsula proper and the scimitar curve of the Keys. From a cluster of pilings, resentful cormorants took flight.

"Look," Eddie said. "Beautiful!" Softly lustrous in pastel pink, three roseate spoonbills flew across the bow. "They seem to be growing more numerous here," Eddie said with satisfaction.

An osprey sailed by high against the blue. Silhouetted in a treetop was one of the untidy clutters of sticks and seaweed that these fish hawks call home. "You wonder how it stays up there in a wind storm," Eddie said. A merganser flew by, going hell for breakfast. "See if those are white pelicans," Eddie said, handing over binoculars.

Ankle deep on a submerged bar stood a dozen big white waders. The white pelican is a poor mixed-up kid, a saltwater fisherman that breeds in the northwest from Minnesota to the Rockies and vacations in Florida along with tourists from Council Bluffs and ball players in spring training. "They don't dive like our brown pelicans," Eddie said. "Just scoop up fish while swimming."

"There seem to be brown ones on each side," the other said, focussing the glasses. "What are they? Native guides or bodyguards?"

"The brown ones live over there on the mainland," Eddie said. "They were bused over here."

He had been cruising past tiny keys, apparently traveling without a plan, but now he pulled up in shallows that looked no different from 10,000 other spots. Might get anything from redfish to snook here, he said. He rigged the rods with little white bucktail jigs.

It was weird. Even for the dude, every other cast produced a fish. Four snook came in furious. Eddie watched one thrash the sea to froth. "He's fighting for something near and dear to him," he said, "his butt."

The same little lure deceived big redfish, alias channel bass, alias red drum. They were overpowered and released. The sport caught a shovelnose shark, a speckled trout and even a sheepshead wearing the prison stripes that used to be de rigueur on Florida's chain gangs.

Sea and sky were alive. There were great white heron, blue heron, one black-crowned heron and probably some kippered heron. Small flocks of snowy ibis cruised by, their hooked noses red as rum blossoms.

"Want to go sightseeing?" Eddie asked. He turned toward the mainland and pointed the skiff up a milky creek meandering through brush. "This is Taylor River. All this brush with the thick-root construction is the common red mangrove. That tree with the rumply bark is a buttonwood and over there is a very large black mangrove. See that big spiny air plant up there? I'm surprised some tourist hasn't cut it down. Those are orchids starting to grow on that limb. All along these banks there used to be alligator lodges. That was one, that hollow there."

They went stalking redfish in the flats. Nature designed the redfish to shore up an angler's shrinking ego. You must hunt him as bones are hunted, but the redfish is patient. Botch up a cast, and instead of spooking off he'll wait around for a second cast, or a third. With such cooperation, failure isn't easy but it can be accomplished.

At length Eddie allowed himself a small sigh. "I know a redfish hole that will restore your confidence," he said. He was right. Casting blindly into the area he indicated, his passenger became once more a mighty angler before the lord.

"Does this jig look like a live shrimp to the redfish?" he asked.

"Nine out of ten of those interviewed," Eddie said, "reported that they didn't know what the hell it was but it was small and they thought they could whip it.

"You cast all right," he said generously, "especially when you can't see the fish you're going after."

"When I get home," his passenger promised, "I'm going to perfect my spin casting on the lawn."

"Won't do any good," Eddie said, "unless you go fishing some more." They were on the way home.

"How long have you been guiding?" Eddie was asked.

"Professionally, 12 years."

"That's a long time to keep your patience."

"It gets easier," Eddie said, "as I grow older."

That evening Ziggy leaned against the wall. "We have some items not on the menu," he said.

# MONEY GAME

*Canadian, Okla.*

T HE first day was windy and seasonably mild, but the next morning bitter rains lashed the fishermen in the $15,500 All-American Bass Tournament. Then a cold front stormed in with gusts up to 35 miles an hour. Within minutes, Lake Eufaula—a "Gentle Giant," in the oleaginous prose of the Oklahoma Tourism and Recreation Department— was throwing things around like a fishwife inflamed by gin. Swells blotted out shoreline and sky. Eleven of the 65 boats wound up on the beach for the night. Two went to the bottom.

Wes Woosley of Tulsa, 69 years old with a history of heart trouble, was in the water for half an hour before other fishermen picked him up. "Better make for the bank," Wes said. "No," his rescuers told him, "we've got a bigger motor than yours. We'll make it back." They made about 200 yards before they were all in the water.

Supported by his life jacket, Woosley was drifting off by himself in the fading light when he was hauled out again. As they loaded him into an ambulance, he spoke from a cocoon of blankets.

"I'm not sure, Ray, but I'm afraid I may have to scratch out tomorrow."

"I'll scratch you," said Ray Scott, who promotes these happenings, "but I'll keep a place open for you."

It would not be strictly accurate to present Wes Woosley as typical of the footloose legions who travel the tournament trail armed with spinning rod and strawberry-flavored plastic worm, but even those whose enthusiasm doesn't match his are creatures undreamt of in Izaak Walton's philosophy.

They are a strange new breed, somewhat like the professional golfer or rodeo hand in that they put up entry fees and compete for cash

111

prizes, but where the rodeo cowboy may tow a roping horse in a trailer, the bass pro pulls a carpeted fiberglass boat rigged with 150-hp outboard, electric stalking motor, sonic depth-finder, bow steering stick, electric fuel gauge, ammeter, tachometer, speedometer, bilge pump, water-temperature thermometer, light-penetration meter, upholstered swivel seats, electric winches, running lights, and enough lures, lines, rods, reels and "lunker lotion" to supply the state of Maine.

Such a rig runs about $4,000, and the fact that there are more than 125,000 in operation reflects the soaring popularity of the black bass. He deserves his high repute, for among freshwater game fish the bass is Joe Frazier without Joe's cheerful disposition.

Compared with the silver elegance of the Atlantic salmon or the radiance of the rainbow trout, the bass is no beauty. He is thick-lipped and pot-bellied; loop a watch chain across his bay window and he would look like a Thomas Nast caricature of Vested Interests. He is a barroom brawler, truculent, greedy and overbearing, the swaggering bully of lake or stream. Of the two main branches of the family, the smallmouth of our northern waters is considered the more aristocratic but it is his loutish country cousin, the largemouth, that the professional angler seeks because tournaments pay off on total poundage.

Competitions are conducted on great man-made impoundments across the southern half of the United States where the largemouth attains the weight and dimensions of a keg of nails. In 1972 Ray Scott's Bass Anglers Sportsman Society (B.A.S.S.) ran its tournaments on Lake Kissimmee in Florida, Lake Keowee in South Carolina, Lake Ouachita near Hot Springs, Arkansas, Watts Bar in Tennessee, Ross Barnett in Mississippi and Oklahoma's Eufaula.

Gross prize money for each was $15,500 with $3,000 to the winner and payoffs scaling down to $150 for 35th place. Points awarded in these events (35 points for first place, one point for 35th) qualified 24 anglers for the Bass Master Classic in late October. If B.A.S.S. is the sport's big league, the Classic is its World Series. Qualifiers are loaded into a plane and not until they are airborne does Scott open a sealed envelope and announce the name and location of the "mystery lake" where they are to cast for $10,000, winner take all.

Entry fee for a regular tournament is $150. Bob Cobb, editor of the society's bimonthly *Bass Master* magazine, says it takes 205 entries ($30,750) to break even. However, B.A.S.S. now has 92,000 members who pay $10 a year ($920,000), for which they receive six copies of the magazine, access to fishing information by mail, a membership patch to sew onto a windbreaker, and a personal letter from Scott.

Scott used to sell insurance in Montgomery, Alabama. Anybody who has heard him summon up organ tones for the prayer that sends the anglers into combat each morning can appreciate what a persuasive salesman he must have been. He ran his first tournament in June of 1967 and the following winter sold his first life membership in B.A.S.S., which then existed only in his mind.

Today the organization has its own building in Montgomery with a staff of 40, and last October the man who bought that first membership, Don Butler of Tulsa, became the top money winner of the year. Butler won the Classic on J. Percy Priest Reservoir near Nashville, Tennessee, and the $10,000 purse gave him $10,975 for the year.

Obviously, the tournament trail offers no rewards comparable with those Jack Nicklaus takes out of golf. The all-time B.A.S.S. champion is Bill Dance of Memphis, who has won $21,490 in Scott's tournaments over five years. He used to sell furniture but now works for a fishing-tackle company like most of the pros.

Still, in theory a man could make a living just fishing. In the six B.A.S.S. tournaments of 1972, Roland Martin won twice with two seconds, a third and a fourth, for $9,550. If he had won the Classic he would have grossed $19,550 for the year. However, a man who knew the secret of doing that year after year would hear a knock on his door some dark night, and his hooded visitors would be carrying branding irons. Bass fishermen have an insatiable curiosity.

Lake Eufaula, an impoundment of the Canadian River, meanders across 102,000 acres of broken hill country near the Sansbois Mountains. This was home to the confederate general Stand Watie and his Cherokee Mounted Rifles. Belle Starr, the lady outlaw, lies buried near the lakeshore.

Today a motorist driving south from Tulsa passes Henryetta and the rodeo school of Jim Shoulders, greatest of bareback riders. He sees white-faced Herefords grazing, reads billboards advertising prize bulls and quarter-horse studs and Creek Nation pottery. On his radio, a bank offers new depositors Little Miss Red, a talking doll that knows five different cheers for the Oklahoma football team. The newspaper hails Mrs. Mike Farino of Midwest City for sweeping all five divisions of yeast breads at the state fair.

The first day on Eufaula, 129 fishermen brought back 259 bass weighing 491 pounds, 15 ounces. Roland Martin had his limit of ten fish and their 30 pounds, eight ounces, gave him a big lead. Martin is a sunburned towhead of 33 who used to be a professional guide on the Santee-Cooper impoundment in South Carolina. He has fished as many as 300 days a year, which explains why he remained a bachelor until last year when he met a girl from Pauls Valley, Oklahoma, on the tournament circuit. Now he and Mary Ann live in Tulsa where he is employed by a firm that makes an electronic depth-finder. Since his first tournament, he has never been out of the money.

That night a hospitality room in Arrowhead Lodge near the village of Canadian offered the anglers refuge from Oklahoma's antediluvian liquor laws. Long before midnight, truth lay bleeding on the carpet.

"Where'd you fish today, Roland?"

"Right in the town of Eufaula among the houses and boat docks. Nobody else bothered to go in there."

"What did you do, Tom?"

"Went for a boat ride. Fella said he knew where some fish were 30 miles upriver so we went. I woulda got fish if I hadn't a rode."

"So he's fishing the bow and before every cast he turns his back and squirts some kinda lunker lotion on his worm but he won't tell what. He's getting all the fish. You think that don't drive a man nuts in the stern?"

"What's your guess on the Classic?"

"I've heard California and I've heard Florida. Would you believe Lake Havasu in Arizona?"

"I left a call and they didn't wake me. So there I was trying to make it for the first flight and I got a $45 ticket for speeding."

"You think Mann will tell you anything? He justs sits and listens and keeps his mouth shut."

To bass pros, Tom Mann is a name like Arnold Palmer or Johnny Bench. He is a strapping graduate of the Alabama cotton fields, six-foot-two, 39 years old, whose strong, bronzed features give evidence of his Cherokee blood. He's a former game warden from Eufaula, Alabama, now a designer and manufacturer of lures like the Little George, named for Governor George Wallace, and the scented plastic Jelly Worms that come in a variety of flavors. Tireless as a machine, he'll work three rods rigged with different lures—casting, retrieving, switching rods, casting, retrieving, switching, casting, retrieving, again and again and again without cease.

"This is John Powell," Scott said. "When I met him he was a master sergeant in the Air Force with about a year to retirement. In his second tournament I got him a little old 12-foot boat with a 20-horse engine. At the start, the big motors went howling past him left and right throwing up rooster tails, and they swamped John.

"It was shallow, so John just stood holding his motor up out of the wet. He got his boat righted, bailed, moved over a little way and started taking bass out of those shallows one after another. Last year he won two tournaments back to back. He's such a shallow-water man, when he wants coffee he orders half a cup."

Powell grinned sleepily. With his round, weathered face, dimpled chin and ears akimbo, he looks like a character in "Sesame Street."

"Where there's oxygen, feed and cover," he said, "there's fish. Where I grew up back in the mountains we had a few acres of red clay to grow cotton and taters, and fish was our meat. Hawgs and chickens, that was for school books.

"We had a 12-foot johnboat with a cane pole and minnows. No motor, so you didn't ride around looking for structure. We'd just work along with a sculling oar, put a minnow in the bushes and take out bass—always in shallow water."

"Were you always competitive about fishing?" he was asked.

"No, and I won't let my kids compete with each other. First few tournaments I tried, I enjoyed the challenge. Now with all these young fellows in the game, it's makin' an old man of me."

In spite of the wild weather on the second day, 163 bass were weighed. Those who didn't get back had no recorded catch, of course. The boats go out in flights of 20 or so and all get equal time on the water. A tardy return costs the angler five percent of total weight for each minute he is late, and after 15 minutes he goes scoreless.

Tournaments have come in for adverse criticism from conservationists who recoil when they read of three-day catches weighing 1500 pounds. As a result, B.A.S.S. contestants get a one-ounce bonus for every live fish weighed and released. On that stormy second day, 92 percent of the catch came in alive.

"And 100 percent of the fishermen," Bob Cobb said thankfully.

The size limit is 12 inches, and if a fish doesn't measure up under official scrutiny a penalty is incurred. If a man with his limit in the live well should catch an eleventh fish of good size, there's nothing to prevent his substituting it for a smaller fish, except that he hardly ever gets the chance. More often luck breaks the way it did for Bob

Ponds of Jackson, Mississippi, in the Rebel Invitational on Ross Barnett. Emptying his live well on the final day, Ponds laid a bass on the 12-inch mark on his gunwale, grinned and shook his head.

"It sure measures 12 inches," he said, "but I'm not going to take a chance." He turned it loose. His eight remaining fish gave him a three-day total of 44 pounds, two ounces—a winning score until Ricky Green of Arkadelphia, Arkansas, came in with nine fish for a total of 44 pounds, three ounces.

Dawn of the third day on Eufaula brought freezing temperatures but the rains were gone and a warming frend was promised. As Scott drove to the marina to send the boats away, a great flight of geese scrawled a wavering V across the red sky. Judging from the number of aromatic cadavers on the highway, the ratio of skunks to people in Oklahoma must be at least 100 to 1.

Swaddled against the cold, members of the first flight steered out to the start and waited with motors idling until Scott's boat pulled up ahead of them. Standing, he addressed the Almighty through a bullhorn, consigning all hands to His mercy. Then he pointed a flare pistol aloft and fired. A score of engines howled like Comanches. Rooster tails flying, the boats raced away, bucking and plunging.

Twice more Scott invoked divine patronage, fired his pistol and led the pell-mell start. As the third flight roared off, Roland Martin's motor conked out. Within moments a mechanic assigned by the manufacturer arrived and started to work. With visible effort, Martin kept out of the expert's way. He was still leading the tournament but these guys reckon every moment wasted is a lunker lost. Motor trouble on the first day had ruined Tom Mann's chances.

It took perhaps five minutes to get water out of Martin's fuel line. He sped off in pursuit of the others, who had fanned out toward waters of their choice in Gaines Creek or North Canadian, Belle Starr Park or Baptising Creek. All of them had studied topographical maps, scouted sloughs and pockets earlier in the week and had charted underwater structure of brush or trees.

The day warmed rapidly. Around the dock, men lied lazily for practice. Bobby Murray showed up from Hot Springs, Arkansas. Winner of the 1971 Classic and the Arkansas National last May, Murray was safely qualified for this year's jackpot and was passing up the All-American on orders. Seems he'd been off fishing when his first child was born so this week he had stayed around home until Mildred brought in a keeper, a seven-pound boy. Then he had driven over to see how the guys were doing.

In the afternoon, spectactors began arriving. The first fisherman to check in found a gallery of 1000 or more on a hillside overlooking the scales.

Jim Houston, an insurance man from Tahlequah, Oklahoma, delivered a plastic bag holding seven live fish averaging a shade under two pounds. "I lost three hawgs," he said. Stan Sloan of Nashville, the $45-speeding-ticket man, had five bass weighing 11 pounds, 15 ounces. Tom Mann had eight. Calvin Hill, Bartlesville, Oklahoma, won a $1500 boat for the biggest bass, five pounds 11 ounces.

Then here came Martin with his limit, all alive. Spectators whooped, watching the scale register 20 pounds, seven ounces. Martin's total for the tournament, 62 pounds, 13 ounces, was the year's heaviest.

Driving back to Arrowhead at dusk, Scott stopped to watch a doe emerge from the woods. Now a buck walked out into the twilight followed by two fawns. A truck came over a hill and the deer retreated. Just short of the lodge, two more deer were silhouetted on a wooded knoll.

"There's another," Scott said. "And two more! This place must be wormy with deer! Tell me, what did you think of the tournament?"

"For me," a visitor said, "proving that I'm as smart as a fish is all the challenge I need. But these guys don't kill fish. They can't do a lake any harm. If they enjoy competition, what's the harm?"

Two weeks later Scott received a letter from Wes Woosley, the twice-dunked. Wes confided that there had been a moment or two among the waves when he was tempted to give up. Then he thought no, a drowning would give bass fishing a bad name. He fought on.

# YOU SHOULDA BEEN HERE IN MARCH

*Port Alberni, British Columbia*

JACK BELL said the king salmon—he calls them spring salmon, or "springs"—would be ganged up in Rainy Bay catching a last snack before the suicidal run up the inlet to make love and die. Pacific salmon always snuff it after spawning, and you'd think a smart fish might decide romance wasn't worth it. Evidently, though, after two years at sea they consider it a beautiful way to go.

"At least," Jack said as he and his brother Bill loaded guests and gear into two small boats, "a condemned fish likes a hearty meal, so they'll be snapping at our herring."

Jack and Bill Bell were born and reared in the logging camps of Vancouver Island. They are on first-name terms with the king and coho salmon, the steelhead and brown trout and sea-run cutthroat that populate this mountainous wilderness, and they planned to introduce some of them to the visitors—Will Yolen, a stray Will had brought west from New York, and Bill Ryan of MacMillan-Bloedel, the forest products giant that logs these woods.

"In about two weeks," Bill said, casting off, "this bay will be full of salmon, but now we have to go after them." He steered southwest down Alberni Inlet, a crooked cleft of blue that makes a 35-mile part in the mountains from Port Alberni to Barkley Sound where the Pacific washes the island's west coast. Green with cedar, hemlock and Douglas fir, the shores rise steeply to craggy peaks still dusted with snow in July.

"Early in the morning," Bill said, "we see black-tail deer sunning themselves on these ledges. Sometimes if a cougar's been running one, we find him swimming, so tired we have to grab him by the horns and help him ashore."

"This stretch, from that light we just passed to the next point, is called Hell's Gate. It's always roughest here, even when it's glassy above and below. Boats that aren't familiar with the inlet can get in trouble. Seems it's always the big, rich 30- and 40-foot jobs that go down. The chop is so short here it can rip a seam clean out of a hull.

"See that tall mountain? Back of there is Nahmint Lake where the rainbow trout run 12 pounds and better. You can only get in by float plane, and if the weather socks in you might not get out for four days. They lose two, three planes a year, but I heard some fellows were in there recently throwing the 6-pounders back."

The boat rounded a point, and now the starboard shore was a desolation of dead brown. From an A-frame of timbers at the water's edge, a cable stretched 2,800 feet to the summit. Once a "gyppo" logger, an independent, worked this slope, swinging his logs down that almost vertical line, but he had three fires in four years. Later, Jack told about one fire.

"I was working over there," he said, indicating the opposite shore a mile away, "and the heat was so intense we had to get out. There was a gale blowing, and the fire sucked the wind off the water, leaving a dead calm on our shore. Stumps and trees were flying straight up, flames were leaping 400 feet high, and the roar you wouldn't believe."

"The gyppo was insured against his first two fires," Bill said, "but the third put him out of business." He lifted a hand in greeting to a passing boat. "That's the fish patrol making sure the gill netters taking sockeye salmon stay in the water allotted to them. There's a gill netter, that boat. That red ball on the water marks the far end of his net.

"That cove over there is the mouth of Coleman Creek. It's just a small stream but loaded with big steelhead in the winter. They average 12 pounds, and you can get 'em up to any size. Not now, though. You should come here in March or in the fall."

There it was again, the saddest of possible words: "You should have been here last week, last March, last year." Still, it is lovely country and this was a lovely day with the sun high in a spotless sky and a delicious breeze on the water. You could say the air was like champagne, but actually it was like air without Con Edison's additives.

The boat swung around Chup Point, threaded past green and rocky islets and was in Rainy Bay. Just outside, long gray streamers of fog were like smoke before the wind. Out there on the west coast, Bill said, there'd be big coho salmon but the weather would be vile.

"Bald eagles," Bill said, and suddenly the birds were everywhere, wheeling and diving, adults with head and tail of gleaming white, the young ones darkly mottled but almost as impressive with their 6-foot wingspread. Somewhere in the depths salmon were slashing at herring; stunned, the herring floated to the surface where the eagles snatched them up. Being a herring is not good.

"American eagles," a visitor said, "the symbol of our majesty. I thought they were almost extinct."

"They are in the States," Will Yolen said. "Most of 'em came to Canada to evade the draft."

The airborne traffic was amazing. There were eagles in the sky, eagles in the trees, eagles on the rocky ledges in such numbers that you'd think this was 2401 West Wisconsin Avenue, Milwaukee, Wis., the grand aerie of the F.O.E.

Now the fishermen split up, Jack taking Will Yolen and his friend into his boat, Bill Ryan riding with Bill Bell. There was no way of knowing how deep the salmon lay, so the brothers rigged trolling gear.

The hook was baited with a strip of herring fitted into a little plastic sheath called a "stripteaser." Above that was a huge lure called a "flasher," a bent plate of chromium brass about ten inches long and three wide. Fifty feet up the line was a tripping device invented by Jack, with an ingot of lead attached. The sinker would carry the bait to the desired depth, and if a fish hit, the tripper would release the lead so the salmon could fight unencumbered by all that weight.

"We'll try a 4-ounce sinker," Jack said, "about 50 feet down." He started the trolling motor, and almost immediately one of his passengers felt something.

It didn't feel like any king of the deeps. There was merely an increase of weight and a tremor of life up the rod. Minimal resistance was felt while reeling up. "A spiky cod," Jack said when the fish appeared. It had an olive complexion, a spiny dorsal and a stupid expression. Jack turned it loose and put on a new bait.

In the other boat, Bill Bell whooped. "Twenty-two pulls," he shouted. He meant that Ryan, measuring out line by stripping it off in 2-foot lengths from the reel to the lowest guide, had found a salmon 44 feet down. The whine of Ryan's reel came clear across the water. This was a king, all right.

Jack's passenger hooked another fish. This didn't run like the salmon Ryan was fighting, but it did struggle resentfully. Over sullen but ineffectual resistance, a brown and ugly critter was dragged to the surface. "A shark," Jack said, trying not to sound amused. "A dog-fish." Across the water came a derisive howl; Bill Bell was baying like a lovelorn beagle.

In about half an hour, Ryan had his fish ready for the gaff, but right alongside the boat the salmon shook the hook. A long time passed without further action. "They're flasher-shy," Jack said. "We'll try mooching gear." He rigged light tackle with a whole herring as bait instead of a strip. He shut off the motor and let the boat drift downwind.

"Not many fishermen here know about mooching," he said. "One time I had my kids out with the commercial fishermen and we were taking springs as fast as we could bring 'em in. Everybody else was getting nothing trolling, and it was four or five days before they got onto our mooching technique. By that time we had the springs thinned out some. At 77 cents a pound, I think it was, we'd been making $180 a day. Hey! Did you see that spring slashing on the surface? They're in here."

Will Yolen's rod tip bobbed. "Wait now," Jack said. "He slapped the herring with his tail. Give him slack until he turns the bait around and starts away with it. Now! Hit him!"

Fifty feet astern, a fish breaking water flung a geyser toward the sky. "He'll go around 25 pounds," Jack said. "Let him run."

Will Yolen is a man of spirit. He is accustomed to handling rod and reel, but usually it is to fly kites. When he has a kite on the line he makes it do his bidding, and he wasn't about to let this fish call the shots. He slammed on the brakes; the reel stopped but the fish kept going, taking herring, hook, line and sinker along.

The day wore on, bright and pleasantly breezy. Eagles soared and screamed. A lone seal stuck his head up near the shore, looked around and went below to snatch some more herring. A black bear ambled out of the forest and worked along the rocky shoreline, apparently feeding on mussels. Bill Bell hooked a salmon 40 pulls down and handed the rod to Ryan, who mastered the fish in 40 minutes.

That was all except that Will Yolen, jumping ashore, pirouetted like a dervish and slid into water waist-deep. He twisted a muscle, which stiffened painfully under his wet clothing. It did not appear to be fatal.

"Looks as though you've thrown a stifle or maybe popped an osse-let," he was told. "If you were a horse, we'd have to put you down."

"The hell with the blindfold," Will said.


A blue grouse stood like a traffic cop in the middle of the road, and not until Jack Bell had brought the truck almost to a halt did she deign to waddle into the underbrush, herding three tiny chicks ahead of her. Around the next bend, a two-pronged buck was posing for a calendar. For a moment after the truck came into view he stood motionless, blocking the trail, then moved with all deliberate haste into the woods.

Jocund day stood tiptoe on the misty mountaintop. On the run down Alberni Inlet, the boat passed two more deer on a ledge warmed by the rising sun. Their coats were curiously pale, as though they'd been to the hairdresser's for a silver rinse.

On the first day of angling in Rainy Bay only one king salmon had been taken and Jack Bell had advised an earlier start. This time we would fish the "morning bite" and return to town, going out for brown trout after an early dinner.

Jack was confident the salmon would be on the feed, loading up on herring before proceeding up the inlet for their rendezvous with love and extinction. Rainy Bay, however, was much quieter than the day before. The bald eagles were fewer and there was a perfunctory quality about their fishing. The salmon were still there, though. Now and then one broke water, and stunned herring kept floating to the surface.

In the next four hours, two or three fish took a slap at the herring offered as bait, then remembered their diets. One made a hog of himself, but when the rod tip was lifted to set the hook, the line snapped. Bill Bell, who had been fishing the far shore of the bay, came over and reported no action.

"Except for this ling cod," he said, lifting a 27-pound salmon. The one caught the day before had been about ⅗ feet long and deep like Sophia Loren. This was more the Lauren Bacall type, a lissome silver torpedo. Bill said it had come in submissively until it saw the boat, then had taken off and fought for 45 minutes.

We draw a veil over the next few hours, passed profitably in sleep. About 7 p.m. Jack showed up with Bob Pennington, a fly fisher on speaking terms with the trout of Cameron River. Driving there was like touring a cathedral, for the road led through a forest of stately firs with trunks 6 or 7 feet in diameter, rising straight and majestic somethng like 200 feet.

"We've had 'em bigger," Jack said. "There was one that scaled out at 165,650 board feet. To give you an idea, a modern house with two bedrooms takes about 12,000 board feet."

Jack produced an assortment of wet flies recommended for the Cameron. In lowering dusk, the anglers struggled through thickets and took up positions at pools which, Bob Pennington said, ought to hold brown trout. Yolen and his friend went to work with flyrods. Bill Ryan had spinning tackle.

One of the first casts with a wet fly brought a strike that was missed. Moments later a hatch of flies showed. As well as could be determined in the fading light, the bugs looked like Hendricksons with pale green bodies. Fish started feeding on the surface.

There was a hasty switch to a Humpy, the dry fly popular with Rocky Mountain trout. It wasn't popular here. A Hendrickson replaced the Humpy and was pitched upstream. A trout slapped at it and was missed.

It was getting frantic, and dark. The Hendrickson hung up in a tree. Five minutes were wasted clawing for a branch just out of reach before the leader was jerked free and another Hendrickson tied on. This brought a quick strike, too, but by now the darkness, the treacherous and unfamiliar footing, the power of the current swirling close to the top of chest-high waders all combined to discourage further adventuring.

Back on the highway waiting for the others, Jack was hailed by a man he knew.

"We lost a faller today," the man said. The faller is the aristocrat of the logging crews, the man who cuts down the trees. Paid according to the number of board feet he cuts, the faller can earn as much as $26,000 a year, but it is dangerous work. Jack recognized the name of the one who had been killed, a veteran.

"Sixty years old," the other said. "He told me last week he wasn't going to work to 65. Just one more season."

The man drove off and the fishermen returned. Will Yolen carried a forked stick hooked through the gills of a brown trout fully 8 inches long. The trout was very dead.

"It was self-defense," Will said.

At breakfast Yolen scowled at his bacon and eggs and demanded: "Where's my trout?"

Fred Warman, maestro of the guest house where MacMillan-Bloedel, Ltd., shelters visiting fishermen and other waifs, was incredulous. "That was a trout? It would take two of him to make one sardine."

"That," Will said, "was a brown trout of legal size who fought me to the death. Nobody would arrest you for cooking him, and anyway, you'd still be a young man when you got out."

So Will ate bacon and eggs and then Jack Bell came around to lead a foray against cutthroat trout and perhaps a steelhead or two. This was the slack season between the spring and autumn runs of steelhead, he said, but there were holding pools in the Sarita River where an off-season loiterer might be found.

En route to the river, he drove past a cluster of wooden buildings in the forest. This was Franklin Division, he said, one of the few old-style logging camps surviving in these times when Paul Bunyan is a commuter who lives with his family in town, rides to and from work not astride Babe, the blue ox, but in a company bus called a "crummy," and with his power saw can easily cut 100,000 board feet of timber a day five days a week.

"As a kid I hunted birds here," Jack said, "and these trees were up to my waist. Now look at 'em, almost ready for logging. Reforestation. See that stand of old timber? That's what they used to call selective logging. They'd leave a line of trees standing like that and, when the wind blew, those trees would reseed the area that had been cut over. Today they give nature a hand."

Today's logger is no French-Canadian bit player in a stocking cap saying, "By gar! She ess one beeg bull moose!" When today's logger talks shop, he uses terms like "sustained yield" and "intensive forestry." The words are music to a guy who grew up in Wisconsin after lumber barons with no thought of the future had stripped that state bare.

For a fly fisherman, there couldn't be a lovelier river than the Sarita, a generous stream, easy to wade and easy to fish, with great pools swift and smooth where a dry fly can ride all day without getting its hackle damp. "You ought to see the bear here when the salmon are spawning," Jack Bell said. "Hundreds of 'em, all fishing. Hey, now you're logging!"

He was applauding the capture of a sea-run cutthroat, a silvery beauty with a rainbow's spots but no other color save for his bow tie of bright orange. If there were steelhead present, they kept quiet about it. The party turned back toward Sproat Lake, home base of the Martin Mars water bombers.

These are huge flying boats built for the Navy during World War II. Their wing spread of 212 feet is 22 feet greater than that of the 747 jet. As troop carriers they had a capacity of 300, more than any other plane before the 747. Of the five delivered to the Navy, one crashed in the Pacific; the other four were bought after the war to serve as flying fire engines.

One crashed fighting a fire. One was "cannibalized" for spare parts. The other two have fought 113 fires here in the last 11 years. Compartments built into their bellies hold 6,000 gallons of water, which they pick up in 25 seconds by skimming over a lake with scoops lowered. The water is thickened with a chemical called Gelgard, but 6,000 gallons of this mixture can't stop a raging forest fire.

The secret is teamwork. When a fire is spotted, a small "bird dog" plane surveys the blaze, checks wind direction, lays out a bombing pattern. Then the big boat comes in low, sometimes through smoke, often in a narrow ravine. If all goes well, the ground crew can handle the job from there.

Bill Waddington, chief of operations, was saying that it took three years to train a pilot for these ticklish runs. Just then the monster roared in for a demonstration, no more than 100 feet above the lake. Its belly opened and water billowed out in misty clouds slashed by a vivid rainbow.

"Do you get much flap from neighbors living around the lake?" Waddington was asked.

"We did at first," he said. "Then we had a big fire over there in the hills. Since then, there hasn't been a word."

# WALK SOFT, WALK COOL

*Andros Island, Bahamas*

T HE cat is tawny and skinny, with pale and wicked green eyes, and for swimming he uses the Australian crawl. Cats hate water but Old Yeller—that is this cat's name—takes a swim every day in the pool at the Andros Beach Hotel.

Todd Clay, who does public relations for the hotel, wanted a picture of Old Yeller coming out of the water with a fish in his mouth. He was confident *Life* magazine would go bananas about it. He brought a photographer over from Miami a fortnight ago. Old Yeller did a duck and stayed out of sight the whole weekend, reappearing only after the photographer left the island. He knew.

He is an elderly cat. Look into his eyes—sometimes they take on a yellowish cast like good chartreuse—and you get the feeling that he has lived for centuries and knows everything. Chances are he knows where Morgan's treasure is hidden, but of course he isn't telling.

People around here take it for granted that Morgan's treasure— that's Sir Henry Morgan, the pirate—is hidden in one of the caves that honeycomb Morgan's Bluff on the northernmost part of the island where the old freebooter had a tower commanding a view for miles and miles. When a ship hove into sight, Morgan pounced. Now and then a stroller or skin diver finds an ancient doubloon, but that's all.

Oh, well, it wasn't to interview swimming cats or to search for pirate gold that this visit was undertaken. There's a troop of bonefish, reported to number either 20 or 2,000, skulking along these shores looking for a fight. They will be accommodated tomorrow.

As most readers know, Andros is the largest and most westerly island in the Bahamas, about 150 miles from Miami and 30 miles west of Nassau. It is a sparsely populated swatch of real estate sliced up by waterways meandering through forests of yellow pine and mahogany.

It is home for a few thousand people and hordes of pigeons, doves, ducks and quail.

Among the people are Bob and Bill Parker, owners of the Andros Beach Hotel. They're brothers out of Miami who came here 15 or 20 years ago, cleared land and planted it to cucumbers. Their operation prospered and they kept expanding until they were producing enough cucumbers to induce indigestion in every stenographer east of Pittsburgh.

They imported farm labor from Haiti until the Bahamian Government put a stop to that. Bill, the farmer, moved the cucumber operation to Haiti where he put in tomatoes and lettuce and now produces complete salads. Bob undertook to develop the Andros property as a real estate project. The hotel was built as part of that.

It is a place of quiet, informal charm which fairly reeks of leisure. The poolside bar with its thatched roof may be as far as 20 feet from the beach. The sea is a pale blue-green where it laps the sand, shading to royal blue as the water deepens, with a rim of whitecaps out near the horizon marking the location of the barrier reef. Beyond that is the bottomless chasm called the Tongue of the Ocean.

It was cocktail time when the resort's 35-foot cruiser came home this evening. The sun was still above the horizon but the breeze off the water made guests in swimsuits reach for jackets.

The cruiser had been fishing over the reef. The catch included barracuda, amberjack, dolphin and yellowtail. As the boat pulled in, two women guests came out of villas back in the pines and hastened to the dock. There was animated discussion, inaudible at first. Then a few words came through:

"All I want is a couple of small pieces I can cook for dinner."

It would have been unmannerly to listen further. They were going to talk price in a moment. Where there are housewives, there is bargain-hunting.


Howling like a soul in torment, the air boat bolted away from the dock in Lowe Sound and Mosser Evans handed each of his passengers a pair of the rubber earmuffs worn by ground crews at jetports. The air boat is a wondrous craft able to navigate on a dewy lawn, but if it weren't for the earmuffs, the motor that drives its airplane propeller would have nerves snapping like rubber bands.

Running before the persistent trade winds, the skiff scooted across waters incredibly varied in color from the palest of pastel greens to royal blue, shining bright green in the channels, translucent mauves, beige with subtle hints of coral. Mosser Evans steered around the tip of a mangrove island, scaring off a big shark that had been loafing in the sun, and throttled down over a plain of sand in clear water about a foot deep.

"This is Candle Cay," Mosser said, and a sweep of the arm took in other patches of forest green. "Long Cay, Rum Cay, Colby Cay, Duck Cay."

Squinting under the bill of a faded red baseball cap, his eyes swept the sea in search of bonefish. "School off there," he said, "and there. Let them settle down."

He wore an old army shirt with the single chevron of a private first class; skinny black legs protruded from yellow bathing trunks. He stepped over the side and waded beside the boat, holding it to retard the drift. Every few moments he stiffened like a bird dog on scent but the bones were always too far away for the passengers' eyes, and retreating. The boat was spooking them, Mosser decided. He signaled the others to join him in the water.

"Walk soft," Mosser said. "Walk light, walk cool."

He prowled downwind. A step or two back came three mighty anglers before the Lord, each holding a spinning rod baited with the flesh of crabs which Mosser had torn apart with his teeth. Every few steps the leader would lift a hand and point. Staring hard, his followers began to perceive dimly what he could see at preposterous range.

There would be a darkness in the wavelets, a sense of something moving through or just below the surface. One cautious step closer and—there. Dark torpedo shapes moved, multiplied, came closer, swerved that way, turned back. Now and then a dorsal fin broke water.

Stalkers crept forward and cast, trusting to the breeze and the power of prayer to carry the morsels to the cruising shadows. The hunters would crouch, tense, not breathing, watching the critters come on. Suddenly the fish would turn and dart away, going like the redball express.

From mangrove key to mangrove key, these sandy flats were wall-to-wall bonefish. Bones trooped by in squads, platoons, regiments, and divisions, and not a freeloader in the whole scaly army would pause to sample a canape. Todd Clay wandered off by himself. Jack Murphy got semidetached. Modesty forbids identifying the genius who stuck close to Mosser and made the first hit.

Truthfully, the hit was just a bunt, or at best a Texas leaguer. Something nuzzled the bait, sending faint tremors up the line. The angler waited, and waited, trembling. Just this side of eternity, the rod tip bent as the fish began to run. Up came the rod, in went the hook, and the battle was joined.

The battle wasn't much until the bone was cranked in close enough to see his captor. Then he cursed and fled with the hissing rush that is the trademark of his breed. The bone isn't bred for the Derby distance but there never was a racehorse that could warm him up at six furlongs.

When this one was licked, Mosser was struggling with a backlash in Todd Clay's line and he paid no attention. "Should I turn this fellow loose?" the angler asked.

"Tomorrow is Sunday, mon," Mosser said without looking up. "Everybody likes stewfish and potato bread on Sunday." In due course he unhooked the silvery sliver and stowed him in his landing net.

Staying close to Mosser, the guy got into a second and larger fish. This one gave him three brilliant runs before subsiding. Within the next half-hour two or three more fish made advances but were not hooked; the angler was striking too soon, Mosser said. Then hell broke loose. The reel sounded like Hook and Ladder No. 2 coming down Seventh Avenue. The fish ran and ran and ran. At last the line went slack.

"He was a big one," Mosser said.

Everybody got back in the boat and Mosser steered off to the left. "Jack Murphy's got to have a bonefish," he was told. "The man came 3,000 miles." Mosser said nothing, but when he had anchored he beckoned Jack Murphy to stay close.

The breeze had picked up, roughening the water, and the sun was behind a cloud, cutting visibility to zero. No mortal eyes could find fish under those conditions. Mosser Evans stiffened, pointing. A tasty little dab of crabmeat splotched into the water. In a moment Jack Murphy had a fish on and running.

The fish may have been smaller than the one that got away but he was bigger than the two that hadn't. When Mosser slid the net under him, Jack Murphy sighed. "I'll remember this all my life," he said.


This is a fair green place of peace completely surrounded by the most truculent fish that swim. Of all the creatures that live in the waters bathing these shores, the bonefish is esteemed by anglers as the worthiest antagonist—shy and timorous as a managing editor, nervous as a network vice-president, swifter than gossip.

Stalking bones in gin-clear water no more than a foot deep calls for craft and stealth, but out beyond the barrier reef that rings this island is the Tongue of the Ocean, a mile-deep abyss where sportsmen of more sedentary bent can drag moribund mullet around with some prospect of attracting a kingfish or dolphin or marlin. This proved a happy circumstance, for on the second day of our visit here we were joined by Morris McLemore, and if we didn't have the word "sedentary" in the language we would have to persuade some Virgil to coin it to describe the new arrival.

Morris McLemore used to be a newspaperman but he has taken his talent and his golden voice to television in Miami. His talent, while by no means as great as his girth, is considerable: the voice has won him acclaim as the Cosell of the Canebrakes.

Mac was an athlete in college, and if need be he can still move with the lithe grace of a pregnant hippopotamus. However, by design and disposition he is more barnacle than barracuda. On the whole, this is good; if he were to plunge into the sea in pursuit of bonefish, the tidal wave resulting would leave hundreds homeless.

Fortunately, the navy attached to the Andros Beach Hotel has a 35-foot cruiser with a skipper named Franklin on the bridge, a mate named Felix in the cockpit, and three stout barber chairs in the stern. In the interests of equilibrium, Mac took the middle chair.

"Five dollars on the first fish," he announced, laying down ground rules, "and another five for most fish."

Though fishing is not and should not be a competitive sport, somebody had to accept the challenge and Jack Murphy wasn't interested. Wading after bones the day before, the man from San Diego had got feet and legs so painfully sunburned that he wanted only to crouch in McLemore's ample shade. Purely on principle, the man in the starboard chair took the bet.

It was his own fault. He should have known that television people are not to be trusted and renegade newspapermen are worse.

On the short run to the reefs and the depths beyond, Felix baited three rods with the corpses of three mullet. Then he brought out three strange dornicks which he attached to a single cord at intervals of a yard or so. They looked like a giant version of the lure called a Hula

Popper—orange, yellow, and green wooden cylinders about the size of beer cans, with rubber skirts slit into ribbons but no hooks. Felix tossed the rig into the wake where it rode ahead of the baited hooks. It was a "teaser," he said.

Twenty or thirty minutes passed before a shout from the bridge made Felix grab for the port rod. Reluctantly Jack Murphy hobbled out of the shade and lowered his barbecued limbs into the chair. He planted the rod butt into the chair's socket and worked it like a pump handle, reeling on the down-stroke. In came a barracuda about the length of a Louisville slugger, Ted Williams model.

Felix lifted the fish by the wire leader and dropped it into a box in the stern. The 'cuda bared its teeth. Jack Murphy curled his lip and retired to the shade.

"First fish," McLemore said. "If you weren't chicken, we'd each owe you five."

By way of reply, Jack Murphy caught the second fish, the third fish, and the fourth fish. These three were dolphin, that many-splendored dude which is so gaudy alive and so tasty dead. The largest of the three leaped three times in an iridescent splendor of green and gold.

For reasons of his own, Felix had reeled in the starboard line and removed leader, hook, and bait a moment before Murphy's third dolphin hit. Evidently the boat found a school just then, for now a dolphin took the only bait available—McLemore's. Curiously excited, Felix tried to gaff the fish before it was played out, lost the meat hook overboard, grabbed the leader and hoisted the catch in.

McLemore's eyes held a look of animal cunning. As far as his bet was concerned, he had the first catch, he led in number of fish, 1-0, and his opponent still had no hook on his line. "Well, what do you know!" Mac said, glancing at his watch. "It's time to go in."

# ⓄN HORSEBACK

*Three years after a pack of impudent colonists de-*
*clared their independence of George III and thus*
*blazed a trail that would lead to Watergate, Lord*
*Derby and his friend Sir Charles Bunbury laid plans*
*to run a race for 3-year-olds at Epsom Downs, a new*
*course southwest of London.*

*They flipped a coin to determine which of them*
*should lend his name to the event. It came up heads*
*and the race was named for his lordship but Sir*
*Charles won the first running with a colt named*
*Diomed, which proves that the breaks even up in*
*the end.*

*It is pleasant to reflect that if that shilling had*
*made another half-turn, the race that draws us all*
*to Louisville each May would be the Kentucky*
*Bunbury.*

# AND BLUEBERRY MUFFINS

*Saratoga Springs, N.Y.*

T HE annual fuel collection in St. Peter's Church on South Broadway will be taken up on the second and third Sundays in August as usual. That's the day after the Alabama Stakes and the day after the Travers when, experience has shown, horseplayers are at their godliest and most generous, especially the winners. Like most of the 15,000 residents of this agreeable city, Msgr. Daniel R. Burns learned long ago to rely on August for the bulk of the year's income, for in August the Beautiful People arrive with their beautiful horses and attractive dollars.

Now that the monsignor is in retirement—at the age of 86 he was still breaking 50 for nine holes on the golf course until his recent stroke—his successor as pastor, the Rev. George A. Phillips, observes the same schedule, but Father Phillips says his appeals for funds lack the perusasive wit with which Monsignor Burns invited contributions.

Saratoga is a one-month town. It doesn't exactly hibernate the other eleven months, for the mineral springs that first brought visitors here flow the year round, the undergraduates at Skidmore contrive to keep their blood circulating from September to June, trotters and pacers at Saratoga Raceway show the way to bankruptcy every weekday evening from April 15 to Nov. 15, and the Saratoga Performing Arts Center offers a summer-long program of pop concerts, ballet and symphony.

There is also a summer-long flow of vacationers bound for the Adirondacks and such tourist attractions as Santa's Workshop, Storytown, U.S.A., Waxlife ("Come meet Marilyn Monroe"), and the Cavalcade of Cars, featuring "The $90,000 Greta Garbo Duesenberg."

Last week when Secretariat, Riva Ridge and lesser members of thoroughbred society were just taking up residence in the stables off

Union Avenue, most motels displayed "No Vacancy" signs. The New York State Republican Women were in convention in the Holiday Inn; finding a place at the bar called for agility and some courage.

"It has been a good July," said Lefty Corsale, who operates the St. Charles Motel on South Broadway, "but let's face it, August produces more than half the city's annual business."

Evidently this was not the case a century or so ago, for when the correspondent for Wilkes's *Spirit of The Times* arrived here to cover the first thoroughbred meeting in 1863 he found all the hotels along Broadway filled, with 2,000 guests in the United States Hotel alone. They had come to bathe in and drink the waters of the medicinal springs, as Indians and animals of the forest had done before them. According to local accounts, the first white man to test the waters' therapeutic qualities was Sir William Johnson, whom the Mohawks dunked in High Rock spring to relieve his gout in 1787.

For the first race meeting, swells and sports sailed up the Hudson on the *Francis Skiddy* by moonlight to Troy, finishing the journey by rail the next day. Describing the crowd that attended the first racing program on Aug. 3, 1863, *The Spirit of The Times* noted that "the elegant and superb costumes of the ladies vied with the blood and beauty of the running horses and the neat but splendid appointments of the various riders."

John Morrissey, who brought the thoroughbreds to Saratoga, was a plug-ugly from Troy who had become an enforcer in New York City political circles, had won the bare-knuckle championship of America from Yankee Sullivan in Boston Corners, N.Y., had prospered as an operator of gambling houses and would ultimately serve two terms in Congress.

The following summer he opened a new course across Union Avenue on the site of the present track. On Aug. 2, 1864, the colt Kentucky was galloped three or four miles on the old course "to warm him out of lameness." Then he crossed the street and whipped four rivals in the first Travers Stakes, named for William R. Travers, the track president who was co-owner of the winner.

The race has been a milestone in the history of the American turf ever since, and an incident in the history of the country. The year 1868, for example, when President Andrew Johnson was impeached by the House of Representatives and acquitted by the Senate, was the year The Banshee won the Travers. Aug. 13, 1920, was the date

Man o' War mowed them down. In 1930 it was Jim Dandy at a preposterous 100-to-1 in a four-horse field, beating the unbeatable Gallant Fox, the good Whichone, the outclassed Sun Falcon. In 1953 it was Native Dancer. Nine years later came the Travers no witness can ever forget, when Jaipur and Ridan went dingdong, head and head, hell for leather every stride of the mile and a quarter with Jaipur's nose in front at the wire.

In 1867 Morrissey built a casino in Congress Park, known as "Morrissey's Elegant Hell." In 1894 it was enlarged and refurbished by Richard Canfield, "The Prince of Gamblers." As Canfield Casino, the building stands today, a mid-Victorian pile of red brick owned by the city.

In Canfield's day, the beauty and chivalry gathered in the United States and the Grand Union Hotels. One block apart on Broadway, these were huge hollow squares, each occupying an entire city block. Victor Herbert conducted the orchestra in the United States, and the legend is that a breathless whisper which he overheard while strolling in the gardens one soft evening was the inspiration for his composition, "Kiss Me Again."

Be that as it may, the garden apartments in both hotels were much favored by gentlemen of substance and their lovely nieces.

Gambling by night as well as day remained a source of amusement for the visitors until recent years. The late Frank Stevens, head of the catering dynasty of Harry M. Stevens, Inc., enjoyed telling of the days when the Harry Payne Whitneys and Harry Sinclairs would go directly from the tables to the track to watch the morning works, and buy more champagne at breakfast than is consumed now at the monthlong meeting.

Before and immediately after World War II, dice still rolled and wheels whirled in clubs like the Piping Rock, Riley's Lake House and Newman's on the Lake. One summer Newman had a belly dancer who took umbrage at a remark by P. J. Bailey, a spirited jockey, and whipped him in fair fight in King's, an oasis across from the track with no clearly defined closing hour.

P. J. felt as Bobby Riggs would feel if Mrs. Billie Jean King beat him at tennis, but he was a firm believer in the theory that a race over the track usually improved a horse's performance. He was consoling himself with a drink and accepting condolences from his friend Pat Lynch, when Bobby Casale, a handicapper, spoke up: "She won going away, P. J., and you better not challenge her again because I got a hundred says she'll whip you right back."

"Take it, Pat," P. J. said. "I give myself a race."

The great hotels are gone and a supermarket occupies the site of the Grand Union. Gone, too, are favored hangouts like the New Worden Bar, where Frank Sullivan, the jewel in Saratoga's literary crown, used to lift an occasional beaker with Monte Woolley, Saratoga's gift to the theater. Canfield's Casino is open only in the daytime, and only to display exhibits of the Walworth Memorial Museum and the Historical Society of Saratoga Springs.

Mr. Sullivan, though, continues to grow in grace in the city that gave him birth more than 80 years ago. A visitor this week found him rejoicing in new petit point carpet slippers festooned with shamrocks, and thinking about the responsibility of the van driver who hauled Secretariat, Riva Ridge, Capito and Capital Asset up from the city.

"You and I," he said, "are worth, chemically, about $1.69. It makes you a little humble to think of $15-million worth of horses in one truck."

Mr. Sullivan's mellow memories go back to the times when he earned as much as $12 a day in nickels, dimes and quarters as the 10-year-old waterboy tending the pump in the betting ring.

"Mr. John Cavanaugh furnished me a stool," he said. "I remember John Cavanaugh with a satchel hung around his neck going through the ring collecting the daily fee the bookmakers paid to set up their slates. I had this stool with a cigar box for tips and three tin cups. I think I invented germ warfare.

"Lillian Russell, that beautiful woman, had a box in the grandstand near a flight of stairs. Sometimes I would go and stand looking at her for two or three minutes. One day a man told me to go take a drink to Miss Russell, but when I started up the stairs a Pinkerton stopped me. 'Miss Russell,' I told him, 'has asked for a drink from the betting ring spring.'

"'Go back and get a glass,' he told me. 'Miss Russell doesn't want to drink from that tin cup.'

"'Oh yes she does,' Miss Russell said. 'Let the little boy through.' She gave me 50 cents."

Today the only gambling done openly after dark is at the Raceway, but the determined visitor can find amusements at the Gideon Putnam Bar or Siro's that will keep him occupied until close to the hour when he should arrive on the clubhouse veranda at the thoroughbred track. If he does not choose to breakfast there on champagne, he can get by with Hand melon, blueberry muffins and eggs not long from solicitous hens while he watches the morning works.

There was just such a morning this week, fresh as the muffins themselves, cool and dewy like the melons. First, though, there were people to see and promises to keep on the backstretch, where the sights and sounds and smells are so good for the soul—the broken drumbeat of hooves as a set of horses pounds by, the voice of an exercise boy crooning to his mount, woodsmoke rising, the scent of open fires under the trees, sunlight rippling on a chestnut coat.

"This Irishman was on his deathbed," Jimmy Conway was saying, "and he could smell a ham cooking in the kitchen. 'Cut me a slice of that ham,' he says to his wife, 'and I'll have a taste before I go.' 'You out of your head?' she says. 'That's for the wake.'"

Not far away a cock crowed loudly. "A day to be alive," Jim Conway said, "and nine chances to get rich this afternoon. Like they say, you never find a man in the river with tomorrow's entries in his pocket."

The rooster crowed again. He had come strutting around the end of Jim Maloney's barn and was pacing back and forth beneath the shedrow, a pure white bird with a tall red comb. Some barns have watchmen, some have watchdogs, and wherever Secretariat goes there is a platoon of armed Pinkertons. The horses trained by Jim Maloney have a watch-rooster to stand guard.

"He joined us at Belmont last year," Maloney said, "and we took him to Aiken for the winter. He's some tough. I've got a Jack Russell terrier—that's an English dog bred to go down in a den and drag out the fox. The dog lifted his leg against the tree and the rooster lit on his hind end. The dog whirled and bit the rooster's tail."

Back and forth the bird paced, back and forth pounding his beat, regarding the world with beady truculence.

"He doesn't make friends," Maloney said. "We got him a couple of hens, but they wouldn't have any part of him. He'll get an old piece of cotton instead, and that rag belongs to him. Watch."

A swatch of soiled cloth lay crumpled at the foot of a big maple. The trainer walked over, picked up a frayed end, and began a Hopi rain dance, stomping on the cloth with measured tread. The rooster shot out from behind a bale of hay like Engine Co. 23 responding to a five-alarm. Neck outthrust, he made straight for the man, leaped and lashed out with both spurs in a double uppercut as Maloney ducked behind the tree.

The trainer popped out, ducked back, popped out, ducked back. Every time he showed, the rooster slashed at him. Hide-and-seek became tag as Maloney took to mock flight, darting right and left again and again. The rooster shifted with him, face to face at every step. The New York Jets should get coverage like that from their cornerbacks.

"I know a pit down in Maryland," a visitor said, "where you could get him a match for big money."

"A good fighting cock would probably whip him," Maloney said, "but he fears no man. We put bandages on him the other day and you should have seen him. Strutting like the heavyweight champion of the world."

Such is Saratoga in the morning. Mark Costello, the track superintendent, loses 30 or 40 trees to Dutch elm disease every year, but he replaces them with maples and preserves the special quality of cool serenity that has always distinguished the dowager queen of American racetracks. So does Saratoga retain something of the grace and leisure of an earlier day, even though the old landmarks pass.

None of it comes cheap, of course. It never has. Shortly after World War II the daily *Saratogian* had an editorial hailing the arrival of August and urging local merchants not to gouge the visitors. The same edition carried an announcement that as of that day *The Saratogian* would sell for 10 cents instead of a nickel.

# MATERNITY WARD

*Paris, Ky.*

**T**HE maternity ward where the Kentucky Derby favorite was born is a black barn with a red roof that stands on a knoll overlooking the sweet green acres of Claiborne Farm. It happened during a visit by Iberia, a mare Christopher Chenery had bought in 1955 from Larry MacPhail, the baseball dervish who had turned to breeding horses and cows after selling his share of the New York Yankees.

Chris Chenery's stallion, Sir Gaylord, maintains a love nest here, and in 1969 Iberia came out from Virginia to keep a date with him. She was in foal to Chenery's First Landing, and on April 13, before her tryst with Sir Gaylord, she bore a bay son. They named the little fellow Riva Ridge, where buddies of Chenery's son-in-law, John B. Tweedy, fought during World War II after the 10th Mountain Division's first landing in Italy.

If Riva Ridge wins the Derby he will join a redoubtable company whose names are like plucked strings. Gallant Fox and Omaha, who not only won the Derby but also the Preakness and Belmont Stakes for the American Triple Crown; Bold Ruler, the prepotent sire of modern times; Round Table, the richest horse ever sent to stud; the brilliant Hoist the Flag, whose shattered leg ended his racing days when they had barely begun—all these and many more began life in this same black barn.

"And there was another I can't help thinking about every year around this time," said Bull Hancock, the master of Claiborne.

"I was a kid of 16 or so," he said, "and my hero was Mr. Fitz, James Fitzsimmons, the great trainer. At Saratoga that summer, I noticed there was a 2-year-old colt in his barn that he paid special attention to. I knew the colt because I'd help to raise him here. He belonged to Mr. William Woodward, who usually shipped his horses to his Belair

Stud in Maryland after they were weaned, but he had left this colt
and others with us as yearlings because of an encephalitis scare in
Maryland.

"I went to John Bogan, the bookmaker, and asked what price he'd
lay on an unraced 2-year-old to win the Derby at 3. He said 100 to 1,
so I bet $10. Then I got thinking. Mr. Fitz really liked that colt. I didn't
have $100, but I asked Bogan if he'd give me 100 to 1 for $100. He said,
'Sure, what the horse's name?' I said, 'I don't know, but I'll find out.
I just know his breeding.'

"The colt's name was Granville. He came around nicely as a 2-year-
old, and at 3 he was coming up to the Derby just the way Mr. Fitz
wanted. If I remember, he was about 15 to 1 in the winter book. I
scraped up every penny I could raise and went over to Louisville.

"There was a good-sized field for that Derby, including a colt from
Canada named Indian Broom. When the mutuels opened on Derby
Day the man who owned Indian Broom socked in $10,000 on his horse.
That brought a shift in the odds that sent Granville's price up to about
20 to 1. I went around borrowing money and bet everything I could
raise.

"At post time Granville was 10 to 1. This was 1936, when we were
just clawing out of the Depression. I was a 16-year-old kid and I stood
to win just short of $11,000.

"I can see it today. I was sitting in a box with my father and Mr.
Woodward. They left the gate, and Jimmy Stout left Granville.
'Where's Granville?' Mr. Woodward said, hunting for those polka dot
silks of his. 'Granville's right up there,' I told him, 'but the jockey is
back there on the ground.'

"In the next couple of weeks I scraped up whatever I could and
went up to Baltimore for the Preakness. Mr. Fitz said he still liked the
colt. 'But I don't know how much of a race he got in the Derby running
with nobody on him,' he said. 'I'm not sure I've given him enough
work.'

"I did what I was there to do. I sent in everything I had. In the Derby,
Brevity had gone to his knees at the start, got up and just missed catching Bold Venture at the wire. In the Preakness it was Bold Venture
again, beating Granville by just this much.

"I had my return ticket on the train, and one nickel for the trolley
to the station."

Bull Hancock fell silent, and here came the voice of a stud groom showing visitors about the farm. "This here is Buckpasser, that's Tom Rolfe in that paddock there and up there is Damascus. Now, Forli here, he win 15 in a row in Argentina. . . ."

"That's Snow telling the tale," Hancock said. "One time he was taking a couple of schoolmarms around. They didn't know which end of a horse ate and he could see they weren't going to tip him anything, and his feet hurt.

"Finally one of them said, 'Haven't you got a horse on the farm that ever won the Derby?'

" 'Yes 'm,' Snow said, 'that one win it twice.' "

# THE BELMONT STARTS WITH GEORGE

GEORGE BENNETT CASSIDY, ruddy, smiling and faultlessly tailored, climbs a short flight of stairs beside the inner rail at Belmont Park and stands watching while assistants lead the horses into the starting gate. The moment the doors are closed, four or five urgent voices rise: "No, boss, not yet!" "No chance, boss!" "Not ready!" Almost immediately, Cassidy's thumb presses the button at the end of an insulated cord. A strident bell rings, doors fly open with a metallic clang, the jockeys whoop like Comanches. They're off in the Belmont Stakes.

"In gate at 5:35," the chart in Sunday morning's paper will report. "Off at 5:35, Eastern daylight time. Start good." With only minor variations, charts have been saying this about every Belmont since June 7, 1930, when Cassidy sent a field of four away and saw Gallant Fox come home in possession of the Triple Crown.

George Cassidy has let horses go from walkup starts, from a belt of webbing stretched across the track, from the Australian barrier—six strands of rope designed to trip horses and strangle jockeys—and from the infernal machines that were the immediate precursors of today's electric gate. Five times while Belmont Park was closed for reconstruction he started the stakes on Aqueduct's stretch turn, where a race of a mile and a half had to begin on a track measuring a mile and an eighth.

"Start good," forty-two of the charts reported. "Start good for all but Determined Man," read the single exception in 1964 when Bill Boland's mount reared just as Cassidy hit the switch.

In Cassidy's time the Belmont has had as few as three starters— in 1931 when only Sun Meadow and Jamestown chased Twenty Grand —and as many as 13—in 1954 and 1971. If Secretariat can add this race to his Kentucky Derby-Preakness double he will become the first Triple Crown winner in 25 years, so Cassidy will take special pains to get a clean start.

He does not anticipate trouble, even though Secretariat is habitually nonchalant leaving the gate. "I can't remember any Belmont that was trouble," he said yesterday, "since the early days before we had the gate. There's just a little more tension than the ordinary race. I guess the year Canonero was here [1971] was our biggest field, plus the fact that there were so many of those South Americans hopping around.

"Canonero was supposed to be a bad actor in the gate. They had to blindfold him and load him last, but in New York we load 'em by post position, from the inside out. We blindfolded Canonero but loaded him seventh, when his turn came. Once he was standing, we took the blindfold off and he never made a move."

It doesn't worry Cassidy that $6-million or more may be riding on the races he starts Saturday. He is a blithe spirit, as patient as he is good-humored, and responsibility rests lightly on those exquisitely groomed shoulders.

Experience has polished a gift that Eddie Arcaro likens to the split vision of a quarterback surveying all his receivers in one glance. "He seems to sense the instant when a bad horse is going to stand," the former jockey says. "Sometimes, sitting on a skittish 2-year-old in the old Widener Chute, I'd marvel at how he could get 28 of us off together."

Maybe this is because Cassidy, like Secretariat, was bred for his job. In 1890 his father, Mars, who owned and trained thoroughbreds and trotters, was pressed into service as starter at Iron Hill, a Maryland track now lost from memory. In 1903 Mars was invited to New York, and he worked the big wheel until his death in 1929.

Mars was distinguished by a high bowler hat, handlebar mustaches, a temper that boiled at 98.6 degrees and a vocabulary that would bring blushes to the foredeck of a Portuguese freighter. All three of his sons worked as his assistants but only George stayed with it. Marshall became a steward and Jockey Club official highly influential on the national scene. A variety of adventures at the post convinced Wendell that his future lay in the oil fields.

Once, as occasionally happens with a horse notoriously reluctant to start, Wendell was assigned to stand behind a sluggard and encourage him with a bullwhip. He slipped his wrist through the thong at the butt of the whip and, on signal, fetched the steed a manly swat. The lash took a half-hitch round the horse's tail.

"Wendell went the first eighth in a little better than 12," George says, "before the whip pulled free."

When George was 22 and schooled in esoteric wiles like biting a rogue's ear to make him stand, the stewards at Saratoga sent word for him to start the first race in the absence of his father, who had been unavoidably detained. In those days, a talent for beating the start was esteemed as the loftiest refinement of the equestrian art. Riding in the first race were Pony McAtee, Laverne Fator, Earl Sande, Mack Garner and Jim Burke, all capable of removing a starter's coat and vest without getting caught.

They walked up to the tape, George shut his eyes and let them go. The stewards couldn't believe their binoculars. It was the best start of the meeting. The stewards didn't know that on the way to the post the desperadoes had made a compact: "Good kid, young Cassidy. Give him a break." After that beginning it was inevitable that George would succeed his father.

Soon after he did, an owner named Reilly demanded that his horse be removed from the schooling list of bad actors forbidden to start until their manners at the post improved. "We had Prohibition then," Cassidy says, "with rumrunners and hijackers, and this Reilly belonged to the armpit artillery. He said he'd make it tough for me. His horse stayed on the list but I had Reilly insomnia for a few weeks."

As far as the jocks were concerned, all friendship ceased when the Cassidy kid officially became The Man. The first to test him was Earl Sande. He tried to beat the barrier and Cassidy gave him a five-day suspension. He tried again and got five days more. This cost him a stakes assignment on Gallant Fox.

"I stopped in a butcher shop," Cassidy says, "and here was this guy with a white apron and red arms, a horseplayer, whacking up a side of beef with a cleaver and saying how he'd like to get his hands on the louse that took Sande off Gallant Fox. I took my business elsewhere."

# SECRETARIAT, POTATOES AND THINGS

*Arlington Heights, Ill.*

IN Canada this is Dominion Day and it coincides this year with the annual Potato Blossom Festival in Grand Falls, New Brunswick, where Ron Turcotte was foaled 31 years ago. Turcotte usually gallops horses on Sunday but he took this one off to return to the home town and be hailed as the most prized local product outside of the Restigouche salmon and the pomme de terre. Town and Provincial authorities raised him to this pedestal because of his ability to ride as fast as Secretariat can run.

In Chicago and environs this is the day after Secretariat Day, an occasion that may be remembered here as long as the St. Valentine's Day massacre. Unconcerned by the purple-and-amethyst prose he had inspired in the Chicago press, Secretariat cropped grass outside Barn 10 at Arlington Park this morning while George Davis, his exercise rider, held him on a long shank. In a few hours he would fly back to New York with Mrs. John Tweedy, his owner, accompanying him.

"The small sizes go down to $6 apiece," a photographer was telling Edward Sweat, the groom. "For a large color one in the winner's circle it's $35."

Secretariat was wearing pale blue bandages on all four legs, concealing his three white stockings. Eight armed guards had surrounded him when he went to the paddock yesterday for the four-horse Arlington Invitational but now that the winner's share of $75,000 was safely his, only two sentries were on duty. Eddie Sweat was asked about Billy Silver, the lead pony who had slipped and fallen on the concrete runway to the paddock.

"He's all right," the groom said. "He's too much in love with that horse, that's why he was raisin' all that sand yesterday. The crowd probably excited him. He shied a little, made a little weave and slipped."

Several other horses were being walked. "How far he win by yesterday?" asked a man in a yellow T-shirt and blue jeans.

"Nine lengths," George Davis said.

"I got a horse here broke the track record," another hot walker said. "That's more'n that big boob did. Come all the way out here and couldn't tie the record."

He plodded on a trifle unsteadily. Sweat and Davis ignored him.

"He's bombed," a stablehand said.

"I feel sorry for his dogs," another said.

Lucien Laurin had got precious little sleep since his midweek arrival. Now, having done his job by winding up Secretariat for a smashing conquest of My Gallant, Our Native and Blue Chip Dan, the trainer was getting some extra sack time, but he would be on hand before the colt's scheduled departure at 10 a.m.

Laurin had noted with interest the weight assignments for Wednesday's Brooklyn Handicap at Aqueduct—128 pounds for Rokeby Stable's Key to the Mint, 127 for Secretariat's 4-year-old stablemate, Riva Ridge, and 126 for Secretariat.

On the weight-for-age scale, 3-year-olds going a mile and three-sixteenths in July get a nine-pound concession from older horses. Thus Kenny Noe Jr., the New York racing secretary, gave Secretariat the equivalent of seven pounds more than he asked the 4-year-old Key to the Mint to carry and eight pounds more than Riva Ridge.

Laurin obviously feels he was wise to give the Arlington field of 3-year-olds a six-pound advantage rather than wait for the Brooklyn and make bigger concessions. Yet, "You bet your sweet life," he said when asked whether Secretariat would take on older horses before retiring to stud in November.

That could happen in the Whitney Stakes at Saratoga, if Secretariat is willing to wait until then. The Whitney is for horses of 3 and up carrying weight-for-age at a mile and an eighth, 3-year-olds getting 119 pounds and the big boys 126.

On the other hand, if Secretariat gets so eager for action he wants to kick the barn down, as he did a fortnight after the Belmont Stakes, Laurin may feel he has to take his chances with the handicap stars in the mile-and-a-quarter Suburban. In any event, the main goal ahead is the Travers, the queen mother of United States classics. Mrs. Tweedy has said she wants to see that sacramental old canoe on Saratoga's infield lake painted in Meadow Stable's blue and white.

The board of strategy has just about abandoned the idea of shipping to France for the quarter-million-dollar Arc de Triomphe. Laurin doesn't want Secretariat skidding on grass wearing the smooth plates required in France.

Not that the trainer has reservations about his champion. It was suggested to him that to call Secretariat our best since Citation would be saying Secretariat could whip Native Dancer, Nashua, Swaps, Tom Fool, Buckpasser, Kelso and Dr. Fager all together.

"Certainly," Lucien said. "What did they ever do that this horse hasn't done?"

# THE RACE OF TWO CENTURIES

$\mathbb{B}$ECAUSE of the considerable popularity of Secretariat, the habit-forming properties of television and the enduring charm of a quarter of a million dollars, the biggest horse race still on the calendar for this year is the invitation handicap in which Secretariat and Riva Ridge are expected to oppose other winners like Key to the Mint, Cougar II, Onion, Tentam and Annihilate 'Em at Belmont a week from tomorrow.

There is, however, "a little group of willful men representing no opinion but their own" who will regard that event as something stale, flat and unprofitable by comparison with a race that will have been run over the same course 24 hours earlier. They call themselves the Baker Street Irregulars and the race that commands their allegiance is the 22d running of the Silver Blaze, named for the favorite in the Wessex Cup of 1890.

As all subscribers to the *Strand Magazine* of 1891 know, Silver Blaze turned up missing a week before the Cup, his trainer was found dead on the Devonshire moors with his head shattered by a blow, and it required the deductive powers of Mr. Sherlock Holmes to clear up the mystery and recover the horse in time for him to win the race.

It was one of the detective's most brilliant coups, for it is known that in addition to solving a case that had defeated the competent Inspector Gregory of Scotland Yard, Holmes fixed the race for Silver Blaze and made a potful. The betting odds were practically the first thing he asked about when Colonel Ross, Silver Blaze's owner, was driving him to the course.

"You could have got 15 to 1 yesterday," the colonel told him, "but the price has become shorter and shorter until you can hardly get 3 to 1 now."

"Hum!" said Holmes. "Somebody knows something, that is clear."

Clearer than he realized, considering that at that moment the only men in England aware that Silver Blaze was still alive were Sherlock Holmes and a man named Silas Brown, who was betting his shirt on the second favorite, Desborough.

The evidence on this point is damning, but the Baker Street Irregulars shrink from it because as a group they are dedicated to the idea that Holmes was, as he seemed to Dr. John H. Watson, "the best and wisest man I have ever known." Like other Americans these days, the Irregulars flatly refuse to believe the man they admire capable of wrong-doing. They will go to Belmont in a body next Friday to offer up their shillings in annual tribute to the Master.

Thomas L. Stix, who got the race included on the New York calendar 22 years ago, is typical of the irregular breed. He believes that if Silver Blaze could win the admiration of an authority as discriminating as Sherlock Holmes, then he must have been a horse for the ages. He feels that if the television people want a show that will really grab the public, they should set their computer to work on a match between Silver Blaze and Secretariat.

There is no shortage of information to feed the machine. At the time of the Wessex Cup, Silver Blaze was 5 years old and undefeated. "He has brought in turn each of the prizes of the turf to Colonel Ross," Holmes said. . . . "He has always been a prime favorite with the racing public, and has never yet disappointed them." Secretariat, at 3, has been beaten three times and disqualified once.

Silver Blaze was a powerful bay with a white forehead and mottled off foreleg. Secretariat is a powerful chestnut with a white star on his forehead; his off foreleg, like both hindlegs, wears a white sock. Secretariat's most spectacular performance was in the Belmont Stakes at a mile and a half, which he won by 31 lengths. Silver Blaze's six-length score in the Wessex Cup at a mile and five furlongs was just another day's work.

Silver Blaze's owner was a well-known sportsman, a small, alert person, very neat and dapper in a frock coat and gaiters, with trim little sidewhiskers and an eyeglass. Secretariat is owned by a syndicate and managed by Mrs. Helen Tweedy, who has become a well-known sportswoman. She is alert, not large, and chic rather than dapper.

Both trainers were jockeys before they became too heavy for the weighing-chair, but there all resemblance ceases. Lucien Laurin, who saddles Secretariat, is a conscientious man of unblemished probity.

John Straker, who handled Silver Blaze, kept a mistress in London who thought nothing of spending $115 on a dress of dove-colored silk with ostrich-feather trimming. To pay for such extravagance, Straker tried to nobble the favorite and make a killing, and was properly kicked to death by his own horse.

Ron Turcotte, who rides Secretariat, is a competent horseman now at the top of his game. All we know of the jockeys in the Wessex Cup is that the nameless boy on Desborough rode the second favorite like a Chinaman. He moved too early and Desborough's bolt was shot at the 16th pole. The fact that Desborough's trainer, Silas Brown, was putty in Holmes's hands may explain the jock's riding orders.

Finally the computer should consider that Silver Blaze always raced on grass and Secretariat never has; that under weight-for-age conditions Secretariat would carry 119 pounds to the other's 126, and that Secretariat's aluminum shoes are lighter than the iron plates Silver Blaze wore. Pending a verdict from the machine, horseplayers among the Baker Street Irregulars were polled as to the probable winner. Their judgment, couched in the stately language of Victorian England, was virtually unanimous:

"Silver Blaze will chew him up and spit him against the fence!"

# LOVE ON THE LAGOON

HIALEAH Race Course is a popular winter resort for wealthy horses, a halfway house providing fast, fast, fast relief for tourists burdened with money, and a sanctuary for overdressed poultry. Probably its most famous residents are the flamingos, those ornate descendants of Cuban immigrants who colonized the infield lagoon almost 40 years ago.

These garish fowl are saluted annually by management, which calls its richest race for 3-year-olds the Flamingo Stakes; cooed over frequently by lady horseplayers in tight magenta slacks; occasionally celebrated in prose by authors with debauched tastes who write of their grace, nobility and beauty.

The truth is they are ostentatious in appearance, antisocial by disposition, and no great success simply as birds. On land they move with arthritic ungainliness, repeatedly falling on their vapid faces. In flight the flamingo resembles no eagle nor lark nor buzzard even, but a starched streamer of confetti in strip-tease pink, long and skinny and blushing like a basketball player without his pants. Seen face to foolish face, the critter is so ill-favored that even a lovelorn boy flamingo can't bear to gaze into a girl flamingo's eyes.

As might be expected in these circumstances, the course of true love in the Hialeah infield does not run smooth. When the female of the species is in the mood for romance, she conceals her ugliness by sticking her head under water, and wades about with what she fondly imagines to be a provocative gait. In much the same fashion do dolls on Miami Beach apply a disguise of war paint, top the bikini off with a mink stole and go swaying past the cabanas where males are playing gin.

If the flamingo plays her cards right, the male of her choice falls into step and follows her in a wolfish courtship dance. If the blonde is successful, she winds up at a table for two listening to Steve and Eydie.

As a rule, romance doesn't ride the wavelets at Hialeah until the race meeting is over. In this warm winter, however, the breeding season started earlier than usual and a shift in racing dates made the Flamingo Stakes later than usual. After a mating it takes about a month for a flamingo to spin an egg and another 30 days for her to hatch it. Right now, the lake is a watery lying-in hospital.

In the early years, Hialeah clipped the birds' wings so they couldn't go helling off into the Everglades. On Flamingo Day these flightless captives were herded up the turf course to flap wings for the clientele. Successive generations hatched in the infield came to regard the place as home. No longer is it necessary to clip their wings, for although the present residents can fly, they don't want to escape. Once each stakes day they are shooed aloft, where they circle the track once and return to the water.

When the Flamingo Stakes came up yesterday, Hialeah's resident birdherd, Angelo Testa, grew concerned about the delicate condition of his flock. He feared that expectant mothers forced to fly might lose their eggs and perhaps the future of the colony would be endangered. Motherhood prevailed; enciente or no, the birds were grounded.

Back in 1966, Buckpasser was such a pronounced favorite for the Flamingo that Gene Mori, who runs the joint, called off betting on the race for fear he would have to dip into the till to pay off a minus pool. Even today, 1966 is remembered as the Year of the Chicken Flamingo. Now this winter goes into the annals as the Year of the Pregnant Flamingo.

# WIND HER UP, SHE TALKS

THE patient wore racing silks instead of a hospital gown, but instead of riding breeches she had a plaster cast from knee to rib cage. She was on the phone when visitors entered the room, and she hung up shaking her pretty blonde head. "I ride for Jack VanBerg," she said, "and they call me between races to tell me how the horses did. Since I've been in here, they haven't won. I just said, 'Those guys are pulling them.' They told me, 'No, Mary, you pulled 'em so long the horses don't know any better.'" Her hoyden grin said: "Some kidders, eh?"

"It was four weeks ago Sunday at 5:15 a.m.," Mary Bacon said, explaining why she was on her back in Physicians Hospital, Queens. "I was in the tackroom shooting the bull with the grooms when somebody yelled, 'Aegean Queen is hung up in her stall!' She's a 2-year-old that I rode as a first-time starter at Aqueduct and I thought, 'That's a potential winner for me!'

"She was one of the horses the boys had tacked up to work in the first set and she must've turned to pull at her girth or something. She had the stirrup iron hooked around her jaw and she was choking. I ran in and pulled it loose.

"She was facing the rear wall with me in front of her when a hot-walker whacked her on the rump. She lunged and smashed me against the wall and then she slipped and went down on top of me. She was cast. She was kicking and trying to get up. When they pulled me out it hurt, but I thought, 'Maybe it's just bruises and I can ride tomorrow.' Then I got here and they told me I had a crushed pelvis, my back broken high and low, and internal injuries."

"What do they tell you now?" she was asked.

"What they tell me is different from what I tell them. I tell them,

'This cast comes off Sunday, X-ray me Monday and name me on horses for Tuesday.'"

Although the *American Racing Manual* gives Chicago, 1948, as the place and year of her birth, Mary says she is an Okie who at the age of 9 was riding quarter-horse races in the home country around Elk City near the Oklahoma-Texas line. "We were migrant farm workers," she said, "picking beans and stuff. No money, no education. If I can fight, it's from fighting to get to the dinner table.

"At 15 I left home. I married a jockey. In Detroit I galloped horses in the morning, worked at a hunt club afternoons, and three nights a week I was a go-go dancer in a club called The Hatrack. I wasn't so flat-chested then before I started making weight. When *Playboy* magazine had that nude picture of me, a guy at Belmont said, 'I kept waiting for it to come out, and then it didn't show nothing.' 'Tell you the truth,' I told him, 'there's not much to show.'

"I'm not Robyn Smith. I'm not a model who became a jockey. I'm a jockey who became a jockey. All's I know is horses. I can't cook, but I can fix a hot mash. I can't keep house, but I can muck out a stall. I always sleep in racing silks, seein' as I don't have any nightgowns. These are the silks I wore on Bold Music in the Derby Trial . . ."

Actually, the race was the 1972 Spendthrift Purse at Keeneland, a prep for the Blue Grass Stakes, which is a preliminary to the Kentucky Derby. Bold Music finished last and didn't go on to the Derby Trial, but Mary hasn't time for small details. This is a doll, you wind her up and she talks. She talks of spills and broken bones, of a race when she was a pregnant jockey on a pregnant mare, of being kidnapped and shot.

"Paul Corley Turner," she said, plunging into the kidnap tale. It was 1969, her apprentice year, when she was second leading rider at the Pocono Downs meeting in Pennsylvania and Turner was a groom who disapproved of women riding races. Capturing her and her 60-year-old agent at knifepoint, he took them up in the hills, telling Mary he was going to kill her, but they broke free. "He threw his knife and hit me in the back. Well, further down, actually, but I couldn't tell the reporters that. I still got a scar."

Turner, Mary went on, was arrested and turned loose, followed her from track to track telephoning promises to kill her, at length caught her and the woman who was then her agent in a Louisville motel room and fired two shots. One bullet grazed the agent and caught Mary in the leg. "He's doing 12 years now in Kentucky," Mary said, "and when he gets out they'll expedite him to Pennsylvania."

Spills? "Last Sept. 15 I hit the Tartan track at Pitt Park—that's The Meadows, the harness track where they were trying to run thoroughbreds. I was unconscious six days with three blood clots on the brain. The 10th day my boss came to see me.

" 'Crafty Cream's going tomorrow,' he told me. 'Name me to ride her,' I said. 'Ride her?' he said. 'You're in intensive care.' They had my hands up here with things on my wrists. 'Name me,' I told him. I discharged myself and rode and she win."

It was a news story when Mary and John Bacon had a friendly divorce because racing authorities had ruled that husband and wife must not ride against each other. (No such conflict of interest is seen between brothers or between father and son.) Before that, they did ride opposing horses.

"The first time in Detroit," Mary said, "I win and Johnie was second. He took a lot of ribbing. Next time, he slammed me leaving the gate. There's a place in Detroit where the film patrol camera has a blind spot, but I forgot about the patrol judge. Man, what I did to Johnie there! He snatched up or I'd a' put him over the fence. He had the best horse, as usual. He took out around the field and got up to win. I was fourth, and they gave me five days. I grabbed Johnie.

" 'You made it look worse than it was,' I told him. 'You snatched straight up. Okay, I got five days. You get five nights.' "

# HOW ORGANIZED CRIME DIED

**T**HE final fatuous platitude fell flat in the concourse of Grand Central Terminal. Waggling beribboned scissors for the television cameras, Honest John Lindsay snipped an orange sash stretched across a window where the bankrupt New Haven Railroad used to sell tickets to Scarsdale. "We're off!" cried Hot Horse Howie Samuels, and a retired post office worker from Brooklyn bet $2 to win on a pacer named Adoras Nicki in the first at Roosevelt Raceway.

Thus came the millennium to Fun City. It is called Off-Track Betting, and let history note that it came to pass at 10:52 a.m. on Holy Thursday, April 8, 1971. Twenty-four hours later it could have served to celebrate the release of Barrabas.

The first legal horse bet ever made away from the racetrack in New York was placed by Philip Gross, 66, who had earned the distinction by planting his stern on a folding chair in front of the windows at 10 a.m. Wednesday. He said he had been a leisure-time horseplayer for 30 years and undertook this 24-hour wait so he could get his picture in the papers and make his family happy.

He was followed to the wicket by Honest John Lindsay, the Friendly Bookie of Gracie Square. Bucking his own game, Honest John bet a deuce on Money Wise in the seventh at Roosevelt.

By this time something like 2,000 spectators had gathered, and as Lindsay left the window some of them queued up to get a piece of the action. With inexperienced help fumbling through a cumbersome manual operation, these transactions were effected at the same glacial pace that has characterized OTB from the outset.

Starting last July when Samuels took over as Lindsay's sheetwriter, it required the full gestation period of nine months and the expenditure of $5.5-million in public funds to take in the first $2. This was the procedure:

Depending on the sort of action he wanted, a player selected from a counter a three-page slip marked Daily Double, Perfecta, Win, Place or Show. Identifying the horse of his choice by letter instead of mutuel number—A for No. 1, B for No. 2—he filled in blanks to indicate the horse, the race and the amount of his wager. Then he waited while the clerk validated the slip in an infrared stamping machine, punched it so the amount bet could not be altered, separated the paper into three parts. One part went to a girl who tabulated the bet, then it was forwarded to the control center; another went into the clerk's cash box; the third went back to the bettor along with his change, if any.

If a bettor filled out the slip incorrectly—using numbers instead of letters, for example—he had to go back and start all over. One got to the head of the line with a fat wad of bets and discovered that he had got a batch of slips with the third page missing. Sorry.

Clerks had to examine each part of each ticket to make sure all carbon copies were legible. The lines moved like wet cement.

One man, starting fourth or fifth in line, got to the window in 20 minutes. Apologetically the clerk set up a sign: Closed. His validating machine was misbehaving. It took five minutes to replace the machine.

Another man who wanted to bet 7 and 7 in the daily double had properly marked his slip G-G. The clerk said he couldn't bet the same letter in each race; if he was betting two different horses, he had to use different letters. It took a while to straighten that out.

"We have a lot of learning ahead of us," Samuels had said during the opening ceremonies.


When social historians of the future inquire into the mores of our time, they will discover that the blow that killed organized crime in New York was struck on the morning of April 8, 1971. That day a Brooklyn horseplayer placed a $2 bet in Grand Central Terminal and the city started up the highroad to solvency, rectitude and respect for law.

For months, Howard Samuels had been promising that his Off-Track Betting Corp. would not only solve the town's fiscal problems but would also wipe the underworld out of existence. Illegal gambling, he explained, supplied the treasury supporting organized crime, and when competition from OTB put the bookmakers out of business, the rogues would be unable to finance such collateral activities as loan sharking, dope pushing and labor racketeering. Oh, we might read now and then of a lady firing a few rounds into her spouse's plumbing, and perhaps an occasional mugger would be arrested for rolling a drunk, but professional enterprises like kidnaping, blackmail and white slavery would be things of the past.

Now Samuels is saying that if OTB's wings are clipped, the bookies he has driven to the wall will prosper once again and a kid at P.S. 89 won't be able to play stickball without tripping over a heroin pusher.

When Governor Rockefeller assigned Charles B. Delafield and eight others to find out what ailed New York racing, Howie said it would be a pleasure to work with "that distinguished body." Later, when the Delafield Commission's scrutiny of OTB made him uncomfortable, he dropped "distinguished" from his vocabulary.

He suggested that M. Donald Grant, a commission member who is chairman of the board of the New York Mets, could hardly be impartial because he worked for Mrs. Charles M. Payson, a horse owner. And as for Fred Capossela, the retired race-caller also on the commission, wasn't he drawing a pension from the New York Racing Association?

Finally, when the commission recommended controls on OTB lest it destroy racing in the state, Samuels called the report "the rape of the city," likened it to recommending welfare payments to bookies, and cried that "the whole aim of the Delafield proposals is to make the tracks rich."

Howie wants to be governor. In OTB he has a hand-tooled political machine supported by the horseplayers, paying millions in salaries and millions more in leases and building contracts and giving employment to many who worked unsuccessfully to make him governor three years ago. He'll give that up as readily as a female tiger abandons her young.

Though OTB hasn't produced anything like the revenue anticipated, it is still John Lindsay's baby and he is not about to yield any loot to the state. Naturally, the Mayor lines up with Samuels to fight the Delafield proposals. "The charge that OTB is hurting racetracks is nonsense," says Honest John. "Tracks are in trouble all over the country."

This kind of poppycock is to be expected from one as uninformed about racing as Lindsay. One does not expect it from men entrusted with direction of the sport. Yet somebody seems to have sold the same can of corn to the State Racing Commission.

In its annual report, the commission cites these figures: In 1970, when there was no OTB, racing at Aqueduct, Belmont and Saratoga produced $82.9-million in state taxes; in 1971, with OTB creeping into action, nine more racing days produced $81.9-million, a loss of 1.2 percent; in 1972, with OTB expanding, the state got $66.1-million, a loss of $16.8-million, or 20.2 percent, during OTB's short life.

The report proceeds to blame this loss on (a) the national economy, (b) "an increasing number of races with short fields which . . . dampen enthusiasm," and (c) inadequate parking.

Fact One: *The Daily Racing Form* lists 84 race meetings around the country where the national economy did not hurt business. One track that showed substantial gains was Finger Lakes, the only thoroughbred course in New York State that is outside the OTB area.

Fact Two: Kent Hollingsworth reports in *The Blood-Horse* that in 1970 at Aqueduct, Belmont and Saratoga, 2,106 races were run with an average field of 9 horses; in 1971 there were 2,187 races averaging 9.1 horses; in 1972 there were 2,087 races and the average of 8.8 horses was one-tenth of a horse below the national average for 59,417 races.

Fact Three: Between 1970 and 1972, daily attendance at Aqueduct, Belmont and Saratoga dropped 22.2 percent, from 28,101 to 21,855. Parking space has not been reduced. The same area that accommodated 100 cars in 1970 is now occupied by 78 cars. The problem is not where to put the customers. It is how to get them back from Hot Horse Howie.

# HELL, HIGH WATER AND PEANUT BUTTER

$\mathbb{P}$OCONO DOWNS is a gambling hell of modest status three miles out of Wilkes-Barre, Pa., on the way to Scranton. It isn't big enough or sinful enough to attract scrutiny by the House Select Committee on Crime, although the concessionaire who feeds and waters the horseplayers there, Sportservice, Inc., has enjoyed that distinction. It's just a vest-pocket sink of iniquity with seating accommodations for 6,500 customers and a horsemen's colony of 850 to 900.

In the dark morning hours of Friday, June 23, the guard at the stable gate got word that the Susquehanna was rising dangerously and additional sandbags were needed to hold back the flood. He put a call out over the public-address system, and everybody in the stable area turned out. A dump truck was loaded with empty feedbags and dispatched. Then trainers, grooms and watchmen flung more bags into pickup trucks and drove into town to help fill the sacks with earth and bank them up against the river.

Daylight came as they worked. About 1 p.m. the dikes gave way. The horsemen retreated to the track. Around 3 o'clock, three helicopters landed in the infield. Each had a refugee aboard, one plucked from the river, one rescued from a treetop and one from a roof. Could Pocono Downs be set up as an evacuation center for other flood victims? Of course, said Ed Gilkey, the track's general manager. Soon there were 14 helicopters ferrying in sick and injured, infants and aged.

The clubhouse was converted into an infirmary and registration center. Every night for a week the 200 cots were occupied, with 24 volunteer nurses working shifts around the clock. Dr. Mario Sindico, the track physician whose home was swept away, organized a medical corps of volunteer doctors from as far away as Philadelphia and Wilmington, Del.

Trucks brought tons of foodstuffs and clothing which the horsemen unloaded and stored in the grandstand area. Horsemen used their cars as ambulances to carry the ill to hospitals, the homeless to temporary living quarters. They helped the Army set up mobile water purification systems in the paddock and the infield. They operated a walkie-talkie communications system. They made sandwiches. And sandwiches. And sandwiches.

One man drove to every drugstore he could reach and bought up 800 hypodermic needles for the vaccination center at the track. Thousands were inoculated against typhoid and tetanus.

Between 3 p.m. Friday, when those first three helicopters arrived, and the following Wednesday, 10,000 refugees went through. There were cardiac cases and pregnant women, lost children and parents hunting relatives, wealthy residents whose riverfront homes had been washed from their foundations, fugitives from shantytown.

A lady of regal bearing stepped from one helicopter accompanied by her maid and three French poodles. Graciously declining assistance, she set up a small compound in a corner of the clubhouse. Her maid did the cooking and walked the dogs. They stayed through to Thursday, July 6, when the track was officially closed as an evacuation center. Departing, the lady thanked Pocono officials for "the simply lovely quarters," adding a hope that wherever they were going, three poodles would be welcome.

A sick woman was hurried off to a hospital and the volunteer who assigned her went off duty without telling the husband what had happened. He was frantic until a Pocono employe located his wife for him. Relieved, he settled in until the last day, and asked if he might stay a week or so longer.

He had grown accustomed to the cuisine provided by Ralph Massias, the maître de clubhouse. For breakfast in the bedraggled misery of Saturday, June 24, Massias contrived mountains of scrambled eggs served from silver chafing dishes onto paper plates. Lunch that day featured spaghetti and meatballs in wine sauce. Sunday luncheon was creamed chicken on toast à la Pocono. For dinner there was ham with pineapple glacé in a champagne sauce.

Always there were sandwiches. By 2 a.m. that first Saturday, stable swipes and security personnel, maintenance men and ticket-takers and secretaries had made 7,000 sandwiches. By daylight, Sportservice's reserves of bread and peanut butter, jellies and cold cuts, had gone into another 15,000 sandwiches which were sent to the Wilkes-Barre-

Scranton airport, another evacuation center. Fresh supplies arrived, including 4,000 loaves of bread, and the sandwich chefs worked on through Saturday and Saturday night, Sunday and Sunday night. By Thursday they had made 250,000 sandwiches.

On Wednesday, even before the track was closed as an evacuation center, Gilkey decided that racing would resume Friday night. Payrolls had been suspended during the flood, so he offered $50 advances to any employes requesting them. Three did. Horsemen on the grounds were furnished two free meals a day.

Supplies were moved out of the grandstand, the clubhouse was cleaned up, the kitchens restocked. Friday night Pocono Downs was in action, admission free.

"I thought people might like to see something besides mud and wreckage," Gilkey said. "Second, I had a responsibility to the horsemen; racing is their living. Third, I wanted to show that business-as-usual was possible in spite of everything. Fourth, the payroll here is important to the economy of Wyoming Valley, and of course our organization was depending on me to get back into business as soon as possible."

Near the grandstand rail, Gilkey was clutched and kissed. The clutcher had been a refugee-in-residence for six days. Now she was back as a horseplayer. "God bless you," she said. "As long as I live I'll never forget landing in your infield."

"Or ever eat another peanut-butter-and-jelly sandwich," the general manager said.

# A MAN NAMED ROONEY

ARTHUR J. ROONEY is a man of such reckless daring that he once entrusted his Pittsburgh Steelers to Johnny Blood, an unfettered soul whose tenure as playing coach Rooney would sum up later in two sentences: "On most teams the coach worries about where the players are at night. Our players worried about the coach."

Evidently Art's five sons inherited their sire's boldness, for even as New York racing cries havoc, they are buying Yonkers Raceway for $47-million. When they take over the world's biggest harness track, the Rooneys' sports enterprises will compare in magnitude with the Roman Empire. They operate thoroughbred racing in Philadelphia, at Liberty Bell Park pending construction of a new track; professional football in Pittsburgh; and dog racing at the Palm Beach Kennel Club. Art still bets blithely on steeds carrying the silks of his Shamrock Farm. He always bet blithely.

"I didn't necessarily know more about horses than the next guy," he said the other day, "but I might have known a little more about playing. I never was afraid to bet."

He was retelling the tale of his big score at Saratoga in 1936, which has become a legend. According to most accounts, he slapped the bookmakers around for more than a quarter-million that day, but when Art tells the story he never mentions the amount.

"I went to Harrisburg," he said, "with Buck Crouse, the great middle-weight fighter, and Harry Earl for a dinner the plumbers' union was giving our friend Charlie Anderson, their international vice president. From there we kept on driving to New York and got to Empire City just before the first race. I bet $20 with a bookmaker in the grandstand ring and won $700 or $800. We'd moved into the clubhouse by that time, so I went back to the grandstand to give the bookie a chance to get even. I had three or four winners and wound up knocking him out of the box.

"That was a Saturday and we went to Joe Madden's restaurant where the football crowd hung out. The next morning Buck and Madden and I were driving to Saratoga in Madden's old car. It broke down three or four times and the radiator kept boiling over going over the mountains.

"Monday, opening day at Saratoga, was a terrible day. If I remember right, a couple of horses were killed by lightning. I had Tim Mara's figures but sometimes I'd see something the charts didn't see, like a change of jockeys or post position, and I'd use my own judgment. I was betting with Peter Blong, who was working in the ring for Frank Erickson that day, and after I'd hit him for about three winners he said, 'That's enough.' Peter was right up there with the big books like Tom Shaw, and very sharp. If Erickson had been there I'm sure he would have kept on taking my action.

"Anyway, I came close to sweeping the card. In those days they ran only eight races, maybe only seven. I was sitting with Bill Corum, the sportswriter, who saw what I was doing and wrote a column about me breaking the books. He did it mostly to needle George Marshall down in Washington. By that time Marshall owned the Redskins and he was a reformed horseplayer. At least, he knew more about horses than any of us, and he was dead against anybody in the league betting.

"After Corum wrote the story it got bigger and bigger. One of the Hearst papers assigned a reporter to go to the track with me every day. On days when I'd lose he'd play it down and when I won he'd make it much bigger than it was. He told me he liked the assignment and had to make me seem like a live guy because his paper wouldn't be interested in a dead one."

The legend goes that Art sent most of his winnings to his brother Dan, a missionary priest in China.

"I sent Dan some money," he said, "but nowhere near the amount I've read about. In those days you could have bought most of China for that kind of money."

This was bread cast upon the waters, and it came back as soybeans. Some years after the Saratoga incident, Art and a Chicago friend, Jerry Nolan, were deep in the commodities market. They were selling soybeans short, gambling on a big crop and falling market.

"Riding home from New York one day," Art said, "I read a little item in *The Times* about floods in China. I called Father Dan, who was the superior in the Franciscan house in Boston. 'You got any Chinese priests in the house?' I asked him. Turned out there were a couple. They got in touch with the bishop in Hong Kong and sure enough, floods were playing hell with the soybean crop. I called Nolan and we switched our position and made a nice score."

Another time Art and a dozen others were trying to corner cocoa. Art confided in a friend who was connected with the Hershey, Pa., hockey team. The friend was aghast. "You've got more cocoa than we have in Hershey," he said. Art took it as a warning and sold out. His partners rejected the advice and got burned.

Then there was Westminster, who won the Double Event Handicap under Art's colors at Tropical Park. This was really two races, run 12 days apart. Westminster won both divisions and legend says Art cleaned up just under a million.

Maybe stories like these explain why his Steelers have never won a championship. Art has succeeded at so many things the law of compensation has to get in its licks somewhere. Son of a prosperous saloon-keeper, Art was a kid football player courted vainly by Knute Rockne of Notre Dame, a baseball player signed by the Chicago Cubs and Boston Red Sox, an amateur boxing champion in both the lightweight and welterweight divisions, a successful fight promoter.

"I could have gone to the Olympics," he said, "but I turned pro. I fought a kid named, I think it was Joe Azevedo on a Pinkey Mitchell-Tommy O'Brien card in Milwaukee and my manager, Dick Guy, talked about matching me with Benny Leonard. But I don't know, the style of fighter I was I might have wound up without all my buttons."

# SUPER BOWL IS A LOVER

IT might surprise Pete Rozelle to learn that there is a Super Bowl that never has a dull moment. For Super Bowl, the horse, things are so exciting that on the day he started his new career he fainted dead away. In his new career he is a lover.

The owner of the world mile record for 3-year-old trotters won his last 18 races, took the triple crown by sweeping the Hambletonian, Yonkers Futurity and Kentucky Futurity, was chosen 3-year-old champion and trotter-of-the-year in landslide elections, was syndicated for $1-million and finally retired to stud on Hanover Shoe Farm near Gettysburg, Pa. His first date was a comely and well-bred lady named Reneged, a daughter of the Hambletonian winner Hickory Smoke. Super Bowl was still just a 3-year-old, a big bashful kid from the country. In his confusion he passed out cold. Hal Jones, Hanover's stallion master, slapped his face until the colt woke up, looking sheepish. Since then, Super Bowl has been attending to duty cheerfully every Monday, Wednesday and Friday.

A typical day begins about 5 a.m. when Super Bowl wakes and has breakfast. As soon as the sun is up he is turned out to romp or loaf as he pleases for three hours or so. Meanwhile Jones checks over the candidates for the colt's attentions.

Ninety mares have been booked to Super Bowl for his first season but about two-thirds of them will be artificially inseminated. Hanover has a horse population of about 1,700 with a dozen stallions besides Super Bowl and at least 300 broodmares. On any given day, anywhere from 10 to 60 mares may be in season; they're all brought to the breeding shed.

About 11 o'clock Super Bowl is brought back to the stallion barn and cleaned up. He knows by now that he'll be having a tryst somewhere between 12 and 1 o'clock, and the routine tells him the time is approaching. When the first stallion is led away, all the others in the barn start raising hell.

If several of the mares booked to Super Bowl are ready, Jones tries to select one he thinks will be compatible, but the colt gets a vote. Stallions, like Broadway producers, have decided views about the opposite sex. The great pacing sire, Tar Heel, for instance, has been holding court at Hanover for years and years and there is no way of getting him to pay attention to a mare he didn't choose for himself. So Super Bowl gets to pick one from the conga line and if others in his harem are in season that day, they're inseminated artificially.

Afterwards the colt is returned to his stall where he gets a dinner of oats spiked with three raw eggs, honey and vitamin E. Unlike some of the other horses who have special friends—Dancer Hanover and Bullet Hanover each shares his stall with a goat—Super Bowl seems contented rooming alone, although he was fretful at first. This worried people who didn't know about his addiction to honey drops.

It seems that Louis Silverstein, whose wife Hilda raced Super Bowl in partnership with Mrs. Stanley Dancer, believes that honey has helped keep him alive since he underwent an operation 40 years ago. A candy manufacturer makes up honey drops for him and he feeds them to the horses. Long before he got to Hanover, Super Bowl was hooked on the confection, just as his sire, Star's Pride, is hooked on Vick's cough drops.

Super Bowl first saw light at Stoner Creek Stud, Paris, Ky., but the story goes back to 1947 when Rachel and Stanley Dancer met in a roller rink in Trenton, N.J. She was fresh out of high school, he was an eighth-grade dropout working as a stable hand. They were married in September and lived with her parents until May, when they were able to buy a used trailer.

When Stanley saw a crippled black gelding named Candor, Rachel took $250 saved for college and they bought the horse. For hours every day they hosed down Candor's bad leg, rubbed and bandaged him. In the next three years Candor won $12,000, and from that stake came Egyptian Acres, the Dancer's farm at New Egypt, N.J., their home near Pompano Beach, Fla., their fame and their million-dollar horses.

Much of their success has been due to Rachel's judgment, or intuition. Two of her earliest purchases were Volo Chief and Titanic, who won about $50,000 between them. Late in 1968, Norman Woolworth sent a yearling colt by Meadow Skipper to Florida for Stanley to train before the January sales at Pompano Park. Rachel thought the horse should bring $30,000; when bidding lagged, she prodded Stanley into buying him for $12,000. His name was Most Happy Fella and he was 2 years old. In 1970 he won the Big Five events for 3-year-old pacers—the Messenger, the Cane, the Little Brown Jug, the Adios and the L. K. Shapiro—and Rachel sold him for $1-million.

That same year she saw a yearling by Star's Pride from Pillow Talk in a field at Stoner Creek. The Dancers had known two full brothers of this colt that weren't much but when Rachel asked Stanley's opinion about this one he said, "He's a different type than his brothers, rangier." They bought him for $20,000 and called him Super Bowl. A few weeks later Rachel offered a half interest to her friend Hilda Silverstein.

To Garo Yepremian, the pass master from Nicosia, super bowl means $15,000. The other Super Bowl paid the ladies $605,609, not counting syndication.

# THE MELANCHOLY DAYS ARE COME

**N**OW is the winter of their discontent, the melancholy days without a thoroughbred running this side of Philadelphia, the cruel times when New York horseplayers are thrown upon the mercy of Howard J. Samuels and his off-track gambling hells.

Beaming through charcoal-gray darkness, yellow lights on the tote board at Aqueduct gave the time as 4:29 p.m. when the winner reached the finish of the 2,187th race of the season. Moments later the reedy voice of Fred Capossela came over the public-address system for the last time: "The result of the ninth race is official. The winner, No. 4, Canning, a chestnut horse by Datour. . . . Thank you, and good afternoon." On laggard feet, 25,380 immortal souls took their leave.

Reluctantly, they would go home. They would note with interest how the children had grown since March. Somehow they would get through 76 dark days squandering their earnings on rent and beer and shoes until the sun would shine again, however bleakly, and the bugle would call the horses to the post on March 1.

In the catacombs below the stands, a man rapped on a door marked "Lady Jockeys."

"Are your eyes gray or blue?" he asked Robyn Smith. "Green," she said, "but right now they're red and green."

She was wiping away mud kicked into her comely face by Canning and Sip Sip Sip, who had burst out of the fog and rain and gloom in the last few yards to finish one-two in the final race and move her back to third aboard Advance Warning.

Robyn had five mounts on getaway day. She won smartly with Princely Margin at 50.40 for $2, was third with Advance Warning and third with Schnappy, an 18-to-1 shot, finishing sixth and seventh with the others. Princely Margin was her 15th winner of the Aqueduct fall meeting. In 51 days she had 124 mounts and finished third or better with 37. Only nine males had a higher winning percentage.

"You've made it in the toughest league in the world," a visitor told her. "You are one girl who has done what the others talked about."

She agreed with a matter-of-fact nod. But she said, "I feel that when I lose my bug I'll be starting all over again."

The "bug" is the five-pound weight allowance an apprentice jockey loses one year after riding his fifth winner, provided he has had 35 winners by that time. Robyn's year expired Nov. 30 but was extended to mid-January to make up for six weeks lost because of a broken hand. Some riders can't win without the weight advantage.

"I notice you like the rail," her visitor said. "That's one mark of a good, unmarried jockey." (In threadbare racing slang, the longer but safer outside route is known as the "Married Man's Highway.")

"I like to save ground when I can," Robyn said, "but I can go outside if that's where the trainer says the horse does best."

"Does it get a little scary on the inside at times?"

"Not for me." Her tone was conversational without a trace of bravado. "What upsets me, though, is to get locked inside with a horse that wants to run. It happened the other day. My horse was full of run and I had no place to go. When I lose by a head or a nose, I always feel I could have done something else."

"Has there been one ride that gave you special satisfaction?"

"The day at Saratoga when I rode Beaukins to a track record for Allen Jerkens. Kennedy Road was in the race, a good horse, and some other good ones that I forget. The boy on Kennedy Road lodged a claim of foul for interference leaving the gate, but I knew exactly what I was doing. I left just enough room inside for Kennedy to go through, but it was tight enough to make the boy wonder. It made him hesitate a little. Then he went through—I knew he'd want to be on the lead—and he really used his horse. I waited, then came around him and won by a length."

Brenda Felicetti, the pretty little trainer of Schnappy, appeared in the doorway. "You rode him beautifully," she told Robyn.

"He was coming strong at the end," Robyn said. "I didn't want to go to the rail, but I had no choice."

"I could see that."

"I think he was a little green going to the turn," Robyn said, "like, 'where am I?' So I snugged him down a little. Then he finished full of run."

"He's young," Miss Felicetti said, "and I think he might prefer a firmer track. I'm taking him to Gulfstream, but I'll probably race him once at Tropical."

"He'll run good at Tropical," Robyn said. "I'll be at Gulfstream for the opening. I'd like to ride him again down there."

# A BAG
# OF WIND

When Rutgers defeated Princeton on November 6, 1869, in the first intercollegiate football match, news of the event soon reached other campuses. Undergraduates at Cornell and Michigan organized teams, challenges were exchanged, and Cleveland was tentatively agreed upon as a neutral site for a game. However, President White of Cornell was something of a wet blanket.

"I will not permit 30 men to travel 400 miles," he said, "merely to agitate a bag of wind."

His words come back to mind sometimes, usually during the shaving cream commercials that flood our autumn weekends, and with them comes the realization that Dr. White's was the wisdom that passes understanding.

# THE NAME OF THE GAME

Well," the coach said, "it took us prettinear all season, but we finally put it all together and for once we got a few bounces so maybe somebody up there thinks we must be doing something right, after all. It was a team effort. It shows what we can do when the horses are healthy and let's hope this is only the beginning.

"The quarterback's not too fast and maybe he hasn't got the strongest arm in the league, but he comes to play. One thing, he can really pick those defenses apart. He knows where it's at. They were keying on the guards, so at halftime we made a few adjustments and in the second half we put it all together like you saw.

"As for those missed kicks, well, that was just one of those things. That's the way the cookie crumbles. You know, the ball takes some funny bounces in this game. I'd have to say that kicker of ours is the gutsiest little guy I ever had. He's played hurt all year and the way he hung in there gave me a good kind of inside feeling, and it really means something to a team.

"That pass interference call? I'd have to see the movies, but you're not going to get me to say anything about the officials. Those guys in the striped shirts have a tough job and it's easy to second-guess.

"I admit we didn't look too good at the start of the season, but at the same time I definitely think it's bad to peak too early. It's a long season and you don't want to run out of gas emotionally. Sometimes if you just hang in there and keep hitting, everything seems to drop in for you.

"As far as this game today, I'd have to say it was the biggest victory I've ever had The whole ball of wax was wrapped up in that one. I told the kids after the game they had done a great all-around job. I told them I was proud of the way they hung in there tough and overcame adversity.

"Next week, well, let's face it, it's not just another game, it's the whole ball of wax. This is a must game for the both of us. The team that wants it most is the team that's going to win, just like I think maybe we wanted today's game a little more than the other people.

"We're just going out there and try to play our game, try to let them make the mistakes. After all, the name of the game is defense. Sure, the other people are tough to defense, but they still put their pants on one leg at a time.

"In this league they can all get the job done. It's just a question of who executes best.

"That wide receiver of theirs, he's got all the moves along with great hands and he can juke you. You just have to not give him any daylight and play him nose to nose. Their fullback can be pretty hard-nosed, but we've been defending against the rush all year, that's where we live.

"That No. 42 of theirs, he's having a super season. He's not the fastest back in the league, but he's strong and quick, got the fastest second step in the league. Get him mad, and he'll reach back for that little extra that can beat you. He's what makes them go.

"No, I haven't talked to Joe and I don't know what he's been saying because I don't read the papers. I'll tell you this, if he wasn't teed off about not playing I wouldn't want him on my club. The guys on this club come to play, or they don't stay around.

"I've been too busy to talk to the owner. One of these days we'll sit down and talk, but if it was security I was after I wouldn't be in this game. I don't need a two- or three-year contract. All we ever had, the owner and myself, was a handshake. I'm not thinking about next year. I'm just thinking about next Sunday and going out there on that field and hitting 'em. That's the name of the game, hitting people."

# WINTER WONDERLAND

A S the second half started, a burly customer with a face like broken crockery arose from his seat at the 50-yard line and stripped to the waist, exposing a fetching tract of meat to God's great outdoors. The chill factor had been figured at 15 below zero when the game started but now the stands were in shadow and cooling.

The hardy soul flexed his muscles, beat his chest and roared. Cheers saluted him. Warmed by the ovation, he unbuckled his belt and unzipped his pants enough to allow a glimpse of white drawers. For five minutes or so he stood acknowledging applause. Then he pulled a plaid lumberjacket over purplish pelt and sat down to watch the game. A little later he added a light windbreaker. He remained to the last play while the seats around him emptied. Some of his neighbors paused on the way out to shake his hand.

At the end, the crowd looked like those the New York Titans used to draw in the Polo Grounds before the Titans became the Jets and made their way up in the world to Shea Stadium. New York is called Gotham, after a fabled city noted for the folly of its inhabitants, yet 17,530 of those who had tickets for New York's last football game of the year had the good sense not to show up. Tickets priced at $8 were being offered for $1 before the game, and before it ended, the clientele had retreated in disorder.

By that time the Jets had succumbed to the Cleveland Browns, 26-10, in a windblown parody that bore a superficial resemblance to football and gave the appearance of being a contest for almost three periods. Breaking out of a tie with an 80-yard touchdown play in the third quarter and adding another touchdown and a field goal in the fourth, the Browns completed a noteworthy salvage job by winning for the eighth time in nine games.

They had lost all six of their preseason games and three of the first five on their official schedule, yet even before they showed up yesterday they had qualified for the American Conference's first round of playoffs.

Chances are some of those who ventured into the climate yesterday would have remained by the fireside if they had known they wouldn't see Joe Namath. That celebrated sex symbol spent the afternoon on the sideline under a hooded storm coat, his classic features concealed by a mask such as goaltenders wear in hockey. Afterward, while reporters waited for admittance to the Jets' locker room, a young woman joined them carrying a parcel in Christmas wrappings.

"You can't go in," the guard at the door told her. "There's 40 naked men in there."

"I don't want to go in," she said. "I just want to leave a package." The guard directed her to another door, grinning.

"Got a package for Broadway Joe," he said after she departed. "When you got it, you get it."

The customers had booed lustily when Bob Davis started in Namath's place at quarterback, and set up a chant of "We want Joe!"

"Did you hear them?" Davis was asked.

"Yes," he said. "They're fans, they can do what they want."

There was a snort from Namath sitting in front of the next locker. "Fine opening question! 'Did you hear the fans?'"

"Get off my foot," he ordered a visitor who wasn't on his foot, and stalked away.

Howling winds that gusted up to 45 miles an hour made passing hazardous, and fingers stiff with cold had difficulty holding a thrown football. Receivers held four of Davis's 12 passes for gains of 44 yards, and one was intercepted. He slipped several times where wet turf had turned to ice.

"They were the worst conditions I ever saw," the young man said.

"Bobby should have worn basketball shoes," said Weeb Ewbank, his coach, "but he thought he could do better with short cleats. Hank Bjorklund wore basketball shoes and had a pretty good day."

Ewbank wrapped up the Jets' season—seven victories, seven defeats —in a sentence: "We never got our team together."

Early in the season Nick Skorich would have said the same about the Browns, especially after their center, Jim Copeland, was disabled. Then they traded a seventh-round draft choice to Miami for Bob

DeMarco, a holdout with the Dolphins who had been traded to Buffalo but had refused to report.

"DeMarco gave us good blocking up the middle and made our offensive line work," the coach said. "On defense our two great tackles, Walter Johnson and Jerry Sherk, carried the load when our ends got hurt. We like our secondary and linebackers."

Last year the Browns had to win their last four games to take the division title.

"It must be boring," a visitor suggested, "coming back to the playoffs year after year."

"I'd like to be bored like that," Skorich said. "Just once, just one easy, boring season."

# AN OFFER PETE COULD REFUSE

THE spectacle of Richard G. Kleindienst twisting Pete Rozelle's arm on behalf of a television buff named Richard Nixon is the most comforting sign we have had from Washington since the eve of the 1972 election when Dr. Henry Kissinger assured us that peace was at hand. It means that the nation's major problems have been resolved; that our leaders are no longer preoccupied with Indochina or the Middle East, with poverty, crime, drug abuse, human rights, space exploration, I.T.T. or school busing; that, in short, matters are so nicely in hand everywhere from Hanoi to Moscow to Watergate that the President and his Attorney General can now direct their attention to the National Football League's infamous practice of blacking out the television area immediately surrounding a game.

Some regard Mr. Kleindienst's statement on the matter as a naked threat, a vindictive display of muscle. However, before releasing it to the press he had the courtesy to tell Rozelle that the boss wanted blackouts lifted on all playoff games that sold out. If the Attorney General considered this an offer Pete couldn't refuse, he was mistaken. Pete refused it.

"I have advised Mr. Rozelle," Mr. Kleindienst then announced, "that as a result of the league's decision, the Nixon administration would strongly urge the new Congress to reexamine the entire antitrust exemption statute and seek legislation that is more in keeping with the public interest."

The captious might say that if the existing legislation is not in the public interest, maybe the man we pay to head the Department of Justice should have been doing something about it before Rozelle told him and his boss to go fry their ears. However, Richard K. is a comparatively new boy around there, so new that perhaps he isn't even aware that there is no such thing as an "antitrust exemption statute" relating to football. Pete Rozelle is keenly aware of it because one of his jobs as football's supreme being is to defend against one antitrust suit after another.

To set the record straight, on at least five occasions from the Toolson case in 1953 to the Flood case in 1972, the Supreme Court has ruled that immunity to antitrust law was peculiar to baseball and was not shared by football. Congress has got into the act only twice, in 1961 to give any professional sport the right to sell its games to television as a league package, and in 1966 to allow the N.F.L. and American Football League to merge.

Pro football's television policies came under direct scrutiny in 1953 when they were challenged by the Justice Department. United States District Judge Allan K. Grim approved them and drew guidelines that are now incorporated in the N.F.L. constitution and the network contracts.

Recently, Superior Court Judge David Eagleson in Los Angeles ruled succinctly in regard to "the public interest," as Mr. Kleindienst calls it. Judge Eagleson said the public had a right to be informed but did not have a right to be entertained.

Incidentally, nothing had been heard from the White House about the "public interest" until this week. When the Redskins played at home and could not be seen on TV by the rest of their Washington public, the games were piped into 1600 Pennsylvania Avenue. This service has not been available to ordinary fans. Somebody felt it was too good for the common people.

Rozelle has frequently stated his reasons for continuing the TV policies that helped pro football to affluence. He remembers with poignant clarity Super Bowl I in Los Angeles, the most avidly awaited, extravagantly publicized and feverishly promoted sports event of our time. Compared with the buildup that attraction enjoyed, the Frazier-Ali fight was top secret. Yet rumors that the blackout would be lifted persisted in Los Angeles until the eve of the game, and 30,000 seats were left unsold.

Two years ago, when the American Conference playoffs were in Baltimore, where the Colts had had 51 consecutive sellouts, there were about 10,000 empty seats for the first round. The next round, when Baltimore householders could catch the conference championship on TV from Washington, the Colts got stuck with $46,000 worth of tickets.

As Rozelle pointed out to Kleindienst, 17,530 Jets fans who cared enough to have laid out their money in advance stayed away from Shea Stadium last Sunday. How many more would have remained in out of the cold if they could have caught the game on TV?

Apart from legitimate business considerations, there is a moral issue involved here, a question of property rights. The promoter of a football game offers a product for sale. Purchase of a TV set does not give the buyer a divine right to receive that product free, no matter what the man in the store says, or even Mr. Kleindienst.

# AULD LANG SYNE

I N the 60th minute of the 13th football game of his 18th season as a professional, compassion softened the flinty old heart of Earl Morrall. The Miami Dolphins had the New York Giants whipped, 23-13, and were in possession two yards short of another touchdown with time for one last play.

Massed around the hog wallow that rains had left in Yankee Stadium, 62,728 witnesses looked on moodily, waiting for the final blow to fall. All through the raw and foggy afternoon they had seen the home forces attack and fall back, attack and fall back, attack and fall back again, frustrating their own admirable efforts by giving up the ball on fumbles and interceptions.

The Dolphins broke from their huddle and hunkered down in the mud. Morrall crouched behind center prepared to turn loose one of the rampaging bulls who have given Miami the most formidable running attack in football. Perhaps at that moment the quarterback remembered his three seasons as a member of the Giants and went dewy-eyed for auld lang syne. Maybe he was aware of the abuse and contumely heaped upon Coach George Allen of the Washington Redskins a few weeks ago when that villainous character stopped the clock in the last half-minute to give his men time to double a 7-point lead over the Giants.

Whatever it was, something stayed his hand. He just crouched there in silence and let the seconds tick away until Miami's 13th victory of the season and New York's sixth defeat became official.

On that clement note, the curtain came down on the season in the Bronx, and the first performance ever given there by the Dolphins. They shouldn't have waited so long; guys like Jim Kiick and Larry Csonka, Paul Warfield and Mercury Morris and Nick Buoniconti were born to play on Broadway.

Last winter when the Dolphins made it to the Super Bowl in New Orleans, they were pictured as faceless, nameless silhouettes. Today they are one game away from the National Football League's first perfect season in 30 years. Already champions of the Eastern Division in the American Conference, they can complete their regular schedule undefeated by beating Baltimore next Saturday.

In 13 games, their runners have gained more than half a mile, and they need only 105 yards against the Colts to replace the Detroit Lions of 1936 as the top rushing team in history. The record is 2,885 yards. Against a recalcitrant defense they made 204 yards on foot yesterday, and the names of those who carried the goods are known to people who never heard of Henry Kissinger.

Biggest of the bulls is Csonka, 6-foot-2, 237 heaving pounds, of whom Bob Griese, the disabled quarterback, says: "He attacks the earth." He had gains of 1,016 yards before this game, and added 30 yards on what amounted to a day off.

Morrall knew what most outsiders did not—that Csonka has done his running this year on feet swollen by gout. Possibly on this account, the quarterback called on him only nine times.

Chances are Miami could have got the job done without using Csonka at all, considering the way Kiick and Morris were operating. The electrifying Morris, who moves so fast he seems to flicker, darted, whirled and fled for 98 yards to bring his season total to 905. If he can do as well against Baltimore, the Dolphins will be the first team ever with two 1,000-yard runners.

Kiick has been troubled this year because Don Shula, the coach, has used him and Morris alternately. There is no animosity between the players, but Jim never had to share his job with anybody during his undergraduate years at Wyoming or in his five previous seasons as a pro.

Yesterday some of his neighbors in Lincoln Park, N.J., came across the Hudson to see him perform. He gave them a show, making an average of 11 yards on every carry in the first half and winding up with 69 yards on 10 rushes for the day. On one play he ripped through the secondary for 26 yards, carrying the Giants' Pete Athas piggyback over the last 10.

Then there was Warfield, the little old pattern-maker whose name used to be a household word in the White House. Last season Richard M. Nixon, helping Shula lay out a game plan for the Super Bowl, recommended using Warfield as pass receiver on a down-and-in pattern. Miami got whomped, and this season Warfield has been hurting.

Yesterday he still had discomfort in the arch of one foot, but a damaged ankle had shown improvement. To celebrate, he caught four passes for 132 yards and one touchdown.

This was a game that meant nothing in the league standings, for the Giants were already consigned to third place in their division and the Dolphins' future was assured. Furthermore, the climate had the color and consistency of a blue point on the half-shell, providing a setting of unrelieved dreariness.

Yet the day furnished entertainment of the first order because both teams responded to the spur of pride. Victory over the only unbeaten team in the league would have made this a successful season for the Giants. Except for their errors, their performance was uniformly excellent. It would have been good enough to beat many teams, but not this one proudly resolved to win 'em all.

# A GUY NAMED ELMER

BACK in the piping times when Knute Rockne coached football at Notre Dame, the 22 players on the first and second teams took their meals at two tables in the dining hall on the ground floor of the Administration Building. (That's the one with the golden dome always shown in photographs.) One undergraduate waiter worked both tables. He wheeled the vittles in on double-decked carts from the kitchen, which was in another building across a courtyard. Because he invariably had to make another round trip for seconds, he was no better than 7 to 2 to get his tables cleared and the dishes back to the kitchen in time to eat with the other waiters, and if he wasn't on time he didn't eat.

When the last mound of tapioca vanished, so did 21 athletes. One stayed to help tidy up so the kid could make the deadline. This was Elmer Layden, all-America fullback and star sprinter on the track team. He wasn't asked to help and he didn't expect thanks. He just was that kind of gentleman.

If today's football fan could see the Elmer Layden of 1924, he would hoot at the notion that this emaciated strip of gristle could play fullback on a high school team, let alone the undefeated, untied national champions and Rose Bowl winners. For that matter no member of the dazzling backfield that Grantland Rice immortalized as the Four Horsemen bore more than a superficial resemblance to the snaggle-toothed monsters of these times. Don Miller was the big man at 164 pounds, Harry Stuhldreher never topped 150, and Layden and Jim Crowley were under 160.

Nevertheless, America half a century ago thrilled to the play of these little guys, and to Granny Rice's prose. As a plunging fullback, Layden made his speed compensate for his lack of weight. He pierced the line like an arrow shot from a bow, often—it seemed—with his whole lean figure leveled out in midair. He was the punter also; Crowley was the drop-kicker; Crowley and Stuhldreher did the passing; and all four, of course, blocked and tackled in that age of the complete football player.

Because of his headlong style, Layden usually went for short yardage. Diving as he did, he would be brought down by gravity if no tackler intervened. Yet if he managed to break loose on his feet, he was gone. In the Rose Bowl game against Stanford he scored with two intercepted passes on runbacks of 78 and 70 yards.

Elmer returned to Notre Dame as head coach in 1934, replacing Hunk Anderson, who had inherited the job when Rockne was killed in a plane crash. In the judgment of many, he did the best all-round job as coach and athletic director in the university's history.

Eligibility rules were stiffened about the time he took over, and Layden was scrupulous to the letter. Athletes had to maintain an academic average of 77, compared with a passing grade of 70. There was no red-shirting, no playing of transfer students. Without cutting corners anywhere, Layden built a won-lost-tied record of 47-13-3—.733 against the best college teams in the world.

He worked with three assistants—Joe Boland, the line coach, Joe Benda, in charge of the ends, and Chet Grant with the backs. Boland scouted Tommy Harmon when that gifted runner was playing high school ball in Gary, and a Notre Dame enthusiast twice brought Harmon to South Bend, putting him up in the rectory of Christ the King not far from the campus. On both occasions the pastor, a Father Corcoran, telephoned Layden to come talk to the kid.

The rules said prospects could be interviewed only on campus. "Tell him I'll be glad to see him in my office," Layden said. Next time Harmon saw South Bend he was passing through en route to Michigan and all-America renown.

Bill DeCorrevont demolished schoolboy scoring records, made headlines all over the country and drew crowds approaching 100,000 to high school games in Chicago. A Notre Dame alumnus took him to hear Layden address a dinner and arranged for the two to meet afterward.

Speaking with quiet conviction, Elmer told the kid how brief was the football player's turn on stage and how fleeting his fame. In choosing a college, he said, a boy should seek the school that would best prepare him for the life he wanted to lead. He never mentioned Notre Dame. DeCorrevont went to Northwestern and wound up in the laundry business.

As athletic director, Layden strove for a balanced program, both intercollegiate and intramural. Football got the same treatment he gave to other games. Midwestern powers like Illinois, Ohio State, Michigan and Minnesota had been reluctant to play and lose to Rockne's teams and in later years they would shun Leahy. When Layden was coach, they probably felt they could sell out with Notre Dame and still have a chance to win. At any rate, Elmer added them to the schedule and flogged them.

Mention Notre Dame's come-from-behind conquest of Ohio State in 1935, and even today some old crocks will begin to babble incoherently. In its most tranquil hours the city of Columbus has often reminded visitors of feeding time at the zoo, and the town really went bananas when a Shakespeare-to-Millner pass made the final score 18-13 for Notre Dame. That night Layden sat in the eye of the hurricane sipping a light scotch and water, unflappable as a seal on ice.

He resigned without pressure in 1940 to become commissioner of the National Football League. He served with quiet distinction through the desperate years of warfare with the All America Conference and when the time came he went quietly—just as he left this world yesterday.

# AMBUSH AT FORT DUQUESNE

IN the raucous streets, Frenchy's Foreign Legion honked at Bradshaw's Brigade, Gerela's Guerrillas hailed Ham's Hussars, and foot soldiers in Franco's Italian Army waved red, white and green flags. Back in the bowels of Three Rivers Stadium, Frenchy Fuqua's muttonchop whiskers twitched rapturously. Art Rooney's cigar was limp. The first postseason football game in Pittsburgh history was over, and not since Braddock was ambushed at Fort Duquesne had the town known a day like this.

Forty years ago little Arthur Rooney, 135-pound playing coach of the Majestic Radios, the Hope Harveys and the James P. Rooneys, paid $2,500 for a franchise in the National Football League. Never in all the cold autumns since then had the Steelers got the whiff of a championship of any kind, and now here they were: half-champions of the American Conference with a date to play again next Sunday for the conference title and a chance to earn $25,000 a man in the Super Bowl. And of all the 478 games they had played before last Saturday, none was more gaudily theatrical than the 13-7 conquest of the Oakland Raiders that brought them to this plateau.

Five seconds this side of defeat, the victory was accomplished on a busted play in which the Oakland defense performed flawlessly.

With fourth down, 10 yards to go, on the Pittsburgh 40-yard line, 22 seconds remaining on the clock, Oakland on top by 7-6, and a horde of predators clawing for Terry Bradshaw's eyeballs, the Steelers' scrambling quarterback threw a pass that Oakland's accomplished safety man, Jack Tatum, deflected out of Frenchy Fuqua's reach. The play was designed to gain about 18 yards—enough to get the ball into field goal range for Roy Gerela—and Fuqua became the target only because the defense wouldn't let the primary receiver, Barry Pearson, get downfield.

Blocked by Tatum around the Raiders' 35-yard line, the ball flew back about seven yards to Franco Harris. The rookie runner fielded it at his knees and crossed the goal line 42 yards away with the clock showing five seconds to play.

"We'll take those little crumbs," said Chuck Noll, the Pittsburgh coach. His tone was devout.

The Steelers reached their dressing room in a daze. Fuqua, who had been knocked down in a collision with Tatum, had thought the pass was incomplete. "When I got up I saw Franco about the 5-yard line."

"I didn't see the ball bounce away," Bradshaw said. "I just saw Franco take off. I thought, 'Man! It musta hit him right on the numbers!' I've played football since the second grade and nothing like that ever happened. It'll never happen again. And to think it happened here in Pittsburgh in a playoff!"

"We're putting the play in tomorrow," Noll promised.

Before Fred Swearingen, the referee, ruled the touchdown official he checked with Art McNally, the N.F.L. supervisor of officials, who had watched the televised replay in the press box and confirmed Swearingen's observation that a defensive player (Tatum) had indeed touched the ball and the pass had not gone illegally from Bradshaw to Fuqua to Harris.

Jim Kensil, the league's executive director, hastily denied that the decision had been made in the press box for fear such a precedent would be cited forevermore by coaches and players demanding that officials consult the instant replay before rendering judgments. However, Noll, who had huddled on the field with all the officials and John Madden, the Raiders' protesting coach, already had reported that the referee had agreed "to check upstairs, I didn't know how."

Heightening the melodrama of the finish was the primeval stodginess of the defensive struggle that preceded it. For 58 minutes the teams played antediluvian football. After a scoreless first half, witnesses were saying, "It took the Steelers 40 years to get here, and they're setting the game back 80." Somewhere in the gray nothingness overhead, Dr. Jock Sutherland must have been watching with a smile of benign approval. When that dour Scot, that rock of conservatism, coached the Steelers he considered the forward pass downright obscene.

Harking back to the days of the Minnesota shift and the flying wedge, the Steelers smothered Oakland's attack so effectively that a 6-0 lead on two field goals by Gerela seemed safe until, with a minute and 13 seconds left, Ken Stabler slipped around end for a 30-yard touchdown run and George Blanda's conversion put Oakland in front, 7-6.

Now Chuck Noll remembered that on fourth-and-two on Oakland's 31 in the first half he had ordered a line plunge that failed instead of a placekick by Gerela. The 3 points he might have got but didn't would have meant a 9-7 lead now. "If I'd had a third leg I would have kicked myself," he confessed.

With a kicker like Gerela around, that would have been another mistake.

# THREE FOR THE AGES

RAYMOND BERRY, Jim Parker and Joe Schmidt were tapped for the professional football Hall of Fame the other day, proving that the ingredients of immortality are manifold. In a single election, the panel of sportswriters that enthrones deities for veneration in Canton, Ohio, chose a genius, a giant and a dragon.

If, as Carlyle said, genius is an infinite capacity for taking pains, then Berry's qualifications are of the highest order. A rather bony individual out of Southern Methodist with 185 pounds on a chassis measuring 6 feet 2 inches, he regarded improvisation as a mortal sin. "No," he would say flatly if somebody tried to make up a play in the huddle, "I haven't practiced it. I'm not prepared."

He was John Unitas's favorite target on passes because he ran his patterns with scrupulous precision and the quarterback always knew where he would be on a given play. He had no great speed, and his patterns were designed like a Swiss watch, the product of endless hours of studying films.

"Can Sally cook?" Billy Pricer, the fullback from Oklahoma, asked Berry shortly before his marriage.

"I don't rightly know," Raymond said, "but she runs the projector." He thought that over for a moment. "I guess we'll eat a lot of sandwiches," he said.

One of his legs was shorter than the other, or he thought it was, so he wore regular cleats on one shoe and long mud cleats on the other. He had a gimpy back, or thought he did, and always wore a leather girdle. He laundered his own football pants so they would feel exactly right, not too stiff, not too tight. His name is Raymond and he hates to be called Ray.

Jim Parker played tackle and guard on the Baltimore offensive line.

He weighed 275 pounds, was approximately as fast, as light, and at least as smart as any of his professors at Ohio State.

"I worked two years on a single move against Parker," Henry Jordan of the Green Bay Packers said one night, "and it fooled him just once." Jordan weighed 250 and thought of himself as small, at least when he was talking about Parker or the 6-foot-8 Doug Atkins of the Chicago Bears.

"I'm nowhere near big enough to handle Parker," Henry said, "so I decided I'd try to use his weight against him, like in judo. I would come up out of my crouch, and as he fired off the ball I would stick my face up in front of him like this, so he'd have to take a swing at me. Then I'd grab his wrist and jerk.

"As I say, there was no way a guy my size could handle him, but we have a film showing me throwing him through the air, over my head. It worked just once, and I never could trap him on it again."

Competitive fire rather than size distinguished Joe Schmidt when he was middle linebacker and unquestioned leader of the Detroit Lions. He was a 220-pound 6-footer, but he said he had stood 6 feet 3 when he played fullback for the University of Pittsburgh. With his pale Teutonic face straight as a string, he would explain that a dozen years of diving headlong into the interference had driven his neck down between his shoulders like a stake.

When George Plimpton was working out as the last-string quarterback of the Lions, he was fascinated by Schmidt, and the linebacker appears prominently in Plimpton's *Paper Lion*. One story concerns the Pitt-Notre Dame game of 1952 when Red Dawson, the coach, asked Schmidt to give the pep talk in the dressing room. "You guys whip Notre Dame," the captain told his playmates, "or so help me, I'll whip you." Pitt won, 22-19. "We were more scared of Joe Schmidt than Notre Dame," one of the players said.

Then there was the 1962 game that is the climax of *Run to Daylight!* the book W. C. Heinz did with Vince Lombardi. Detroit was leading Green Bay, 7-6, and with less than four minutes left Paul Hornung missed a field goal that would have put the Packers in front, 9-7. Coming off the field as the offensive unit took over, Schmidt told Milt Plum to call running plays to eat up time. He was confident that if Detroit had to kick, the defense could contain the Packers on their side of midfield.

Instead, Plum mixed passes in with the running plays. Two were completed for first downs, on the Detroit 34-yard line and on the 47. On third and 8 with a minute and 46 seconds to play, Plum tried another pass, Herb Adderley intercepted and ran the ball back into field-goal range. This time Hornung's kick won the game.

"It took Joe Schmidt a long time to get over it," Plimpton wrote, "and perhaps he never did. For many games thereafter, when Plum and Schmidt passed each other on the field as the defensive unit came off and the offensive players were taking over, Schmidt would say disdainfully: 'Pass, Milt, three times and then punt.'"

Plimpton protested that this sort of talk from the captain couldn't have done much for Plum's morale, or the team's.

"The quality that makes Schmidt a leader," Bob Scholtz, the center said, "is his absolute honesty. The guy never said anything, ever, he didn't believe in. Schmidt took that for a dumb call in that Packer game, and there's no way in his book it can be rubbed out."

# ELINOR'S LIB

J UST when we get to feeling that things are looking up in the family of man, along comes word of some injustice so appalling in its stupid brutality that hope gives way to despair. For example, how can the man of good will rejoice over the prospect of Arthur Ashe's playing tennis in Johannesburg when the edition that carries this news also has a photograph of Miss Elinor Kaine, a victim of apartheid right up the pike in New Haven?

Elinor is a spirited lady who may or may not be good at crocheting a cozy for a tea caddy but does know her way around football fields and horse parks. She knows what color a gelding is and which linebacker has primary responsibility when the end crashes and the fullback flares right.

As a member of the Professional Football Writers' Association of America, Elinor applied for working press credentials for the New York Jets' impending confrontation with the Giants in Yale Bowl. She was turned down by somebody who didn't realize that Yale no longer regards being female as a capital offense.

Chances are one phone call to Pete Rozelle would have resolved the difficulty, but Elinor is, as mentioned, spirited. She bolted into a court of law and filed suit against Yale, the Giants, the Jets, and Bill Guthrie, a New Haven sportswriter in charge of press credentials for this exhibition.

It goes without saying that she'll win her point, for the day is long past when the rule against dames in the pressbox made sense. Once it was a good rule, neither discriminatory nor unchivalrous.

That was back in the days before women had infiltrated the sports-writing dodge to any noticeable extent. If you saw one in a pressbox you knew she belonged to one of the working stiffs, or vice versa. She might be highly ornamental but she was a nonproducer taking up space needed for the laboring classes. Hence the misogynous ruling: No broads.

Well, we all know what hell hath no fury like. "Banzai!" cried the daughters of Eve and sisters of Susan B. Anthony, and down came the barricades one by one. Yale was one of the last to capitulate. The surrender was a dramatic reenactment of Appomattox with Charley Loftus playing Lee to the Ulysses S. Grant of Miss Ann Morrissey.

Charles Loftus, now an enterprising public relations counsel in New Haven, was chief drumbeater for Yale athletics when Miss Morrissey was chosen sports editor of the *Cornell Sun*. On Monday of the week when the Cornell football team was to play in New Haven, Charley telephoned Miss Morrissey to tell her that although no female had ever set foot in the pressbox, her qualifications were beyond question and would be honored. She said she didn't want to cause trouble or embarrassment, and he begged her not to worry her pretty head about that.

Charley wasn't telling the exact truth when he said there had never been a woman in the pressbox. Between halves of a Dartmouth game one rainy Saturday, he had heard that Mrs. A. Whitney Griswold, wife of Yale's president, was getting drenched, and on his invitation she had watched the second half from the coop. Moreover, the noble breed of Morse code telegraph operators was dying out, and Western Union had started assigning women to handle teletype machines at the games.

In other words, Charley was prepared to cite precedents if anybody objected to Miss Morrissey's presence, but no flak flew. Instead, the Connecticut Sportswriters' Alliance came up with a corsage for their visitor. Loftus had the foresight to plant her next to Allison Danzig of *The New York Times*, an old-school type from Cornell who could have a hangnail and still be polite and helpful to Dracula if they were sitting together.

All went swimmingly until United Press International tried to make a test case by assigning one Faye Lloyd to do a feature on the Yale-Army game. Recognizing this as a trick play, Loftus seized the chance to grab a few headlines.

"Miss Morrissey was here on a legitimate mission," he declared. "But this is an invasion and it shall not succeed. We will fight on the beaches, we will fight on the field, we will fight to the last booth in the pressbox men's room."

Miss Lloyd had asked for a pressbox seat. Charley had a number painted on a 14-inch plank and sent it to her, explaining that she was getting four inches more than he allotted to males. He also sent her a ticket for a seat in the top row of the stands, directly in front of the pressbox. Mimeographed statistics, lineups, and play-by-play sheets were lowered to her in a basket. She took it like a good guy.

That was the last time sex reared its tousled head in Yale Bowl until Elinor Kaine rushed into court. To renew the battle of the sexes at this late date is ludicrous, especially now that Yale has gone coeducational. The university will enroll 500 girls this fall.

The next step will come when some Old Blue puts his daughter up for membership in the Yale Club on Vanderbilt Avenue. "She's finishing Davenport this year," he'll say. "I had hoped to propose my son, too, but he's at Sarah Lawrence."

# HOPELESS CAUSES

A RECENT item on the obituary page reported that Capt. Reaves Baysinger, quarterback for the United States Naval Academy in 1946, 1947 and 1948, had died of Hodgkins disease at the age of 45. The item said his football career had "included two of the most famous Army-Navy games in history," an understatement.

On Nov. 30, 1946, Glenn Davis, Doc Blanchard, Young Arnold Tucker and their accomplices played their last game for West Point. Army had gone undefeated through 27 games over three seasons, scoring 1,158 points to 143. In the war years of 1944 and 1945 the cadets had horsewhipped Notre Dame, 59-0 and 48-0. There were no doubts about the outcome of this match with Navy. The question that intrigued fans was whether West Point could have beaten the Chicago Bears.

The high point of Navy's season had been a 7-0 conquest of Villanova. Everybody else, even Columbia, had flogged the midshipmen.

Secure in the knowledge that they had all the guns, the Cadets took an early lead with the mercurial Davis carrying the ball. Late in the first quarter Leon Bramlett, Navy's captain, carried a pass by Baysinger to the Army two-yard line and Baysinger scored on a sneak, exciting nobody outside the Annapolis cheering section.

"Reaves Baysinger," said a man in the pressbox. "Is that R-double-e or R-e-a?"

"The guys call him Ribs," the man was told, "or sometimes Slats."

That Army team did not take kindly to lese majesty. Blanchard burst through the middle and boomed 53 yards for a second touchdown. He took a pass from Davis for a third. The half ended with the score 21-6.

Halfway through the third quarter, customers in Philadelphia's Municipal Stadium felt the first prickling sense that something extraordinary was taking place before them. Nothing had changed on the scoreboard, but Army no longer had control on the field. Bill Bartlett, Lynn Chewning, Bill Earl, Pete Williams, Bill Hawkins, Al McCully— the supply of Navy backs seemed inexhaustible and Army couldn't handle any of them. Now and then, if the running attack sputtered, Baysinger would throw a strike to Art Markel or Phil Ryan.

Navy pounded 78 yards to the end zone. For the second time the conversion kick missed. The Army lead was 21-12, still safe enough, but the Army kids panicked. Unwilling to trust their defense, they gambled on keeping the ball, sending Blanchard into the middle on fourth-and-one at the West Point 35. Dick Scott flattened Blanchard for a loss.

Navy went in from there, but the last yards had to be hammered out on an anvil. On fourth down from the two-yard line, Baysinger pitched out to Earl, who threw on the run to Bramlett in the end zone. Army 21, Navy 18.

The last Army punt was downed on Navy's 33. The remorseless hammering resumed. With a minute and a half to play, Chewning swept left end to the Army three-yard line. Crowds had poured out of the stands and were massed along the sideline, and as the seconds drained away Chewning was smashed down at their feet. To this day Navy men swear that he was out of bounds and the clock should have stopped.

It didn't stop. Time ran out with Navy a stride or two from the goal line. The losers from Annapolis, beaten eight times in nine starts, had lost to the greatest of all Army teams by the margin of three points-after-touchdown.

Baysinger's first two Navy teams won one game each. The third didn't win any. Coming to the Army game of 1948, Navy had lost 13 straight. Bookmakers made Army the favorite by 21 points, and that's exactly what Army scored. So did Navy.

Pete Williams started it, taking one lateral from Baysinger 59 yards and another 15. Baysinger sneaked across and Navy was in front. Army went 55 yards for a tie, with Arnold Galiffa passing to Dave Parrish for the key gain. A similar series was good for 54 yards, and the half ended with Army leading, 14-7.

Starting the second half, Navy went 81 yards for a tie, Bill Powers gaining 30 on one bold burst. Running the ball himself, Galiffa got the lead back for Army, 21-14. Then Navy's Hawkins, fresh out of a hospital after a long siege of acute infectious mononucleosis, went absolutely crackers. Head down, cleats digging, he butted defenders aside for a 10-yard gain, then ground out 12. He slanted through tackle for four, bulled over the middle for a touchdown. Roger Drew kicked his third exta point.

It was 21-21, and in the boxes near the 40-yard line 50 Secret Service men fidgeted. They were responsible for the safety of the President. With less than two minutes to play, they wanted him out of there before the whole crowd of 102,000 started moving.

This was Nov. 27. Just 25 days earlier, Harry Truman of Independence, Mo., had gone in against a 21-point favorite named Tom Dewey and got better than a tie. A noted fancier of hopeless causes, he wasn't budging until this one ended.

# ROYAL AND ANCIENT

*Picking up a ball in a sand trap and hurling it onto the green may be, in the aseptic lexicon of Joseph C. Dey Jr., "conduct unbecoming a professional golfer," but it is a mere reflex action for any man of spirit whose days are spent in angry pursuit of a dimpled pill not less than 1.680 inches in diameter and weighing no more than 1.620 ounces avoirdupois. Since he took on the job of housemother to golf's performing seals, Joe Dey has learned some four-letter words he never heard in the United States Golf Association's ivory tower.*

# MASTERS AND MEN

SOME years ago, Cliff Roberts, who runs the Masters golf tournament in Augusta, Ga., asked a newspaperman up to his New York apartment. Over drinks he confided that he had a problem. He said "the people down in Augusta" had warned him that if he ever had a Negro in the Masters it would be the end of the tournament. On the day he told about this, the scores had come in from the first round of the National Open championship and two black men were among the leaders. (Their names elude memory now, but the chances are Charlie Sifford was one.) What should he do, Roberts asked, if one of them should finish among the 16 leaders in the Open and thus qualify for the Masters?

"If you think having a black man in the Masters would spell trouble," the newspaperman said, "try ignoring a black man who qualifies. Believe me, it would not remain a secret, and then you would learn what real trouble is like.

"For your own good, Cliff, if a black man qualifies, you invite him. In fact, see that he gets the very first invitation."

Roberts didn't express his own racial attitudes and he wasn't asked about them. At the time he was just worried about his tournament, unnecessarily as it turned out, for no blacks qualified that year. In fact, no black has ever qualified under the terms laid down for this 39-year-old tournament. This has prompted Herman Badillo and 17 other Congressmen to write that "it is probably time that your regulations be subject to a careful review and reconsideration."

Describing the qualifying standards as "subtle discrimination," the Badillo group asked that a special invitation be extended this year to Lee Elder. Roberts refused, saying that inviting Elder merely because he was black would be "discrimination in reverse."

This is an unprofitable argument, just batting the word "discrimination" back and forth like a shuttlecock. Rhetoric aside, the fact is that some hundreds of golfers have been invited for a variety of reasons, and none was a black man.

The prospect of becoming the first black in the Masters is a burden no white man has to bear. This makes it harder for a black man than for a white to meet the qualifying standards. Lee Elder is asking for no special favors, but it can be argued that an exception ought to be made if only to eliminate unfair pressure on one particular group. That is not discrimination in reverse. It is simple justice.

There is nothing sacred about the qualifying regulations. Indeed, they didn't exist in 1934 when the tournament began as the Augusta National Invitational. In those days the tournament committee could invite anybody it chose and it did not choose blacks. Qualifying standards came later, have been changed many times and will be changed in the future.

The rules distinguish between United States citizens, who must qualify in one of 13 published categories, and foreign players, who can be invited on Cliff Roberts' whim. Acting on what Roberts describes as "our judgment of their ability to provide competition for American players," the committee has invited 16 professionals and two amateurs from abroad for this year's tournament. Not all are white. Maybe Elder or some other black should be invited as an African.

Chances are Herman Badillo never heard of John Shippen, though Cliff Roberts probably has. He was a black caddie at Shinnecock Hills on Long Island and when the second United States Open was held at the club, he entered. Some of the British and Scottish pros muttered about a boycott. "We'll miss you," they were told by Theodore Havemeyer, the sugar king who was president of the United States Golf Association, "but Mr. Shippen plays."

Mr. Shippen did, and tied for fifth place. This was 1896 and John Shippen died only recently, great with years and grace.

# RIP MANN'S DAUGHTER

WHEN she started playing she was known around the Country Club of Maryland as Rip Mann's daughter. Now Rip is Carol Mann's father. Carol is a professional golfer, the United States Open champion of 1965, leading money-winner in 1969, with a bagful of records like the 30 she shot on the Sunset Club's front nine in St. Petersburg, Fla., like her 66, 66—132 in the Lady Carling open at Palmetto, Ga., where she added a 68 in the third round for a 54-hole total of 200.

"Not to mention the first round I ever played as a pro," she said. "It was at Sea Island, Ga. It was raining, I had a cold with a temperature of 104, and my score wasn't a lot lower—89."

Carol was in New York between tournaments. She is a stunner, tall and trig and wholly unaffected, with honey-colored hair, candid blue eyes and a smile that would light up a coal mine.

Last weekend she collected $15,000 for winning the Sears Classic at Port St. Lucie, Fla., and she is taking a fortnight off before shooting for the $25,000 first prize in the Colgate-Dinah Shore Winners Circle in Palm Springs, Calif. With a gross of $154,000, this is the most opulent tournament ever laid on for the girls. It is being called the women's Masters, although Mistresses is probably the proper usage.

The financial figures tell what has been happening in women's golf. In 1948 Babe Didrikson Zaharias "unloosened the girdle," as she said, and led the Ladies Professional Golf Association by winning $3,400. In Carol Mann's rookie year, 1960, Louise Suggs showed the way with $16,892. Carol won $49,152 four years ago, and last year Kathy Whitworth's official take was $65,064.

"In the beginning," Carol said, "there were Patty Berg, Louise Suggs and Babe. Louise's father was a golfer. I don't know what motivated Babe, except that she was an athlete who'd played all games. I think when Patty was a tomboy in Minneapolis her family decided golf was more ladylike. 'You've got to stop playing football in the street with Bud Wilkinson,' they told her.

"With us in Baltimore, golf was a family activity. My mother played, and my four brothers, who are all younger than me. My father was in sales and away all week. When he came home weekends he played golf. I wanted to be with Daddy, thought if I took it up I could play with him. Actually, I don't think we've played two dozen rounds together. Now when he'd like to play with me, I don't have time.

"I had a partial golf scholarship at the Women's College of the University of North Carolina in Greensboro. After two years I decided I didn't want to be a phys ed teacher, after all, and I called my father. 'I think I'll turn pro,' I told him.

"For the first year and a half, Janet Olson sponsored me. She was a great friend of Babe's. Our family had moved to Chicago when I was 14, and in the club out there I won an irons competition that she sponsored. Janet paid me $600 a month—in those days you could get by on the tour for $150 a week—and it came to $7,500 altogether. When I talked to her about paying it back, she said, 'No, just do the same for somebody else sometime.' That's still ahead of me.

"My trouble as a golfer is, I don't have a strong stomach. I think too much. I get knotted up in my head instead of playing on sheer guts. I was playing Las Vegas and doing well, in contention. On the 15th hole, I said, 'Janet, walk with me.' She was an older woman, affectionate. She died not long ago. We walked hand in hand.

" 'Oh, Janet,' I told her, 'how I wish I had your stomach now!' 'I'll lend it to you,' she said. I can't tell you how that bucked me up. I played well and finished third.

"In 1969 I led the money-winners. When it was over I came home and said to myself, 'Well, it was quite a year. But is this all there is?' It had been a satisfying year, but not complete fulfillment. I had no close relationship with a man, with anybody.

"Yes, when it came to dates and dancing my height got in the way. I'm 6-foot-3 and sometimes the guy was self-conscious about being shorter. And I was suspicious. When I wasn't doing well, nobody asked me out. Then when I started to win I was afraid they just wanted to be out with a champion.

"I'm 32 now and I think I've grown up. And I met a man in Baltimore, a wonderful man. Our relationship has done so much for me. Yes, I hope we get married, but we haven't worked it all out yet. How much does each have to give to satisfy the other's needs, and what can each keep for himself? He has his life, and I'm not ready to give up golf altogether.

"Since 1969 I've tried to find interests outside of golf—music, which I've always loved, photography, and people. I try to talk to people, most of all to listen if I can. But for that you have to be anonymous. The world is full of anonymous people walking around, but to get them to talk to you you can't be a celebrity."

# 70 IS TWO UNDER PAR

§TEALTHY as a Mohican, Gene Sarazen's 70th birthday crept up on him yesterday. He tried to ignore it, rising early as he would any other day, pulling on fresh knickers for his daily round of golf. "Don't make opera of it," he had told Fred Corcoran by phone from Marco Island in Florida. "When you get down here you and Nancy and Mary and I will have dinner, that's all."

"I've got an idea," said Corcoran, whose success as a golf promoter is due to the fact that he never lacks ideas. "We'll announce that anybody who shoots 70 on Feb. 27 gets a free set of Gene Sarazen clubs."

"Like hell!" Corcoran, sitting at the phone in Manhattan, could have heard the scream even without help from Alexander Graham Bell. Since he left off carrying members' clubs at Apawamis in Rye, Gene Sarazen has never concealed his admiration for solid American and Italian virtues like thrift. There was that time back in the nineteen-twenties when he won a tournament in Agua Caliente and they delivered 10,000 silver dollars to him by wheelbarrow. Years later, some of his locker room colleagues recalled the occasion.

"One thing is sure," one of them said, "Gene still has every one of those dollars."

"Hell," said Walter Hagen, who loved the little guy, "he still has the wheelbarrow."

It was 50 years ago this summer that Sarazen burst upon the headlines by winning both the United States Open and the Professional Golfers' Association championships. A cocky 20-year-old not long out of the caddie hut, he shot 288 in the Open at Skokie outside Chicago to beat Bobby Jones and John Black, who were in the clubhouse with 289's. He won the P.G.A. at Pittsburgh's famous Oakmont course.

Half a century has worn a hole in the slicked-down haircut, but otherwise the years have left few traces. The Piping Rock tan is as deep as ever. The Mr. Kleen grin still starts under this ear and stretches clear to that one, crinkling the face so that wrinkles of merriment fan out from squinty eyes. The half-column britches are still de rigueur on the course, and he moves with the same purposeful strut that could get him through a whole round in the Masters championship in an hour and 56 minutes.

Even from demigods, however, age exacts a toll. When Gene shot a 69 at Marco Island last week it took him more than two hours.

Sometimes it bugs him that fans seem to remember only one shot out of all the brilliant rounds he has played. That's the wood he holed out for a double-eagle 2 on the 15th at the Augusta National Club. With one swing he gained three strokes to tie Craig Wood, who was in the clubhouse accepting congratulations on winning the Masters; Sarazen won the playoff.

"Show me the plaque marking the spot," said a guy at a later Masters.

"Plaque hell," Gene said. "They just threw a handful of Italian rye in the divot."

He made a face. "You know, I won the U.S. Open and the British Open and the P.G.A. and I don't know what all, and yet wherever I go you'd think I'd made only one shot in my life. Even in Japan they ask me, 'How about the dubber eager?' "

A few months ago Gene went to Boston to play for the Francis Oiumet Caddie Fund at Charles River Country Club. On the par 5 seventh hole he sank his second shot for a double eagle. He used a No. 3 wood.

"What did you hit at Augusta?" he was asked.

"A 4-wood," he said, "but 35 years later I needed more club."

Gene will celebrate the golden anniversary of his first British Open when the tournament returns to Troon in Scotland. Barely able to hold his feet in a gale off the Firth of Clyde, the 21-year-old shot 89 in 1923 and failed to qualify.

"Impossible," Alan Gould, sports editor of the Associated Press, cabled when the score came in. "You mean 69." The answer was prompt: "Sarazen's score 45-44. You add it."

Champion golfers don't celebrate 89's. "But I'll be there if I'm walking," Gene has told the Scots.

He is a world figure with a strong peasant strain, an inborn love of the soil. When he first got into the big money he bought a Connecticut farm.

"It was stone walls and fruit trees and I sold it," he said. "After I did, I felt lost, like I had no rights in this country because I didn't have a piece of ground. Driving up the Hudson one day, I stopped and bought two farms at Germantown, N.Y."

That was home for him and Mary until they sold out last year. Now they live in Florida and summer in New Hampshire, and they have rights everywhere.

# IT ISN'T CRICKET

I N this holy season it is reassuring to note that Ladbrokes, the reliable London house that caters to Britain's bettors as Howard Samuels would like to service the sporting gentry of New York, has been declared persona non grata on British golf courses, not to say nux vomica.

After a brief flirtation with the bookmakers, the Royal and Ancient Club and the Professional Golfers' Association have concluded that gambling on the greens is not cricket. From now on, anybody who wishes to risk a few quid on Tony Jacklin or Bob Charles will have to phone his bookie up in town. There'll be no more investment counselors setting up their slates beside the 18th fairway. The decision will gratify godly golfers such as Arnold Palmer and Gary Player, who were scandalized when they saw Ladbrokes doing business in a tent at Turnberry, Scotland, during the $134,750 John Player tournament last September.

"We don't have this in the U.S.," Palmer said then, "and my feeling is that it is not necessary. Wherever there is gambling, there must be at least a danger of something underhanded."

"It is not traditional to have this on the golf course," said Gary Player, who owns a stable of racehorses.

"It lowers the standard, the whole image of golf," said Neil Coles of the British Ryder Cup team.

So speaking, they settled their Nassaus, relaxed with a few hands of gin, and were off to the greyhound races.

Palmer is a regular participant in the Sahara Invitational in the churchly climate of Las Vegas. The Sahara is one of our holiest events, so sacred that when Jack Nicklaus was asked to represent the United States in the World Cup matches in Australia this year he declined because, he explained, he owed it to American golf to stay and compete in the Sahara.

For that one, the odds are posted in the hotel lobby between the craps table and the blackjack game, just beyond the slots.

The fact is, golf has been a gambling game since Mary Queen of Scots was batting a leather ball stuffed with feathers across the dunes beside the Firth of Tay. When one duffer asks another, "What's your handicap?" he doesn't mean has he got a speech impediment or something. He's setting up the guy for a royal rooking.

You don't have to go to Las Vegas to find a Calcutta pool and it is common practice for a bettor to cut in the player he is backing. Sometimes in events as insignificant as a club championship, the Calcutta compares favorably with the national budget.

Al Besselink may have quit the tournament circuit before Palmer arrived, so perhaps Arnold never heard of the time Al bet on himself in Vegas, won and collected a potful. Chances are Arnold never met Titanic Thompson, but he undoubtedly knows some of the players who were in Titanic's stable.

The celebrated Titanic was the most famous, and gifted, of all the golf hustlers. His dodge was to get entree to a club where he wasn't known, pump up the self-confidence of high-rolling members and then arrange a match.

"I'll take some caddie for my partner," he would say. "That little kid over there, for example."

That little kid would be a ringer whom Titanic had planted in the caddie yard weeks ahead of time. If necessary, the bashful tyke would shoot a sheepish 70.

There has been a book on the British Open for years and years. When Tony Lema won in 1964 he was 15 to 1 because he had never played the St. Andrews course. Three years later Roberto deVicenzo brought off a 25-to-1 chance. At Turnberry this year, Scotland's Harry Bannerman bet on himself and collected $2,000 when he finished fifth.

Harry approved of Ladbrokes' attendance, but there were dissenting views. Keith McKenzie, secretary of the Royal and Ancient, said: "We felt too much of the betting was on the horses." Seems Ladbrokes took action on the races as well as the golf and most of the enlightened British observed the ancient injunction "Never bet on anything that can talk."

# TEN INTERESTING YEARS

*Harrison, N.Y.*

THE 12th hole on the West Course at Westchester Country Club measures 500 yards if you stretch the tape across the old quarry in front of the green, or approximately nine miles if you're careless. Jack Nicklaus hit a No. 3 wood off the tee and decided he could get home with a 4-iron. The ball stopped just short of the green, so with his sand wedge he chipped it into the cup for an eagle 3.

He had begun on the 10th tee, so the 12th was the third hole for him. On the next 15 he shot five birdies and never yielded a stroke to par, bringing in a score of 65.

It is downright immoral to say that a 65 can be easy, but Nicklaus made it look that way. His drives were true, his irons generally accurate, and on the few occasions when he missed a green he was able to chip up stiff. He never had to sink a putt of more than six feet.

"On the four par-5 holes," he said, "I was five under—an eagle and three birdies." When he is on his game, that's what he does to the long holes. When he is on his game he is the best golfer in the world. This has been true for a long time, but until this year there were many who resented the truth and rejected it.

Until this year he was an upstart and an interloper, the crasher who had dared to expose Arnold Palmer as merely human. Ten years ago, in his first season as a professional, he beat Palmer in a playoff for the United States Open championship and won the undying enmity of the rabble they called Arnie's Army. Undying, that is, until he set out this year on a hunt for the four top titles in professional golf—the Masters, the United States Open, the British Open and the Professional Golfers' Association. He won the Masters, he won the United States Open, and even those who had hated his guts were saddened when he missed by a stroke in the British Open.

215

"You know," a man told him today, "you've been Gene Tunney. You whipped Jack Dempsey." Then, seeing Jack's puzzled frown, the man explained: "You beat Arnie, so the mob hated you."

The expression cleared. "It's been a very interesting experience, these last 10 years," he said. "And especially interesting this year, by contrast.

"I've had more mail this year than ever before," he said, "all of it warm. Not that I ever got many crank letters. Just once in a while. But everybody I've known in golf told me they were rooting for me. And so many players. You know, when the fellows in the game, who are trying to win themselves, when they're pulling for you to win, that's something special."

After losing to Lee Trevino in the final round at Muirfield, Scotland, Nicklaus played twilight tennis with an Irish friend, Jim Fitzgibbon. A former Davis Cup player, Fitzgibbon beat him.

"You may be the only internationalist to lose at two different games on the same day," a guy said.

Jack laughed. "I didn't want to sit in the hotel and have everybody come up and tell me they were sorry I lost and have to say thanks, I was sorry, too. So I got Jim and we played an hour and a half and I released my frustrations."

The Decade of Nicklaus offers an example of how passionately involved sports fans often get, and how unfairly at times. On and off the course, Jack is all class. Never once over the years did he utter a word of complaint about an unfriendly gallery, and some were outrageous.

The sports fan is an odd bird, anyway; in a theater it would not occur to him to hoot when the star makes his entrance, but he abused Roger Maris for his assault on Babe Ruth's home run record and booed Joe DiMaggio for being too good.

Gene Tunney fought the best, lost one bout in his life, and retired a villain because he had whipped the beloved Dempsey. Johnny Goodman won the United States Amateur and United States Open titles but never got a nod for golf's Hall of Fame. He made the mistake of beating Bobby Jones.

# A STRAIN OF POETRY

IN 1954, friends of Fred Russell converged on Nashville, Tenn., to help readers of *The Nashville Banner* celebrate Russell's silver anniversary on the paper, which he serves as vice president and sports editor. Bobby Jones had already undergone surgery twice for the spinal disorder that would one day leave him helpless, yet he made his painful way up from Atlanta.

When diners were seated for the dinner in the Vanderbilt gymnasium, the special guests filed in to take places on the dais. As Bobby hesitated almost imperceptibly at the lowest step, two men immediately behind him closed in, each put a shoulder at his back and eased him quickly up the stairs. It was done so unobtrusively that only a few following in line saw it happen and they felt a sudden inward warmth. Bobby's volunteer bodyguards were Jack Dempsey and Red Grange. There should have been a caption above the tableau reading: "Golden Age of Sports."

It was inevitable that when Bobby Jones died the obituaries would bracket him with Dempsey and Grange and Bill Tilden and the others whose extraordinary talents endowed the 1920's with a glamour that has endured for 40 years. Whether Bobby was the greatest golfer of his decade is a question to be debated with disciples of the Walter Hagen persuasion. There can be no doubt, however, that he was one of the most gifted craftsmen who ever swung a stick, incomparably the finest amateur player of any era, and a gentleman unafraid.

Much has been made of the hot temper young Bobby brought to tournament golf. Probably too much. Many who read of his performances in the 1916 National Amateur championship at Merion, outside Philadelphia, must have put this pudgy 14-year-old away as a petulant brat, spoiled rotten. He was decidedly in the public eye, a kid in his first long pants who had led the entire field in the first qualifying round, so everything he did made news.

For his opening match, he drew Eben Byers, a seasoned tournament player who had been national champion 10 years earlier. They took turns missing shots and throwing their clubs away in rage, but it was the child prodigy's tantrums that made the headlines. Bobby raised no protest then, but years later he put the incident in proper perspective.

"Mr. Byers and I played very wretchedly," he wrote in collaboration with O. B. Keeler, "and I think the main reason I beat him was because he ran out of clubs first."

Kindlier and more understanding than the American press was the great chronicler of British golf, Bernard Darwin.

"Bobby did hate missing a shot," Darwin wrote. "Perhaps that was why he missed so few, for in the end that highly-strung nervous temperament, if it had never been his master, became his invaluable servant. In his most youthful and tempestuous days he had never been angry with his opponent and not often, I think, with fate, but he had been furiously angry with himself. He set himself an almost impossibly high standard; he thought it an act of incredible folly if not a positive crime to make a stroke that was not exactly as it ought to be made and as he knew he could make it."

Today's tournament golfer moves through a round with stately deliberation, as though celebrating high mass. One evening during a tournament Roberto deVicenzo was encountered in a restaurant just finishing his dinner.

"How's the food here, Roberto?" somebody asked.

"Like Jack Nicklaus," said the gentleman from Argentina. "Very good, and very slow."

A few years ago Jones was asked how he felt about the glacial pace of some players. "If I had thought it would help my game," he said, "I would have taken as much time as I needed. But I thought I played my best when I could sustain a sense of fluid, continuing action."

"There could be no more fascinating player to watch," Darwin wrote, "not only for the free and rhythmic character of his swing, but for the swiftness with which he played. He had as brief a preliminary address as Duncan himself, but there was nothing hurried or slapdash about it, and the swing itself, if not positively slow, had a certain drowsy beauty which gave the feeling of slowness."

The stories could go on forever, like the telegram Bobby received at Oakmont near Pittsburgh in 1925 when he was going for his second National Amateur title. He had been spraying his shots and this had him upset until the wire came from Stewart Maiden, the Atlanta professional whose style he had copied as a boy.

"Knock hell out of them," the message advised. "They'll land somewhere." Bobby did and they did. He smashed Watts Gunn in the final match, 8 up and 7 to play.

"The steady-going and unimaginative," Darwin wrote, "will often beat the more eager champion and they will get very near the top, but there, I think, they will stop. The prose laborer must yield to the poet, and Bobby as a golfer had a strain of poetry in him."

# CHI CHI

As the putt ran down, Chi Chi Rodriguez sheathed his putter in an imaginary scabbard at his left hip, then drew it with a flourish and struck a fencer's pose, en garde. The gallery was delighted.

Galleries usually are delighted by Chi Chi but he does not always amuse the professionals who play golf with him. Some of them, over-privileged and overdressed, fail to realize, as Chi Chi realizes, that they are public entertainers, and they complain that his blithe caper-ing shakes their concentration. Chi Chi understands.

"There was this fellow had a baby gorilla for a pet," he said, "and he was rocking him in a cradle. 'When he has grown full size,' they asked him, 'when he is too big for the cradle, where will he sleep?' 'Anywhere he wants to,' the fellow said."

Chi Chi paused, his cameo features at peace. "I have won tourna-ments," he said, "but never a championship like this one. My biggest was the Western Open. Now, Lee Trevino does about the same things I do on the course, but he is the big gorilla." Trevino, of course, has won a United States Open.

This was in the locker room at the Merion Golf Club between rounds of the National Open. Does he play as he does out of pure high spirits, Chi Chi was asked, or is it a calculated performance?

"Some people have the wrong idea about Puerto Ricans," he said gravely. "We are supposed to be hot-tempered, troublemakers. If I can show people a happier picture of my people, that is a victory. If I concentrated more I could win more tournaments but if I can do good for my people that is a bigger victory than the Open.

"That is why I want to go into politics someday. My people are a minority group, many are poor, there is so much to be done for them. It will not be before another eight or ten years, but I want to be gov-ernor of Puerto Rico. I'll start at the top."

220

Because he declines to talk about it, nobody knows how much of Chi Chi's earnings from golf have gone to help poor kids in Puerto Rico. However, he doesn't mind talking about the poverty of his own childhood.

"My mother and father were divorced," he said, "and when I came home at noon— I went to school only mornings—the house would be empty, locked, so I would go to the golf course and caddie. I missed lunch for two years. I had sprue from malnutrition, that is why I am small. Sprue is almost like rickets; the only reason I did not get rickets was the vitamin D in the sunshine.

"With sprue you must not eat any gluten or flour but all I could buy was that yellow flour that I would mix with water like a gruel. The sprue still comes back on me.

"I worked with my father in the sugar cane fields when I was six. Then I became a fore caddie and when I was nine I was a regular caddie full time. I would get from 35 to 75 cents a day and a kick if you lost a ball. I didn't lose a ball in 13 years. I was very lucky shooting craps. What I won I brought back to my father. And throwing coins. At a distance of 90 feet there is nobody in the world can throw a half-dollar closer to a line.

"I was a very good pitcher in Class A baseball. My father would say, 'I know you can play baseball but you could never make it in golf.' So I would have to be a golfer to prove myself to my father. Afterward he told me he always wanted me to be a golf pro.

"When I was 19 I went into the Army, to learn English and manners, which I had already but did not know it. My father had a stroke and could not work. It makes my knees weak now to wonder how we lived, my brothers and sisters. I sent home $50 a month—my salary was $72, I was a private—and at Ft. Sill in Oklahoma they put me on the golf program where I could play with officers. If I won $3 I sent that home.

"When I came home after two years, I got the best job I ever had, in a psychiatric clinic. I got $20 a week and I fed the patients and bathed them and played dominoes with them. Play dominoes with them and you would not think they were mentally ill.

"When Laurance Rockefeller opened Dorado Beach, my sister said I should try for a job there. I told her they would not want any poor people, but I applied to Ed Dudley and we played a round to try me out. I shot 89 and I told him, 'With you to help me, I think I could play good golf.' He made me assistant pro and caddie master and starter at $400 a month and let me give lessons at $3 for half an hour.

"One day I gave six lessons and I brought home $18. 'Where did you steal this?' my father said. I told him I made it in one day. 'It used to take me a month to make $18,' he said."

Chi Chi stood up, slender, wiry, erect. The sweep of a hand encompassed the crowded scene. "This is my office," he said. "I like to get away from the office. I will go now to Liberty Bell Racetrack."

# NATURAL HISTORY DEPT.

*In September, monarch butterflies move down from the North to meeting places on the Atlantic coast. Assembling by the million, they take off in clouds that may require two days to pass a given point. Although they have never been far from the milkweed where they were hatched, they find their way over ocean and forest to the Gulf Coast or Central America, spend the winter there and fly home in the spring to lay their eggs and die.*

*Human ingenuity needed all the centuries from Icarus to Lindbergh to the Concorde jet to accomplish what these wisps of orange and black do in a few months of life. Yet man persists in manufacturing lipsticks and razor blades in the foolish belief that he can improve on nature.*

# SUPER SQUIRREL

*Martha's Vineyard*

AS this is written a gray squirrel is batting his brains out against an inverted pie-plate designed to keep him from filching goodies from a bird-feeder on the lawn of Thomas L. Stix. For the time being the pie-plate has the squirrel licked, but he knows his frustration won't last. He knows that even if he bats half his brains out he'll still be smarter than the adversary who set up that baffle-iron.

This contest was a mismatch from the day it was made, and if Ruby Goldstein were the referee he would have stopped it in the first round. By human standards, Tom Stix is a pretty hip guy. He can read and write and count his change without facial contortions. Before he quit work to concentrate on his battle of wits with the squirrels, he trained a string of writers, lecturers, and radio spielers that include such unlikely stablemates as Eleanor Roosevelt, Walter Cronkite, Elmer Davis and Phil Rizzuto.

However, Stix is merely a Bachelor of Arts from Yale, Class of 1918. Every squirrel on this tight little isle is a Ph.D. and a lot of them wear Phi Beta Kappa keys.

Love laughs at locksmiths? These varmints are in stitches watching the Yalie's pitiful efforts to keep them out of the sunflower seeds.

There was a time early this summer when no fewer than four feeding stations operated simultaneously in an area smaller than the Madison Square Garden boxing ring. All were squirrel-proof, by the naive standards of the manufacturer.

Two were windowed boxes set on 6-foot stakes. Each had a perch affixed to a rocker-arm with a counterweight just heavy enough so the perch would support a bird up to the size of a bluejay. Anything heavier caused the perch to tilt, bringing a wooden slat across the feeder's mouth and shutting off the source of supply.

Chuckling indulgently, squirrels dropped out of trees or shinnied up the stakes and gnawed away the wooden blinds. They left the lawn looking like a slum with chewed-up feeders sagging like abandoned sharecropper shanties.

A third feeder was the metal and plastic ball which the manufacturer calls a "satellite." Suspended by a thin wire, it had a small round opening with a little plastic lip as a perch for clinging birds like nuthatches, chickadees, titmice and finches. Larger birds couldn't hang on and neither would squirrels, Stix fondly imagined, until he saw one swing by the knees from the supporting branch like a trapeze performer, grip the little perch between his teeth, and tilt the satellite until the contents poured out.

Cursing, Stix stormed off to Edgartown to shop for more sophisticated weapons. He came back with two more feeders-on-sticks which he set up at a safe distance from the trees. Around each stake was a wide metal collar shaped like a coolie's hat to serve as a roadblock for any rodent climbing the pole. Adjusting this about two feet above the ground, Stix retired to his converted cowbarn to spy on the enemy through a picture window.

Soon a manic giggling was heard. A squirrel started up the stick, bumped into the obstacle and dropped. Gloating, the triumphant Yalie turned away to pour a victory toast. While his back was turned, the squirrel stood off a few feet, sprang to the top of the baffle-plate, and scurried aloft to start ripping the new feeder apart.

As of now, Stix is five feeders down and going for six. To move the satellite away from the trees, he has driven two stakes in the ground and hung the little feeder from a line stretched between them. The first line he put up was monofilament stolen off his grandson's spinning reel—too fine for a tightrope act, he reasoned. He was right. Instead of walking the line, the squirrel bit it in two.

There is also a suet container of wire with a little wooden lid. Unable to push their faces through the mesh, the squirrels learned to raise the lid and lift the suet out in one chunk. Yesterday Stix thrust a long spike through the suet, pinning it in its cage. The squirrels are thinking this over.

Nearby is a metal pole supporting the newest feeder. Near the top is a hole through which Stix has thrust a second spike to keep the baffle in position. He swears he chased a squirrel that was scrunched up there, clinging to the pole with its hind feet while he lifted the plate with one hand and tugged at the nail with the other. Tom Stix is a truthful man.

He is also a discouraged man. Today he saw a redwing blackbird on the feeder. It would pick up a few seeds, then sweep a quarter-pound to a squirrel waiting below. Stix is sure there's been a payoff.

# FINE FEATHERED FRIENDS

*Martha's Vineyard*

EDWARD L. CHALIF chatted amiably while his flock fluttered into the Chilmark Community Center, starting point for the regular weekly bird walk. The flock included young as well as adults of both sexes, and plumage varied, but all wore the distinguishing field mark—binoculars on a strap around the neck.

"There'll be a phone call about some great rarity," Chalif was saying, "and I'll rush over and it will be a baby towhee or something. But one day Mrs. Epstein called—some of you met Mrs. Epstein Thursday at Roaring Brook—and I went over and there in a tree was a white-winged dove. Now, the white-winged dove is almost never seen east of Texas. While I was looking, here came a black-headed grosbeak, another that is strictly Western."

"Two birds with one phone," a voice mumbled, regrettably. Through a window behind Chalif, a squadron of Canada geese could be seen crossing the gray morning sky in tight oblique formation.

"If we were going to Katama Bay," Chalif was saying, "you'd see what looked like a baby goose, but if you think it's a goose you'd better take another look because it's a brant."

"Bad day for birding," a man said as the flock moved outdoors. "It's going to rain." All got into station wagons.

At a lane leading to an arm of Tisbury Great Pond Chalif gathered his flock. It numbered 57. He hoped nobody would push ahead of him when they approached birds.

"What should we look for?" asked a male in a black beret. Chalif smiled.

"Everything. This is indigo weed. Takes its name from the seed, not the yellow flower. See these seed pods, beginning to develop the indigo color. This is sweet goldenrod."

"Indigo is black, isn't it?" a female said.

"Dark blue," an adult male said.

"This is the Jimson weed I told you about," Chalif said, "with the purple stem and trumpet flower. It's called purple thornapple. This is the only place on the island where it grows, far as I know."

From a meadow sloping down to the water, a herring gull could be seen perched on a tiny rock island. A tern was in flight. On the near shore, sandpipers and killdeer plover were feeding.

"The killdeer," Chalif said, "gets its name from two sources—its cry of 'keel, keel, keel' and the fact that it has more or less the color of a deer. Look at those peeps. From here I think we see four species— the lesser yellowlegs, the spotted sandpiper, the least sandpiper, and —I think from here—the Western sandpiper. The swallow is a barn swallow, of course, and in the distance there's a towhee singing. Come along slowly.

"The Western sandpiper—no, the bill isn't long enough, unfortunately—it's only a semipalmated sandpiper. Look at the legs. If they're yellowish, it's a least sandpiper; if they're black it can be any of four species. That one has found a little territory of his own and he's chasing everything away. That's another semipalmated sandpiper he just chased. Yes, they're often antisocial like that. He has himself a good spot and he won't share it with anybody.

"A kingfisher just flew by. If you were looking at that heron or stake or whatever it is on the far shore, that was a kingfisher you saw flying."

"The stake's head moved," an adult male said, "so it's got to be a heron. A small green heron."

"There's a red-tailed hawk in the air," Chalif said. "Watch as he turns and you see the red tail."

"If you can see a red tail you're good," a male told a female.

"That small green heron on the far shore," Chalif said, "is a stake with a kingfisher sitting on top. Those are least tern down here. They were born on this island and they'll go all the way to Argentina and won't be back for three years."

Sheep were grazing nearby. A female in pink slacks with baby blue shoes scooped handfuls of dried manure into a plastic bag.

"Two black ducks on the water," Chalif said.

"They've disappeared," a male said. "Dove out of sight."

"They can't," Chalif said. "If they don't come right up, then something grabbed them and pulled them down. Snapping turtles account for most such deaths."

"What a shame!" a female said.

"Unless you're a turtle," a male said.

"There's another black duck," Chalif said. This one splashed noisily, took off in flight, skidded to a splashy landing. "No," Chalif said, "it's not one of that other pair. This is a female trying to draw the dog away from her young." He had seen a small dog working along the shoreline.

"A kingbird," Chalif said, turning up through the meadow. "See the white edge of the tail. There's a goldfinch overhead somewhere. The goldfinch—there he is—always announces himself and he flies like a roller coaster. 'Watch me go,' he says as he climbs and then he swoops down."

"The sun is coming out," an adult female said. "I want to get to the beach. Not that I don't love nature."

Everybody in the car had binoculars and as the Banker drove past the airport, the Ballet Master said: "Let's go by way of Katama. Maybe we'll see short-eared owls flying." He turned to the others. "This," he said, "is where we had one of the biggest concentrations of golden plover on the Atlantic coast. As a rule, they migrate nonstop from Nova Scotia to Bermuda and only come down in a storm. But one year we counted 250 and the next year 125."

"What's that flying?" the Banker asked.

"Meadowlark. See how he flutters his wings and then sails. We could always bring visiting birders to this field to see the upland plover. When Roger Tory Peterson and James Fisher were doing their book, *Wild America,* Fisher saw his 600th bird here, and it was an upland plover. Haven't found the bird here lately, maybe because the field has been planted to corn. Peterson and Fisher invited me to make that trip with them, but I wanted to go to Carolina and look for Bachman's warbler, which hadn't been seen for two years. So they went their way and I went mine and rediscovered Bachman's warbler."

A sparrow hawk on a telephone wire worked his tail like a pump handle. The absence of short-eared owls disappointed the Ballet Master. The other day, he said, he had seen two of them giving a marsh hawk hell, really dive-bombing him. The goal for this day, though, was Chappaquiddick and its slender barrier beach, Cape Poge, so the Banker drove onto the ferry at Edgartown. Across the channel the Doctor was waiting in his jeep.

First stop on the island was a pretty grove of evergreens and oaks around a pond. A pair of yellow-shafted flickers took flight as the jeep pulled in. The Ballet Master whistled a warbling trill punctuated by a kind of hiss. Somewhere in the tree tops a pine warbler spoke. A chickadee identified himself. A pewee stated his name, rank and serial number.

At the next stop the Ballet Master struck off through waist-high marsh grass to find himself a seaside sparrow. "I'll believe it when I see it," the Doctor said.

Fish were rising all over Poucha Pond. A herring gull stuck his head underwater, brought up a crab, dropped it, snatched it up and struggled into the air. From across the pond came the raucous cursing of crows. "They're after a short-eared owl," the Banker said, focusing his glasses. "He just lit in that bare tree top."

The hunt proceeded north along the sandy shore of Cape Poge Bay past Whistler Point, Simon Point to Little Neck and Shear Pen Pond. Out of the grass burst 10 Hudsonian curlews which circled back, alighted at water's edge and dutifully displayed their great down-curved bills.

"There's a black-bellied plover," the Ballet Master said. "See the white in his tail when he flies? If that were a black-tailed bird, he'd be a golden."

"Black-crowned night heron straight ahead," somebody said. Knee deep in water, the bird stood frozen in a round-shouldered crouch staring down into the tide with a baleful red eye, his heavy bill poised like a lance. "A reptilian eye," the Banker said.

A little farther on, an oyster-catcher ran along the beach like a woman in a hobble skirt. He wore a black hood that came clear down to make a dickey meeting his white vest. His bloodshot eye and huge red nose marked him as a rip long gone in debauchery.

"A laughing gull," the Doctor said as that blackheaded showoff sailed past. "They used to nest by the thousands on Muskeget Island, but the herring gulls seem to have displaced them."

"Two dowitchers coming in," the Banker said.

"Come see this snowy egret doing a dance all by himself," the Ballet Master said. "I'm afraid the skunks are doing terrible damage to nesting egrets."

Swallows dipped and swooped, making a nosh of airborne insects. Most were barn swallows but here was an occasional bank swallow, there a tree swallow. The Doctor told of watching a vast flock of tree swallows in migration harassed by a duck hawk that would swoop in, pick out one bird and devour it. There was a sweep around the Cape Poge lighthouse where seedy-looking eider ducks rode the waves. Then the Doctor drove down to the tidal flats at the southeastern tip of the island.

En route the Ballet Master spotted a horned lark sitting on a heap of dried seaweed. A marsh hawk with something like a mouse in his talons flew over, and a flock of swallows drove him off.

At low tide, the flats were like the Automat. At least 15 black-bellied plovers queued up in one puddle. There were dowitchers and curlews, egrets and gulls, yellowlegs and semipalmated plover. A pair of knots still wore rusty shirtfronts, the plumage of spring. "Look at the eye-line on that one, Eddie," the Doctor said.

"A stilt sandpiper," the Ballet Master said. "First of the year, and the first two knots." There was triumph in his tone.

# LOBSTERS IN LOVE

*Martha's Vineyard*

T HIS is about love among lobsters, a topic singularly appropriate on this romantic island where the tender passion has long been esteemed by the very best people. There was Miss Nancy Luce, for example, who lived at the head of Tiah's Cove on Tisbury Great Pond with her hens and her cow. She wrote love poems about the hens, and when they cackled their last she had marble headstones cut for their graves.

The news that lobsters make love will come as no surprise to the birds and bees, but what is unique about Martha's Vineyard is that here and here alone they have made it a spectator sport.

From the dawn of civilization and probably earlier, the ritual of courtship and marriage was practiced only in strict privacy at the bottom of the Atlantic until about five years ago. Since then, boy lobsters on Martha's Vineyard have been persuaded to chuck their New England inhibitions and cuddle with comely crustaceans under the benign gaze of John T. Hughes, director of the Massachusetts State Lobster Hatchery and Research Station.

One result has been the hatching of lobsters that seem to be blushing. They aren't really embarrassed though. Their bright red complexion, like that of Warren Giles or a lobster already cooked, is a triumph of selective breeding that could lead almost anywhere. It isn't impossible that selective breeding could someday produce a quick-hatching, fast-growing lobster that an ordinary Joe could buy boiled, broiled, or thermidored for a blonde without first visiting the Morris Plan.

Since the hatchery got going in 1951, several million lobster fry have been hatched, reared to the age of three or four weeks, and turned loose in coastal waters to augment the supply for commercial fishermen.

"We can't be sure what effect the stocking has had," John Hughes told visitors. "In waters where we had released fry, lobstermen have reported good catches in sizes corresponding to our year classes, but the power of suggestion is strong with both commercial and game fisherman. If they know you've been putting fish into an area, they'll work it harder and perhaps take more."

John Hughes is a scientist who makes no claims that he can't support, but the odds seem to be with the restocking program. It is estimated that, under natural conditions at sea, one-tenth of 1 percent of the hatch survives for a month—say, 60 lobsters out of 60,000 fry. The hatchery survival rate runs about 28 percent—one year it topped 40—so it figures to increase the population.

"We think research is the more important part of what we do," Hughes said. "We've bred lobsters successfully here; it hasn't been done anywhere else. We've ascertained the gestation period—18 to 24 months—and learned that by raising the water temperature we can shorten it to 11 months. We want to know whether the inshore and offshore lobsters are close relatives."

Except for a few old bucks wearing 16-ounce gloves, all the working lobsters in the hatchery are females captured after mating at sea. After a tryst, a lady lobster carries her eggs inside for nine months or so, then extrudes them and glues them under her tail where they are carried until hatching.

From a big old girl wearing maybe 60,000 eggs like an amber girdle, Hughes took a pinch of eggs and placed them under a microscope. "Some people eat this like caviar," he said, "but look at the eye of the embryo." Each egg, smaller than a pinhead, had a big blue eye of bulging compound construction.

When a lobster quits the egg en route to the gourmet's table, he has the size and general appearance of a retarded mosquito. These minute critters are transferred to rearing tanks where the water circulates constantly to prevent the larvae from clotting up, because even a day-old lobster loves other lobsters—as we love them, not as boy lobsters love girl lobsters. If the larvae accumulated, they'd eat one another up.

In three weeks they're about an inch long and ready to go to sea. They will need four to six years to reach a pound, and nobody knows how many years a lobster can live. The recognized heavyweight champion of the world weighed 43 pounds.

Once they got affectionate decapods breeding in captivity, the hatchery people started collecting lobsters of unusual color, the rare red, blue, yellow, or albino freak that occasionally crops up among the green. By mating these parents, fry have been produced that are all red, albino, or lemon spotted. This suggests that selective breeding might develop desirable characteristics like rapid growth, tender meat, and a sense of humor.

Many of the big egg lobsters for the hatchery are taken from water 100 to 300 fathoms deep by dragger fishermen working the edge of the continental shelf with otter trawls. These are nets shaped like stocking caps which are dragged large end foremost to catch bottom-feeding fish.

"Once," said John Hughes, "our lobsterman caught the submarine Nautilus."

"Did he land it?"

"No, his boat started moving backwards and he had to cut loose."

# A HUNTING MORNING

*Martha's Vineyard*

T HE professor is a mighty hunter before the Lord but a man of peace. He hunts for food yet he does not kill. His quarry is the untamed mushroom—the elusive Tricholoma, the Blushing Amanita, the humble Agaricus campestris, the wary Amanitopsis.

"No," he told his pupil, "we won't be starting out before daybreak, it's not that kind of sport. In some countries they go to church the day before, but that's just a local custom like blessing the bull in Spain or the fleet at the Biloxi Shrimp Festival."

It was 10 a.m. when the Professor led his pupil along a footpath into the woods.

"I root for the Baltimore Orioles," he said, "but this is real, a blood sport. If you make a mistake, the next thing you hear is the ambulance siren. However, there are only two poisonous mushrooms on this island—the fly and the angel. Learn to recognize these, and your greatest danger is poison ivy.

"There are 38,000 known varieties but we'll divide them into two main types—those with ribs, or gills, on the underside of the cap and those with spores that look like sponge rubber. Later in the season the puffballs will show up.

"Here you are. This bright orange job is the fly, the little beauty that killed Czar Alexis, Peter the Great's father. They use its poison in laboratories to stop the growth of certain organisms. The angel is pure white—here it is. You see, the gills and stem are white—it has a frill or skirt on the stalk and the bottom is an onion-like bulb.

"There is no known antidote for the destroying angel or—oops, here's what we're looking for, this russet number, the Amanita rubescent, called a 'blusher.' You sauté it in butter and eat it on toast. People are afraid of it because it looks so much like the poisonous variety, but you see the brown gills, reddish brown stalk, and the ball on the bottom instead of the onion. Delicious.

"See the fungus on that dead tree. They tell you anything that grows on wood is safe to eat, but who'd want to? All non-poisonous mushrooms are classed as edible, but that doesn't mean they taste good. A book calls this one 'choice' but we've cooked it and dried it and mixed it in salads and it still tastes like library paste.

"This hollow oak, by the way, is a honey tree. See the bees around the entrance? At certain times they cluster there and hang way down, 'bearding,' it's called. I brought a bee man in here and he said there was about 200 pounds of honey inside the tree.

"Pardon? That purple mushroom? It's called a bolete. It won't poison you but you might wish it did, it's so bitter. I mixed one up with some blushers once and my daughter said the taste stayed with her the next day.

"See how the snails have been eating this? And this one with the cap gone, probably a field mouse has been at it. Hey, squat down here and see if you can spot some more of these little black trumpets. They're mushrooms but they don't have the toadstool shape. Barbara dries them and makes a delicious soup with cream and butter.

"Never mind, I'll send Barb. She has the patience to stare at the ground until she begins to see these little trumpets. I don't. That's why you need husband-and-wife teams for proper mushrooming.

"Here's a variety the book calls choice, but I haven't the guts to try it because it is so like the fly. And isn't that pretty, that bright blue? It's good but it's a solitary and there's no use bothering with mushrooms that you see only occasionally as singles. Can't get enough for a meal.

"Now, Margaret Boni's lawn here is covered with fairy rings, sometimes called Scotch bonnets. After a rain you can gather a bushel in an hour. They have a nice nutty flavor raw or dried. They're very bland if cooked.

"First time I came on this field I was following a deer's track. Now I come here once a month. See this yellow plant that looks exactly like coral on the Great Barrier Reef. It's a mushroom, called coral. We use it to garnish salads. That's another coral over there, the black thing shaped like a little club, and if we looked hard enough we'd find pink coral and white.

"What? Those buttons? Those, my friend, are deer signs, not mushrooms. Maybe we've had enough for one morning. Come on home and I'll cook you an appetizer for lunch."

# TIME AND TIDE

"IN Wisconsin there occasionally occurs a peculiar fluctuation in the water level of Green Bay. On a perfectly calm day with not a ripple and the surface glassy, the water will gradually rise three or four feet, then slowly return to its former level. The cycle may be repeated several times and each cycle may take about 10 minutes. The phenomenon is called a seiche.

"People in the area all pronounce it as though it were spelled 'seech' to rhyme with peach, beech, and so forth.

"Both World-*Webster* and the *Pronouncing Dictionary of American English* give it as 'saysh.' Merriam-*Webster's Third International* agrees, as does *Funk & Wagnalls*. So the preponderance of learned evidence seems opposed to the local pronunciation. Nonetheless we hope that the people of Green Bay will continue with 'seech' because this is the established regional pronunciation and anything else would sound false and affected."

Those paragraphs are from the third volume of the *Dictionary of Word and Phrase Origins* by William and Mary Morris (Harper & Row, $7.95). Because games are part of the culture of America and England, both the English and American languages are rich with expressions that have their roots in sports. This dictionary deals with many of them, from "aesthete's foot" (John Chapman's term for gout because it seems to pick on the upper classes) to "vigorish," a word familiar to bookmakers, horseplayers and other lowly types.

There are enough sports references in the book to fill a dozen columns, but if the reader will indulge an old Wisconsin bass fisherman, it is proposed to deal here with the Door County variety of the seiche, or "seech."

As far as can be testified from personal experience, the phenomenon occurs not in Green Bay itself but in Rowley's Bay, a tiny bight on the Lake Michigan shore of the Door County peninsula. (Door County is a spear of limestone dividing the waters of Lake Michigan and Green Bay. The rocky shorelines are nicked like a razor which a wife has been using to sharpen pencils. Rowley's Bay is one of the nicks.)

About halfway across the peninsula, a swamp gives rise to Mink River, which makes its mosquito-ridden way through marsh and meadow to empty into Rowley's Bay. It is a pretty poor excuse for a river, with only two distinctions: (1) early in the fishing season, smallmouth bass of noble proportions and evil disposition congregate at the mouth, or used to; (2) it's where that seiche happens.

You'll be fishing from a boat and suddenly you'll realize that a tide is running out, faster and faster until little whirlpools gurgle like a severe attack of indigestion. Gradually the flow slows down until it stops altogether. After a brief period of slack water, the current starts moving upstream, picking up speed until once again whirlpools are spinning past the boat. From ebb to flood to ebb takes 20 minutes.

There is, or was, an inn at Rowley's Bay where fishermen could rent rowboats. The old pappy guy who tended the boats had grown up in the neighborhood. We asked him about the curious behavior of the water and he grunted. "Yup," he said, "20-minute tide." His tone suggested that this was a fact of nature like the sun rising in the east.

He didn't call it a seiche or seech. Neither did anybody else encountered in a decade or more of summer sojourns on the peninsula. First to use the word within hearing was Dr. Dan Merriman, the oceanographer of Davenport College at Yale. Told about the Mink River tide, he said maybe it wasn't a tide but a "saysh."

This was a few years ago, and a dictionary consulted at the time wasn't encouraging. It said a seiche was something left over after a storm, but this kooky thing out in Wisconsin happened all the time, in the mildest of summer calm.

However, a recent consultation with *Webster's Third International* was more helpful. It defines seiche as "an oscillation of the surface of a lake or landlocked sea, varying in period from a few minutes to several hours. It is thought to be initiated chiefly by local variations in atmospheric pressure, and perpetuated by the oscillations of the water surface after the inequalities of atmospheric pressure have disappeared."

Well, now, there are some pretty wild atmospheric variations in Door

County. It can be hotter than the rivets of hell on the Green Bay side, and just six or eight miles to the east the breeze off Lake Michigan will raise goose pimples the size of grapes.

So maybe that's the explanation of the 20-minute tide in Rowley's Bay. As for the local pronunciation, Bill Morris needn't worry. Across the peninsula is a town name Fish Crick. It was Fish Crick when Jean Nicolet arrived in 1634, and it will be Fish Crick when the hydrogen bomb makes differences in pronunciation academic.

# THE AMATEURS

*On August 26, 1972, President Gustav Heinemann of West Germany proclaimed open the Games of the 20th Olympiad. That day it was written from Munich:*

*"The weather was brilliant, the color exuberant, the great crowd obviously enchanted and the whole occasion free — outwardly, at least — of political, racial and social undertones. When the pageantry ended, the feeling seemed to be general that perhaps the next two weeks of competition would help heal some of the wounds of the past, blurring the memory of the 1936 Olympics in Berlin which Adolf Hitler's propagandists made into a Nazi carnival, giving a happier meaning to the name of this city which for 34 years has been synonymous with appeasement."*

# AVERY'S ADVENTURES IN WONDERLAND

*"Let the jury consider their verdict," the King said, for about the
twentieth time that day.*
*"No, no!" said the Queen. "Sentence first—verdict afterwards."*
*"Stuff and nonsense!" said Alice loudly. "The idea of having the
sentence first!"*

Without a hearing, without a defense and without appeal, Karl
Schranz of Austria has had his buttons cut off and been drummed off
the ski slopes of Sapporo, Japan, by the self-appointed, self-perpetu-
ating kangaroo court that calls itself the International Olympic Committee. Never has that clutch of overripe playground directors brought
off a more transparent exercise in face-saving and never in all his
years as Defender of the Faith has Avery Brundage, the noblest badger
of them all, been in finer form.

Schranz, at 33 the senior member of Austria's Alpine ski team, ranks
third in the world this winter in the art of sliding down hill, which
makes him a national hero. His crime was cashing in on his fame by
endorsing ski equipment. This puts him in a class with ladies of the
peerage who advertise that they wash their faces with a certain soap,
movie stars who shill for deodorants on television, and practically
every other schussboomer who ever cracked a fibula.

Indeed, Brundage, doubling as chief justice and prosecutor, went
into the star chamber with a list of about 40 skiers whom he considered
guilty of violating the amateur code. Had the I.O.C. cast them all into
outer darkness, the millions Japan spent getting ready for the Winter
Games would have gone down the drain and the slopes would have
been stained by the blood of National Broadcasting Company vice
presidents falling on their Scout knives.

Quailing from such a responsibility, the vestals of the Olympic flame made an example of Schranz and found all other defendants without sin. Brundage said the Austrian was singled out because he was "the most blatant and verbose," which is pretty bad, and also "disrespectful of the Olympic movement," which is unforgivable.

Schranz, it seems, wasn't content merely to sell his name and photograph to advertisers. He compounded his misbehavior by denouncing the Olympic fathers to the Associated Press for their "nineteenth-century attitudes" and charging that they favored "rich competitors over poor ones."

Brundage characterized these remarks as "very ill-advised," and he was right. Schranz should have said eighteenth century.

Avery Brundage is both the president and symbol of the I.O.C. He is a rich and righteous anachronism, at 84 a vestigial remnant of an economy that supported a leisure class that could compete in athletics for fun alone. His wrath is the more terrible because it is so sincere and unenlightened.

It goes without saying that Karl Schranz is a professional. So are all the state-supported athletes of many countries, so are the American kids who are hired to play games for colleges, so are all those Olympic runners who took bribes from manufacturers of track shoes during the 1968 games in Mexico City.

Several years ago the custodians of amateur morals in United States skiing circles decided that the way to keep athletes pure was to beat them to the loot. A firm of agents was employed to sell official endorsements for every item of winter sports equipment from thermal underwear to skis. Price lists were drawn up for manufacturers wishing to advertise that the United States ski team used their mittens or boots or goggles.

An interesting rationale operates here. If a manufacturer pays an individual skier for using his product, it is dirty money. If the same manufacturer pays off the national association, the swag is as clean as new powder.

The simple truth is that the whole concept of amateurism is archaic, as the dear old doyens of lawn tennis came reluctantly to admit at long last. Brundage is not the only hardshell who refuses to recognize this. He is just the godliest, the most intransigent and the loudest. He isn't going to change but perhaps one of these days younger and more flexible minds will reject the outmoded ideal of the gentleman sportsman and come around to the realization that open competition is the only kind that is practicable today in any sport.

A man is not unclean because he earns his living with his muscles.


Willi Daume, president of the Olympic Organizing Committee and thus promoter-in-chief of this summer's muscle dance in Munich, says Bobby Lee Hunter will not be welcome as a member of the United States boxing team because "an Olympic athlete should be an example to youth." Hunter is a flyweight doing time for killing a man in a knife fight.

Avery Brundage says "there is a basic regulation that athletes must live in the spirit of the Olympic rules, the Games, and the Olympic ideal." Nowhere in the rules is manslaughter mentioned with approval or otherwise.

Presumably what applies to Hunter applies equally to Gene White, a high jumper who is doing a bit for forgery. Accompanied by a prison guard, Hunter went to Colombia last summer to win a bronze medal in the Pan-American Games and this year competed in Britain and the Soviet Union as a member of a touring party of United States Olympic candidates. White represented the United States against Russia in a dual meet in Richmond, Va., last March, clearing 7 feet 2¾ inches.

The conclusion to be drawn from these facts is clear: Pan-American athletes and American representatives in international competitions less widely publicized than the Olympics are not required to live in the spirit of the Olympic ideal.

It says here that Olympic officials, no less than Olympic athletes, should be an example to youth and that qualities they ought to exemplify include understanding, helpfulness, clemency and faith in the essential decency of mankind. If sport is the instrument for good that the high priests of the playgrounds profess to believe, then they should welcome the opportunity to help pluck a couple of brands from the burning. Especially brands that can jump 7-2 or take an adversary out in the first round.

Judging from their public statements, Daume seems less disposed to compromise than Brundage. When the press quizzed Brundage about Hunter in Munich, he took refuge in the comment that "Rule 26 of our Olympic code says that each participant must have adhered to the Olympic spirit and the Olympic ideals and that he has lived accordingly."

This must be the first time in his many years that Slavery Avery avoided taking a stand on an issue involving the Olympics, be it Eleanor Holm's preference in vintage champagne or rumors that Karl Schranz didn't always pay his laundry bills in European ski resorts. A granite tower of rectitude where infringement of the amateur code is concerned, Brundage seems to have a slightly more flexible view of manslaughter and forgery.

If this is the case, then Avery is to be applauded along with the South Carolina authorities who have given Hunter leave from prison, and the warden, judge and others in Pennsylvania who have encouraged White. There has been no indication that the United States Olympic Committee would bar Hunter from the Olympic trials. White is in Seattle now for the National Amateur Athletic Union championships and expects to go to Eugene, Ore., for the Olympic trials.

In the interests of humanity, it is devoutly to be hoped that both young men qualify and compete in Munich. There but for the grace of God go Avery Brundage and Willi Daume.

*Munich*

For practice, they bilked a kid from Uganda early in the program but it was petit larceny, like lifting a piece of costume jewelry in Woolworth's. The bright and airy cockpit called the Boxhalle wasn't more than two-thirds filled when Degratias (Thank God) Musoke, a Ugandan featherweight, punched Finland's left-handed Jouko Lindberg around the ring and lost a unanimous decision.

Two bouts later a stubby Mongolian named Palomarj Baatar took out after Bulgaria's Kountcho Kountchev and the crowd howled with laughter watching the tall Bulgar flee as though all the Mongol hordes were in pursuit. In a daring daylight burglary, three of the five judges swiped victory for Kountchev. They weren't the same characters who had jobbed Musoke. On the theory that six heads are worse than three, the Olympic brass assigns a nonvoting referee and five judges to each bout and keeps them circulating so their incompetence won't stagnate.

By this time, perhaps 6,000 of the 7,200 seats were occupied. It sounded more like 60,000. The whistles alone could have brought blood but there were also boos, hoots, shouts, chants and bellows. They drowned out the public address system introducing the boxers for the next bout.

As the tumult ebbed, Baatar reappeared in the gallery and the thunder swelled again. The victim was plucked off his feet and lifted high, and all over the hall spectators sprang from their seats shouting and beating their palms, ignoring the ring, where a Canadian kid was losing to a Colombian.

This was only the warmup. They didn't bring off the big caper until Reggie Jones of Newark had whacked the whey out of Russia's Valery Tregubov, two-time European champion in the light-middleweight division (156 pounds). Now Reggie knows how the Brink's people felt after that job in Boston.

It required mathematical acrobatics worthy of Olympic gymnasts to contrive the decision for the left-handed Russian. On the 20-point must system, the judge from Liberia, one E. Khalife, gave all three rounds to Jones for a score of 60-57. T. Foo of Malaysia called the American the winner, 59-57. D. Ivanovic of Yugoslavia voted for the Russian, 59-58, and the other two, Niang Malik of Niger and J. D. Krom of the Netherlands scored 58 points for each fighter but checked Trebugov as the winner.

Thus the cumulative score gave it to Jones, 293 to 289, but Reggie was eliminated by a vote of 3 to 2.

"I'll probably stop fightin' now," the young man said. "This ain't the first time or the last. The Olympics are as far as you can go, and I'll probably just sit back now and watch."

"What went through your mind when you heard the decision?" he was asked.

"There was a big blur. I closed my eyes for a second. I knew this was not no dream. I knew I was not gonna get no medal. There was no sense startin' anything, getting mad. I just left the ring. The best man win it, that's the way it always go."

Invited to describe the bout as he had seen it, Jones proved himself a better judge than the guys with the scorecards. He felt the first round was his. It was. The second was "on the edge," he said, might possibly have been scored for Tregubov by a shade. He was being modest.

"Before the third round my coach [Bobby Lewis] told me I had to go after him. I fought harder so there wouldn't be no doubt. The guy was just in there in the third. I had him hurt. I threw the punches and they all connected and he was staggering. There was no doubt in my mind. It wasn't close."

In the judgment of the crowd, he understated it. When the decision was announced, crumpled paper and assorted trash rained on the ring. Even while the boys were being introduced for the next bout, debris kept falling. Fans were on their feet, bawling, whistling, stomping. A young one with a beard waved an American flag. Outstretched arms turned thumbs down. A thunderous chant began:

"Schieber! Schieber! Schieber!"

"Schieber," a young German said: "It means like one of the judges is taking money?" He spread his hands palms up.

"Aufhören!" the crowd chorused.

"Aufhören! Aufhören!" ("It is finished. Enough for today. Get lost.")

It went on and on, through the three two-minute rounds that followed and into the bout after that. The American coaches got Jones out of the hall. "We were afraid there'd be a riot," one said.

*Augsburg, West Germany*

The canoe bucked like a bronc with a burr under his tail as Tom Southworth and John Burton steered through the concrete gorge past the boulder called Brundage's Nose—it is a hard nose, not a soft nose—plunged headlong into the Washing Machine and brought up against the rock in the middle of that maelstrom. The canoe rolled over once, rolled again, righted itself with both men still aboard and lurched on, burying its nose in white water diving down the Zoom Flume, twisting, careening, whirling through the Spin-Dry Cycle to surge past the finish line where the torrent empties into the river Lech.

The wetbacks from Media, Pa., had maneuvered the 30 gates at a cost of only 40 penalty points, but that underwater detour in the Washing Machine had eaten up seconds they couldn't afford. Their time for the voyage of 1,968 feet—call it two-fifths of a mile—was 6 minutes 27.4 seconds.

With the penalty points added, their score for the run was 7 minutes 7.4 seconds. In the canoe slalom that doesn't get you arrested for loitering, but it was only tenth best among the 14 pairs that stayed afloat through the whole wild run.

Six teams went overboard on the first run and three would be racked up on the second. On their second trip, Southworth and Burton would cut 20 seconds off their score and finish 12th in the field of 20 with Russ Nichols of Huntington, L.I., and John Evans of Sylmar, Calif., 14th.

This was the last event in the canoe and kayak slalom, a slightly suicidal undertaking new to the Olympic Games, which combines the best features of skiing down the Matterhorn, shipwreck, and going over Niagara in a barrel.

The sport, if that is the word for it, is a hasty search for a watery grave, with rules. It is an outgrowth of white-water racing, which appeals to people whose idea of fun is to be flung down the rapids ears over appetite, hurled against rocks and submerged until the coroner arrives.

On the international level it is dominated by the two Germanys, possibly because of some macabre streak in the breed. West Germany alone is reputed to have 100,000 kayak paddlers and there must have been 25,000 spectators massed along the banks for the two days of Olympic competition.

The course here, the world's only man-made white-water river, is a cement-walled canal 39 feet wide that twists along an old river bed. The water rushes down the chute, varying in depth from a few inches to six or seven feet, boiling around concrete boulders constructed with evil cunning at strategic points, sloshing and churning against the walls.

As in ski slalom, the gates are skinny barber poles, red and white on one side of the course, green and white on the other. They must be negotiated in numerical order, always with the green at the paddler's right. That means that sometimes he must whirl his craft around and go down backward, sometimes he must find an eddy below the gates and struggle through against the current.

If he happens to capsize and be swept through a gate upside down, that's perfectly all right. It impairs breathing but gets him no penalty points. Penalties for touching poles or missing gates vary from 10 to 50 points. Skull fractures and deaths by drowning are held to a minimum by headgear, life jackets and a rescue crew.

On the first day of competition, Jamie McEwan of Silver Spring, Md., got a bronze medal in the men's canoe singles, finishing third behind an East German and a West German. That day a Dartmouth student, Eric Evans, was America's top man in the kayak singles, taking seventh place.

The second day opened with kayak singles for women, and when the first run was over a tall man with a beard wandered into the press center. This was O. K. Goodwin of Newport News, Va., who had been watching his 19-year-old daughter, Cynthia. How, he was asked, had Cindy got into this dodge? He ducked apologetically.

"My fault. I got into it through the Boy Scouts. Had an Explorer troop in Newport News. We had to travel 80 miles to find fast water. Then we got going to the annual races at Washington, D.C."

"You mean there's fast water in Washington?"

"Oh, yes. Below the falls eight or nine miles up the Potomac. That's a good course—Wet Bottom Chute, Yellow Falls, Difficult Run, Stubblefield Falls."

Cindy took up the sport about five years ago, her father said. In the first run here she had made brilliant time but amassed a gang of penalty points and finished 15th.

Competitors count only their better run, and Cynthia's second trip moved her up to 14th place. Lyn Ashton of Kensington, Md., finished ninth and Louise Holcombe, Cheverly, Md., 15th.

"How does Cindy build up the strength for that upstream paddling?" her father was asked.

"By paddling," he said.


*Munich*

Olympic Village was under siege. Two men lay murdered and eight others were held at gunpoint in imminent peril of their lives. Still the games went on. Canoeists paddled through their races. Fencers thrust and parried in make-believe duels. Boxers scuffled. Basketball players scampered across the floor like happy children. Walled off in their dream world, appallingly unaware of the realities of life and death, the aging playground directors who conduct this quadrennial muscle dance ruled that a little bloodshed must not be permitted to interrupt play.

It was 4:30 a.m. when Palestinian terrorists invaded the housing complex where athletes from 12 nations live, and shot their way into the Israeli quarters.

More than five hours later, word came down from Avery Brundage, retiring president of the International Olympic Committee, that sport would proceed as scheduled. Canoe racing had already begun. Wrestling started an hour later. Before long competition was being held in 11 of the 22 sports on the Olympic calendar.

Not until 4 p.m. did some belated sense of decency dictate suspension of the obscene activity, and even then exception was made for games already in progress. They went on and on while hasty plans were laid for a memorial service.

The men who run the Olympics are not evil men. Their shocking lack of awareness can't be due to callousness. It has to be stupidity.

Four years ago in Mexico City when American sprinters stood on the victory stand with fists uplifted in symbolic protest against injustice to blacks, the brass of the United States Olympic Committee couldn't distinguish between politics and human rights. Declaring that the athletes had violated the Olympic spirit by injecting "partisan politics" into the festival, the waxworks lifted the young men's credentials and ordered them out of Mexico, blowing up a simple, silent gesture into an international incident.

When African nations and other blacks threatened to boycott the current Games if the white supremacist government of Rhodesia were represented here, Brundage thundered that the action was politically motivated, although it was only through a transparent political expedient that Rhodesia had been invited in the first place. Rhodesia and Brundage were voted down not on moral grounds but to avoid having an all-white carnival.

On past performances, it must be assumed that in Avery's view Arab-Israeli warfare, hijacking, kidnapping and killing all constitute partisan politics not to be tolerated in the Olympics.

"And anyway," went the bitter joke today, "these are professional killers; Avery doesn't recognize them."

The fact is, these global clambakes have come to have an irresistible attraction as forums for ideological, social or racial expression. For this reason, they may have outgrown their britches. Perhaps in the future it will be advisable to substitute separate world championships in swimming, track and field and so on, which could be conducted in a less hysterical climate.

In the past, athletes from totalitarian countries have seized upon the Olympics as an opportunity to defect. During the Pan-American Games last summer in Cali, Colombia, a number of Cubans defected and a trainer jumped, fell or was pushed to his death from the roof of the Cuban team's dormitory.

Never, of course, has there been anything like today's terror. Once those gunmen climbed the wire fence around Olympic Village and shot Moshe Weinberg, the Israeli wrestling coach, all the fun and games lost meaning. Mark Spitz and his seven gold medals seemed curiously unimportant. The fact that the American heavyweight, Duane Bobick, got slugged stupid by Cuba's Teofilo Stevenson mattered to few besides Bobick.

Even the disqualification of 16-year-old Rick De Mont from the 1,500-meter free-style swimming, in which he has shattered the world record, slipped into the background. This may be unfortunate, for it appears that the boy was undone through the misfeasance of American team officials and if this is so the facts should be made public.

The United States party includes 168 coaches, trainers and other functionaries, which seems like enough to take care of 447 athletes. It wasn't enough, however, to get two world-record sprinters to the starting blocks for the 100-meter dash and it wasn't enough to reconcile young De Mont's asthma treatments with Olympic rules on drugs.

After the boy won the 400-meter free-style, a urinalysis showed a trace of ephedrine, a medicine that helps clear nasal passages. A list of forbidden drugs, released before the Games, includes ephedrine. The fact that De Mont uses it for his asthma appears on his application sheet for the Games.

Why didn't the American medical staff pick this up and make sure there would be no violation? Efforts to get an answer today were unavailing. Dr. Winston P. Riehl, the chief physician, couldn't be reached. Dr. Harvey O'Phelan declined to talk.


There used to be an advertising slogan for a chewing gum: "The flavor lasts." For a gum manufacturer, this is a proud boast. When it is said of the 1972 Olympic Games, it is an unhappy truth. It would be a relief to forget the fortnight just concluded, to pretend it never happened. Perhaps an ostrich could manage this, or a member of the Olympic hierarchy. For everybody else, those sorry days must be remembered always as a time of bloodshed, bungling and bitterness.

Neither the Games nor the governing heads of the International Olympic Committee were in any way responsible for the bloodshed. On the ground of common decency, however, the brass is faulted for blundering on with the frolic while the world stood aghast. As to conduct of the sport, never since these global clambakes got started in 1896 has there been one remotely comparable with this for official misfeasance, incompetence and stubborn arrogance. Chances are it would never be possible to bring together thousands of young people from widely dissimilar backgrounds and cultures and throw them into competition for two weeks without creating some friction. Even so, by comparison with past gatherings, Munich was a disaster.

The first loud cries of outrage were heard in the boxing arena when the Soviet Union's Valery Tregubov took a three-round licking and a 3-2 decision in a match with America's Reggie Jones. This should have surprised nobody familiar with the dark ways and peculiar rules of amateur boxing on the international level.

All of us are influenced in some degree by our prejudices, our likes and dislikes. In the fiercely nationalistic climate of the Olympics, judges are frequently swayed by national, political, ethnic or religious prejudice. Evidence of this crops up in every game that is scored by judgment—boxing, figure skating, diving.

In the Olympics, judges are supposed to give a boxer credit for defensive skill when he makes his opponent miss, but at the same time he is penalized for ducking below the waist. He can win by a knockout, but a clean blow that drops a man for nine seconds is no better than a light jab, for the rules say no extra credit shall be given for a knockdown. It is not uncommon for honest, competent, professional judges to view a fight differently. What, then, should we expect from amateur judges who work only occasionally and then under idiotic rules?

Even so, the job they did on Jones was something special. Afterward, some judges were disqualified and others warned. By that time, of course, Jones was out of the competition.

The Jones decision started it, the basketball caper wrapped it up and there was an unappetizing array of exhibits in between—the last-minute decision to take Bob Seagren's vaulting pole away from him at the insistence of East Germany's Wolfgang Nordwig, who won the event; the disqualification of an American swimmer because he took his asthma medicine; the banishment of two quarter-milers because of their demeanor on the victory stand.

Sometimes it requires conscious effort to preserve a sense of proportion. It doesn't matter at all, for example, who wins a basketball game, but it does matter if there is cheating. For at least 40 years the United States has been sending coaches around the world to teach basketball in other nations. If the coaches were any good, it was high time somebody beat an American team in the Olympics. Now it has happened, and the kindest thing that can be said about it is that officials erred.

To many viewers, Vince Matthews and Wayne Collett cut an unattractive picture on the victory stand after running one-two at 400 meters. Some witnesses considered their inattentiveness disrespectful to the American flag and the national anthem.

The young men gave cause for complaint, but this in no way justifies the star-chamber ruling of the I.O.C. brass, who flung the pair out of the Olympic family with no pretense of a hearing.

If the I.O.C. booted every other play, the chiefs of the American delegation did no better. When Rey Robinson and Eddie Hart, world-record sprinters, showed up too late for their qualifying heats in the 100 meters, somebody put forward a half-hearted fiction about their getting caught in traffic. The fact was Stan Wright, a coach, had misinformed the runners about their starting time, and he was man enough to admit it.

Nobody yet has admitted responsibility in the disqualification of Rick De Mont, the 16-year-old swimmer. Efforts were made to find out why he was allowed to go on taking medication that was forbidden in the international rules, but nobody would talk. Later it was suggested that the doctors were keeping silent "to protect the boy."

Somebody ought to tell somebody that suppressing the truth protects nobody.

# SWEET DREAMS

*Philadelphia*

T HE runners lined up for the mile on the gray-green Tartan track. One wore a white jersey with "Villanova" in blue block letters, another had his Olympic Games suit with "U.S.A." on the bosom. The others could have been naked, for all the 22,000 witnesses in Franklin Field knew or cared.

This was Marty Liquori and Jim Ryun in the match race that was two years in the making. Four years ago as a sophomore at Kansas, Ryun ran a mile in 3 minutes, 51.1 seconds, faster than any man before or since, and in the same race the Villanova freshman, Liquori, broke four minutes for the first time.

Two years ago Liquori, lighthearted, light-footed, and gaily combative, literally ran the moody Ryun into retirement. Outrun eight times in eight earlier engagements, Liquori beat Ryun for the National Collegiate Championship in Knoxville, Tenn., then made it two straight in the National Amateurs in Miami where Ryun walked off the track and out of competition.

While Liquori romped blithely on, Ryun married, became a father, and settled down as a breadwinner in Eugene, Ore. Not until January of this year did Ryun feel the competitive fires burning again, and encouraged by his wife Anne he started a comeback as an old crock of 24. Ever since then, track fans waited for the pair to hook up again, and it happened at the third annual Martin Luther King International Freedom Games. Rains which had fallen all morning subsided just before the meet opened, but puddles still stood on the track when the milers lined up.

Through the raw afternoon, Ryun had been a spectator and leading player in a family scene that attracted half the photographers on the

255

Eastern seaboard. In the front row of seats just off the first turn, Jim sat wearing a yellow rain jacket. Anne was beside him with her parents, Mr. and Mrs. Monroe Snider, of Bay Village, Ohio. On Grandpa Snider's lap was Heather Ryun, aged 10 months, wrapped in one blanket and much admiration.

When at last the field of 11 peeled down to lingerie and straggled up to the starting line, the customers were true to Philadelphia's sacred traditions—they booed Marty Liquori, the local boy. Moments later they were cheering him wildly, saluting a victory achieved on the kind of guts few athletes are called upon to show.

Liquori had conceded from the outset that he couldn't match history's fastest miler in speed or strength. That left him only one avenue to victory; if he couldn't outrun Ryun, he would have to outrace him. He did. To do it, he had to run more than two seconds faster than he had ever run in his life. He did that, too.

He took the lead from Ryun on the backstretch of the third quarter, held it down past the starting point and into the gun lap, held it under increasing pressure in the final rush down the back and into the last big turn, and as Ryun moved up on his right shoulder straightening for the tape, Liquori hurled back the challenge with a rally that was one part physical and nine parts pure spirit.

It isn't often that a sports event which is awaited so long and so eagerly fulfills all expectations. More often than not, events that are billed as the race or fight or game of the decade turn out to be an anticlimax.

This was magnificent, a thing of wildly beautiful perfection. Liquori had hoped for a fast pace and he got a pretty smart one from Joe Savage of Manhattan, who took the lead at the start. Running fifth through the first lap, Liquori did the quarter in 61.1 seconds, three-tenths faster than Ryun, who was seventh or eighth.

Both did the half in 2:03.3 and Ryun forged into the lead as the second lap ended, holding first place only around the turn. Witnesses had started screaming when the gun cracked, and by now the rivals were racing through a roaring tunnel of sound. Liquori's clocking for three-quarters was three minutes flat.

At the end, both were caught in 3:54.6. In all his life Liquori had never beaten 3:57.3. He went the last lap in 54.6, on guts.

"Event No. 25," the program read, "Dream Mile Run," which goes to show the force of habit. A year ago the adjective was valid. A year ago it really was the sort of footrace that track and field buffs see flashing over the counterpane at 2 a.m. It was the perfect match, the first confrontation between Jim Ryun and Marty Liquori since the world record-holder began his comeback after an 18-month sabbatical to "learn how to lose," and on a raw and rainy Sunday it drew 22,000 customers to the International Freedom Games.

Today Liquori, the blithe spirit who ran Ryun into his temporary retirement, was looking on from a television tower and Francesco Arese, the European champion, was home in Italy. On the same wet Tartan track in Franklin Field, with the same showery, gusty weather, attendance may have been slightly more than half as large as last year.

Ryun was running again, but the situation that made last year's match a happening no longer obtained. In the real "dream mile," Liquori fought off Ryun's closing kick to win by five feet in 3 minutes 54.6 seconds. Then he raced on unbeaten through the year. This year an injured heel has immobilized him.

Because he lives no more than 20 minutes from the stadium, Marty came over this afternoon as a spectator and on arrival was dragooned as a commentator on TV. He wore a double-breasted jacket of mod pattern, a pink-striped shirt with white collar and a necktie depicting sunrise over a lumberyard.

His straw-colored mustache drooped when he was asked what would be going through his mind while he watched Ryun run. "I can't tell till it happens," he said reasonably. "Right now I feel pretty detached from the sport."

"That doesn't mean you're retired?"

"For today I am."

Liquori said he would be packing tomorrow to go consult Dr. Robert Kerlan, the California orthopedic surgeon who worked on Sandy Koufax's elbow, various tracts of Wilt Chamberlain, and the ailments of other celebrated athletes.

"What do you expect from Dr. Kerlan?" somebody asked.

"A miracle. I guess," Liquori said.

He listened incredulously when told about the mystery man of the mile field, Tim Fergerson, a student at California Polytechnic of Pomona who runs for the West Coast Jets, coached by his father. An absolute unknown in major track circles, Fergerson was said by his father to have done 3:52 in practice (nine-tenths behind Ryun's world record) but never in his life had he started in an open mile.

Rain had been falling steadily for perhaps an hour—rain in which Madeline Manning Jackson, the Olympic champion, matched the world record of 2:02 flat in the half-mile—but it subsided to a barely perceptible drizzle as the field lined up for the mile. God, it seemed, was doing what He could for Ryun, but the young man would be on his own once the gun barked.

Indeed, Jim was soon on his own and practically all by himself. He was up with the others for two of the four laps, then all of a sudden he was empty. Before the third lap was over, everybody had passed him save the mysterious Fergerson, who had dashed away on top but folded inside a quarter.

"Fergerson's father said he could beat Ryun," a man said as the world champion faded, "and maybe he will." He didn't though. The mystery man ran last and his clocking of 4:33.2 deepened the mystery of why he was on the track.

Ryun had finished 19 seconds earlier, ninth in a field of 10. Up front, big Dave Wottle of Bowling Green came on to win by inches from Howell Michael, the former national collegiate indoor champion. Both were clocked in 3:58.5. Ken Popejoy of Michigan State might have broken four minutes, too, but he eased up when beaten and was clocked in 4:00.2 in third place.

Bundled in a warmup outfit, Ryun's wife Anne joined him in the infield as he finished. They walked together to the top of the home-stretch, Anne smiling resolutely for photographers. There they crossed the track, Jim helped her over the outside railing and departed without a word. The dream mile had been a nightmare.

# THE TIGERS

Terry Daniels played freshman football at Southern Methodist and was nine credit hours away from a degree of Bachelor of Science in Government when Joe Frazier batted him bubble-eyed on the eve of the 1972 Super Bowl football game. Terry lost the fight but won a singular distinction as the only challenger for the heavyweight championship of the world who was skilled at needlepoint.

"A girl showed me," he said. "It's relaxing. I can push the needle through back and forth and think about other things."

Here was a wedding of the arts: a practitioner of the Sweet Science who exalts the needle; Nat Fleischer's Boxing Encyclopedia crossed with Godey's Lady Book; a modern John L. Sullivan announcing to the Home Economics class: "I can whip any seamstress in the house!"

# THE BIG FIGHT

ARLY in the 15th round a left hook caught Muhammad Ali on the jaw and it was as though Joe Frazier had hit him with a baseball bat, Frank Howard model. Several times earlier Ali had sagged toward the floor. This time he slammed it like a plank. He went down at full length, flat on his back.

He rocked back on his shoulder blades, both feet in the air, rocked forward to a sitting position and pushed himself wearily, sadly, to his feet. He was up by the count of four but Arthur Mercante, the referee, counted on for the mandatory eight seconds. He stepped aside and Joe came on, bloody mouth open in a grimace of savage joy.

Another hook smashed home, and Ali's hands flew up to his face as if to stifle a scream. When they came down, he had an advanced case of mumps. The comely visage he describes with such affection—"I'm the prettiest; I'm the greatest"—was a gibbous balloon, puffy and misshapen.

"Broken jaw," somebody said at ringside, but the diagnosis was not confirmed. As the 15th round started, Angelo Dundee, Ali's handler, had said the jaw was broken. But x-rays taken later showed there was no fracture.

On one point there was no shadow of doubt. Joe Frazier, whom they had called a pretender, was heavyweight champion of the world—the only champion of the only world we know.

Though he was on his feet at the final bell, Ali took a licking in the ring and on all three official scorecards, his first defeat in 32 bouts going all the way back to the days when he answered to the name of Cassius Marcellus Clay.

Losing, he fought the bravest and best and most desperate battle he has ever been called upon to make. In all his gaudy, gabby years as a professional, he had always left one big question unanswered:

Could he take it? If ever he was hit and hurt, how would he respond?

He not only took it, he kept it. Each fighter got $2.5-million for his night's work, and earned it. At least they did in the estimation of 20,455 witnesses, but those beautiful people have so little respect for money that they paid $1,352,961 at the gate.

This was not only the biggest "live" gate for any indoor fight; the loot was almost twice as great as the previous record, established in the same Madison Square Garden by a double-header featuring the same Joe Frazier (with Buster Mathis). Chances are it will be weeks before the swag from television is counted up, for the match was shown on closed-circuit all over the United States, Canada and Great Britain and on network TV in 32 other countries.

It was the most hysterically ballyhooed promotion of all time, and not only because of the obscene financial figures. If these men had been fighting on a barge for $500 a side it would still have commanded extraordinary attention, for never before had a single ring held two undefeated heavyweights with valid claims to the world championship —Ali unfrocked but still a champion because he had never been whipped for the title, Frazier his rightful successor because he had whipped everybody else—both at the peak of youth and strength.

So great was the interest that a bad fight would have left the Sweet Science sick unto death. A performance that left any shadow of suspicion behind might have destroyed boxing. This one destroyed nothing but Muhammad Ali.

It didn't do a thing for Frazier's health either. It did, though, prove Joe just about as close to indestructible as a fistfighter can be. He walked into hundreds of clean, hard shots, flashing combinations that drilled home with jolting force, and never for an instant did they halt his remorseless advance.

Outpointed as expected in the early rounds, he hurt his adversary in the sixth, batted him soft in the 11th, knocked him into a grotesque backward slide along the ropes in the 12th, and wrecked him in the 15th. Not many men could have survived the attack. But then not many athletes have Ali's armor of arrogance. Even in his deepest trouble, the loser pretended he wasn't losing, shaking his head to deny that a punch had hurt him, beckoning Frazier in to slug him again, trying by every trick of the theatre to support the "secret" he had confided just before the start to a closed-circuit microphone:

"I predict, first of all, that all the Frazier fans and boxing experts will be shocked at how easy I will beat Joe Frazier, who will look like

an amateur boxer compared to Muhammad Ali, and they will admit
that I was the real champion all the time. Frazier falls in six."

Before these men ever saw Madison Square Garden, the English
music critic Ernest Newman wrote of something he called the magic
chemistry of genius:

"What is the artistic faculty? Is it just a knack, which some people
are born with and others are not, for moving the counters of art—
words, sounds, lines, colours—about in a particular way? We do not
expect of a great billiards player or boxer that he shall have read Kant
or Aeschylus, or understand the political problems of the Balkans. We
do not even expect Mr. Joseph Louis to have studied the rudiments
of that science of the impact of forces upon moving masses, upon the
correct application of which his success depends. Indeed, were he and
his like to try to get their results by reason, by 'culture,' they would
find themselves in the company of Mr. Belloc's nimble water-insect:

*If he ever stopped to think*
*how he did it he would sink."*

Joe Frazier has now fought 27 boxing matches as a professional and
won 27. The Olympic heavyweight champion of 1964 has won the
championship of the professional world three times—by knocking out
Buster Mathis when Cassius Muhammad Ali Clay was ostracized as
a draft-dodger, by knocking out Jimmy Ellis, whom the World Boxing
Association called champion, by knocking Muhammad Ali down but
not out.

All his fights were cut to the same pattern, yet he could not tell you
how he does it any more than Beethoven could.

Joe can talk a little about tactics, about "cutting the ring," which
means advancing obliquely on a circling opponent to cut off the escape
routes. As for his own bobbing, ducking attack: "I'll be smokin'," he
says. "Right on." A witness within earshot of his corner Monday night
could have heard his manager, Yank Durham, enlarge on this:

"Down, Joe, down... for the body, Joe, the body... bring the right
over... don't wrestle him, Joe; let the referee do the work."

What Joe says and Yank says merely brushes the surface. These
two don't begin to explain what makes Joe the best fistfighter in the
world at this time. Neither truly understands it. Yet one thing they
do know.

If they fought a dozen times, Joe Frazier would whip Muhammad
Ali a dozen times. And it would get easier as they went along.

# MR. SHRIVER JOINS A WINNER

*Kingston, Jamaica*

SARGENT SHRIVER, Democratic candidate for Vice-President of the United States last November, was chatting with a dozen sportswriters when George Foreman appeared on the far side of the swimming pool. In five seconds, Shriver was alone except for Barney Nagler of the *Daily Racing Form.*

"You've been deserted by the people," Barney said, rising to follow the crowd.

"Not for the first time," Shriver said.

He, too, got up, and he stood behind Foreman when the new heavyweight champion of the world took a seat at a table facing the press. They are friends and Shriver had rejoiced last night when George pounded Joe Frazier to the floor six times in four and a half minutes, detaching Joe from the title. It's good to be with a winner now and then.

"I felt pretty good wakin' up this morning," Foreman said. "I thought it'd feel different, but I'm the same old George."

The same old George didn't look or sound quite the same. As challenger for the title he had walked erect and talked with every appearance of confidence, but now there was a new assurance about him, an attitude of command and even a touch of arrogance. "O.K.," he told the world press, "if you have any questions you can direct 'em to me so we only have to say 'em once." When several voices rose at once, he rapped sharply for order. "You want to fight, you shoulda been on the card last night." Once when his lawyer was talking he interrupted. "I want to answer questions and get out of here.

"Right now I've got no plans for a title defense as yet," the new champion said. "I been training for three months and I haven't saw my family. I'm not lookin' for anybody. I'm the champion and they got to challenge me."

He said that after joining his wife, Adrienne, and Michi, the two-week-old daughter he has never seen—they are in Minneapolis—he would like to "travel around and let the kids on street corners see the new champion."

George said that before Arthur Mercante, the referee, stopped the fight, he (Foreman) had suggested to Frazier's manager, Yancey Durham, that he intervene.

"About just before that last knockdown," he said, "Frazier was looking for help. I couldn't help him, I was too busy, I looked at the corner"—He stretched out a long arm as if pointing at Durham—" 'You better stop it.' He say, 'You reckon?' "

Of his swift and generally unexpected victory he said, "It was quick, but it wasn't easy because I was fightin' one of the greatest fighters there ever was. He beat everybody. I was fortunate to land some of the punches I'd been practicin'. No, I wasn't surprised it was so quick. I told some guys out in California, there's no way Frazier can hurt me. I'd look at myself in the mirror and say, 'There's no way. He'll have to tiptoe through the tulips.' "

The inevitable question—had Muhammad Ali taken something out of the champion back in 1971?—annoyed him. "If Frazier had lost something he wouldn't be heavyweight champion of the world," he said. "What you tryin' to say—that I fought a little girl or something?"

He rejected a suggestion that it had been reckless of him to throw right hands as early as he did. "I am the boss," he said. "I been knocking guys out in two-three rounds. Frazier wasn't no different except he was the champion."

It was pointed out that the fight public, who had been awaiting a Frazier-Ali rematch, would now be speculating about a Foreman-Ali fight. Would George be receptive?

"The public makes these fights," he said. "Let the public demand what it wants. The public will get its demands. I am the champion and all the others are contenders."

"What did your wife say when you talked on the phone last night?" the new champion was asked.

"She said, 'Congratulations.' "

That left one point to be noted: Before the bout, police had an anonymous warning that a bomb would go off in the stadium; the caller should have warned Frazier.

# THOSE ORGAN TONES ARE STILL

I F a person who did not know Yancey Durham heard him talking in the next room, he would assume that the voice belonged to an actor or preacher or con man or politician, if that isn't a distinction without a difference. As a matter of fact, Yank was a little of each. He was a fight manager. He made his entrance on the national scene with the 1964 Olympic heavyweight champion, Joe Frazier, he guided Joe to the championship of the professional world, and when he died last Thursday after a stroke he left the former champion desolate, feeling that he had lost a father for the second time.

Yank was only 52, had added Bob Foster, the light-heavyweight champion, to his stable, and was laying plans to maneuver Frazier into a return bout with George Foreman, who knocked Joe loose from the title.

If Hollywood were looking for an actor to play the fast-talking, side-of-the-mouth, angle-shooting stereotype of a fight manager, Yank Durham would be the last candidate Central Casting would send around. He was a stately man, well-fed but not fat, graying at the temples, conservative in dress and dignified of bearing, who spoke in slow, measured accents. He took speech lessons for years to enrich his supple and sonorous voice and would carry sound equipment to training camp so that when he wasn't occupied with his fighter he could talk onto records that he would send to school for grading. When a sportswriter called him "the black Everett Dirksen" he was delighted.

Yank didn't teach Frazier to fight, he had no voice on the boxing commissions that ostracized Muhammad Ali and lifted his title for refusing to do military service, and he wasn't responsible for the controversial and magnetic qualities in Ali which made a match with Frazier worth a $5-million guarantee. But he made the decisions and charted the course that put Joe in a position to move in as champion when the title was vacant and that ultimately led to a $2.5-million purse.

Some managers cheat their fighters, some take half the fighter's earnings and consider themselves underpaid. Yank did his job for 15 percent and it was he who initiated the arrangement that has made the fighter worth $2-million.

Occasionally Yank made some passing reference to his own days as a boxer but he laid no claims to fame in that area and his unmarked features suggested that his career must have been brief. Apparently he had a few amateur bouts growing up in his native Camden, N.J. He was also casual to the point of vagueness about the injury that left him with a slight limp. He was in the service in World War II, and the story is that a jeep ran over him during an air raid in England, breaking both legs. He drew disability pay as a veteran and had a pension from the Penn Central Railroad, having worked as a welder for the old Pennsylvania Road.

As a fight manager Yank fitted neither of two common patterns—the oldstyle boxing man who grew up in the game or the cloak-and-suit tycoon who comes in for an ego trip or seeking a quick buck.

He enjoyed working with kids in Police Athletic League gymnasiums in Philadelphia. He got to know Frazier when Joe was learning the rudiments of boxing from Duke Dugent, a police sergeant who doubled as instructor in the 22d P.A.L. Gym at 23d Street and Columbia Avenue.

Dugent was Frazier's tutor in the amateurs but when the fighter went to the Tokyo Olympics there was an understanding that Yank would handle him after his return. Joe came back with his gold medal, and Yank set out to get a grubstake.

He consulted the Rev. William H. Gray, pastor of the Bright Hope Baptist Church—the church incidentally, from which Yank will be buried Thursday. The result was Cloverlay, Inc., the managerial firm whose original stockholders paid $250 a share to underwrite Frazier's expenses. Cloverlay paid all expenses and took 25 percent of the income, with Frazier getting 60 percent.

Cloverlay, not Yank, was the manager of record but Yank made all the boxing decisions. His official title was trainer but for big fights he always brought Eddie Futch in from California to supervise training.

Perhaps Yank's wisest decision was to keep Frazier out of the television tournament in which Jimmy Ellis won World Boxing Association recognition as champion during Ali's enforced absence. While that charade dragged on, Frazier won the New York version of the title by flattening Buster Mathis, and later he stopped Ellis, paving the way for the big one with Ali.

During negotiations for that match, a plague of lawyers descended on Philadelphia. There were attorneys for Jack Kent Cooke, who bankrolled the promotion; for Jerry Perenchio, who had closed-circuit television rights; for Madison Square Garden; for Cloverlay and probably for the Marquis of Queensbury.

"All you lawyer guys stay here," Yank told them. "Herbert and I are going to talk." He and Ali's manager, Herbert Muhammad, conferred in private for almost three hours. When they emerged Yank said: "Herbert and I know what we want. Now you guys put it in law language."

That's how the fight was made—not by Cooke or Perenchio or the Garden or Cloverlay. By Yank and Herbert.

# IN SOLITARY, YOU SLEEP ON A BED

IN solitary, Ron Lyle said, you sleep on a bed, get three square meals a day and take a shower twice a week, but never leave your cell otherwise. The Hole is smaller and there is nothing in it but the slab you sleep on. At least, that's how it was in the Colorado State Penitentiary in Cañon City, where Lyle did 90 days in solitary and 20 in The Hole for the fight in which he was knifed.

Technically, he was stabbed to death. Twice during the seven and a half hours while surgeons searched for the artery that had been cut, his heart stopped and he was "clinically dead."

"That's what the doctor told me later," he said yesterday on the telephone from Denver. They gave him 36 pints of blood by transfusion and had him on the critical list for 14 days. When at last it was clear that he wasn't going to die again, they sent him to The Hole.

"What about the other guy?" he was asked. "What happened to the con who stabbed you?"

"He got the same; they were a little fair about it, I guess."

This was back in 1965, when Lyle was doing 15-to-25 for murder in the second degree. In November, 1969, he was paroled after serving seven and a half years. Today at 30, he is a professional fistfighter, ranked fourth among heavyweight contenders by the World Boxing Association and by *The Ring* magazine.

Ron Lyle was the third of 19 children of William and Nellie Lyle. His father, a minister in the Pentecostal Church, was a steelworker in Dayton, Ohio, when Ron was born. Eight years later the family moved to Denver.

Of the 17 children who survived (one son was killed in Vietnam), only Ron had trouble with the law; two of his brothers are ministers.

He was 17 when he shot and killed a man in a street rumble. He had already done nine months in a reformatory for burglary of an ice cream stand. After a mistrial on a charge of first-degree murder, he was in jail for 16 months before his conviction on the lesser charge.

At Cañon City, sports were an outlet for his hostilities. He batted .400 as a catcher on the baseball team, scored an average of 20 points a game in basketball, was quarterback on the football team. A con named Texas Johnson whipped him in his first amateur bout and that was the last time he lost. As the best athlete in the pen, he was a wall-to-wall celebrity, but he rebuffed the prison athletic director, Lieut. Clifford Maddax: "Man, you're a screw, I'm a con."

This changed after Lyle was knifed in a fight with a fellow worker in the prison laundry. When he regained consciousness he saw Maddax at his bedside. "He was white and he had a badge, but he cared. I cried."

Bill Daniels is head of a cable television company, president of the American Basketball Association and owner of the Utah Stars in the A.B.A. In 1969 he sponsored the Denver Rocks, a team in the short-lived International Boxing League. He is also active in rehabilitation work with addicts, criminals and alcoholics. He visited Lyle, helped him get a parole, gave him a job when he got out and invited him to join the Rocks.

"He won most every title an amateur can win," Daniels said. "He won 25 bouts and lost four, never was knocked down or cut. In April of 1971 he turned pro." Daniels bankrolls him; Irwin Rosee of New York is manager of record and adviser; the United States Olympic coach, Bobby Lewis, is the trainer and actual manager.

Manuel Ramos, the big Mexican whom Joe Frazier knocked out in Madison Square Garden, and Leroy Caldwell, a loser from New Orleans, are the only opponents Lyle hasn't knocked out.

"Caldwell moved a lot," he said. "It was in the Playboy Club in Lake, uh—Lake Geneva, Wis., and we were supposed to go eight rounds, but they run out of time or something and stopped it after five. With Ramos, I think Bobby wanted me to go 10. He made me just box."

Although he stopped huge Buster Mathis in two rounds, Lyle didn't meet anybody ranked in the top 10 until he knocked out Larry Middleton at 2:34 of the third. Known for his heavy right hand, he dropped Middleton twice with hooks.

"They're always saying this guy has got no left or that one's got no right," he said. "Just shows if a fighter's got two hands, you better watch both of 'em."

"He is a beautiful person," Daniels says. "Doesn't smoke and never has, doesn't drink and never has, and spends his time heading the March of Dimes, visiting the Boys' Ranch out here and Juvenile Hall, where we keep kids who need help. He is the single most popular athlete in Colorado. And he knows he can't be beaten."

"I asked him about Joe Frazier," Irwin Rosee said. "I told him Frazier hits pretty hard. 'No harder than them screws with clubs,' he told me."

# A BIG MARSHMALLOW

*Houston*

$\mathbb{B}$USTER MATHIS is big as Texas is big, and it has been said that in this state a man can drive farther and look longer and see less than anywhere else in the nation. There may be more peaceable prizefighters than Buster, but none his size; pound for pound, he probably is the mildest gladiator in circulation.

He is a decent, sensitive monster with one attribute that makes him seductively beautiful by fight-mob standards. The late Don Skene described this trait in a novel called *The Red Tiger.* "He was kind of a marshmallow," Don wrote, "but at least he was a big marshmallow."

Buster is back in Houston for the first time since Feb. 6, 1967, when he performed in a preliminary with one Tugboat Thomas, a canvas-back from North Carolina. At first sight of Mathis undraped, Thomas genuflected, Buster struck him in the middle of his haircut, and Tugboat was one with Nineveh and Tyre.

In the main event that evening Cassius Muhammad Ali Clay disposed of the title pretensions of Ernie Terrell, then recognized by the World Boxing Association as heavyweight champion, stabbing, hacking and taunting Terrell over 15 rounds. Now the preliminary boy and the former champion are here to meet Wednesday night in the feature of a show the promoters hope to sell on theater television. With a display of courage as stirring as any likely to be seen in the ring, the promotional firm of Top Rank, Inc., has contracted to pay Ali $300,000 for the engagement.

To Ali and almost everybody else, the tryst in the Astrodome is a mere pause on the way to a second match with Joe Frazier for the world championship. To Mathis it is a new start in a profession he forsook two and a half years ago when, after a dismal defeat by Jerry Quarry, he went home to Grand Rapids, Mich., to brood and eat and

272

play a little semipro football and eat some more until his weight hit 320 pounds and his savings account scraped bottom.

Trained down now to a svelte 260 pounds and theoretically imbued with new confidence—he says rehabilitation set in last March 8 when he watched Frazier whip Ali and decided he had more talent than the pair of them—he keeps reminding himself that he is the only man on earth who ever beat Frazier.

Ali, of course, seldom opens his mouth without whipping Frazier, but Buster beat Joe twice with his fists in trials for the 1964 Olympics. Four years later they met as professionals and fought on fairly even terms for about eight rounds, until Frazier picked a suitable site and began digging. In the 11th round the avalanche came down.

Now Buster roughs up sparring partners named Dave Matthews and Dick Hall, sits through interviews with monolithic patience, and charms everyone with his unfailing, gentle courtesy.

Tracy Forest, the small daughter of the manager of the Travelodge motel where Buster is staying, had a consignment of candy to sell for her Brownie troop. Buster was her first customer at a table her father set up in the lobby. Buster gave her a $5 bill for one box, then gathered up her entire stock and walked into the cocktail lounge. (Parched travelers who haven't visited Texas lately will be cheered to know that booze-by-the-belt has at last reached these plains.)

"I'm Buster Mathis, the fighter," he told patrons in the bar. "Don't you want to buy some candy?"

In five minutes he had sold $24 worth for the happiest Brownie in the Southwest.

"You're a sensitive man," a reporter said, "and you must be aware that everybody regards this fight as just a whistle stop for Ali. Everybody looks on you as a victim, an exalted sparring partner. How does that make you feel?"

"If I lose," Mathis said, "I'm just batting par. But if I win, that's something else. That's a real upset, man, and a whole new life."

During his two and a half years of soul-searching, Buster and his wife Joan and their baby son lived on what was left of his ring earnings.

"It was hard," he said, "but I guess everything is hard. I know I never got nothing easy."

He grinned, showing a gap in the middle of his smile.

"I thought it'd be easy. I'd be a fighter instead of gettin' a job."

The rueful tone said he knew better now. It is a hard business he chose. It could be the wrong one for him.

# IN WITH JOE LOUIS, 16 TIMES

THIRTY-FIVE years after his seconds threw in the towel, Max Schmeling will climb back into the ring with Joe Louis and Arthur Donovan, the referee, Thursday evening. The three principals in two of the most memorable fistfights of this century will lend their mellow presence to an amateur tournament between teams from West Germany and the United States in the Nassau Coliseum. There won't be many in the hall who saw both bouts—the one on June 19, 1936, when Schmeling, the former heavyweight champion of the world, knocked out the unbeaten youngster from Detroit in the 12th round, and the single round on June 22, 1938, when Louis destroyed the German in defense of the title he had won from Jimmy Braddock.

Arthur Donovan saw them, from an arm's length away.

"What I remember about the first bout," Donovan said yesterday, "Louis got a bad break but you couldn't stop it. The bell rang ending the fifth or sixth round and I was moving toward them when the German hit him a terrific punch. It was after the bell but you can't withhold a punch once it goes. The way I saw it, Louis never recovered from that shot.

"The German had trouble with his feet and couldn't retreat. I think he had fallen arches in both feet. He carried his right hand on his chest and his stance was odd. Louis let go a hook that turned into a swing, it had to because on account of that odd stance you had to punch wide to reach the head. Schmeling moved inside the hook with that short right, and that's what started it.

"The second fight Louis started out jabbing. He had the most vicious jab I ever saw on a fighter. If Max Baer was alive you could ask him, 'Max, what did Joe's jab feel like?' He'd say, 'What did it feel like? Like a bomb bursting in your face.' Well, Louis jabbed him and jabbed him and let go a straight right that started the German backwards, but bad as he was hurt he still threw a right that Louis was lucky it landed high on his cheek or it woulda knocked him out right there. After he missed that, Schmeling had no chance.

"They complained later about a kidney punch but they weren't in a clinch. Schmeling was holding onto the ropes, got his arm tangled in the ropes, and that's why the punch hit him in the kidney instead of the head. Max let a groan out of him and geez, it scared me because I never heard anything like that before. One of the German's seconds threw in a towel, it almost hit me in the face and I threw it back in the press row.

"I knew then I couldn't be wrong stopping the fight, they were admitting defeat. But they weren't gonna take the play away from me, saying they stopped it. It was my responsibility and I was the one stopped the fight and they agreed, with the towel. Louis had a man in his corner, Jack Blackburn, who was a great fighter and one of the few great fighters who could explain things to help a fighter. I'm sure he must've told Louis about Schmeling's stance.

"I worked about 16 of Louis's fights and they called me Joe Louis's referee, but I never spoke to the man in my life in public. Remember the night Tami Mauriello hit Louis the first punch and if it hadn't of been for the ropes Louis would of gone down? That Italian boy could hit. They blamed me, said I got in the way, but what was I supposed to do? Go take him by the arm and say, 'Hit him again'? He was so shocked himself he didn't know what to do and just stood off five or six feet. Finally Joe came off the ropes punching, and that was that.

"Tony Galento, too. If he had of won that night it would've ruined boxing because he was no ornament. He knocked Louis down. If he'd of been an inch taller Louis would've got up and flattened him but he was so short Louis couldn't reach him with the final punch. Finally in the fourth Joe nailed him and Galento went down with his feet sticking straight up in the air, funniest thing I ever saw. I tried to pick up one leg but I dropped it quick.

"Before I got into boxing I was at sea four years in the Merchant Marine. I went through training school at Fort Schuyler. We made a summer cruise to England on a gunboat, a barkentine, square-rigged forward, fore-and-aft on the main and mizzen. We were in Plymouth Harbor and some English cadets came aboard. Their skipper said did we have any boxers and our skipper said he guessed we could oblige and they made up a tournament.

"I was 117 pounds when I went in but climbing that rigging I built up to 157 and I was strong. I was boxing this English fella and I threw a jab and he ducked it. I thought, that's a funny thing. I fiddled around a little and threw another jab. He started to duck and I brought up an uppercut and knocked him clean overboard. The water was full of cadets pulling him out.

"In Havana Harbor a big English mate slapped me in an argument. He was about 250 pounds with a black mustache but him being English I couldn't take that. I hit him a hook and flattened him. They told me, 'You can punch like that, better get yourself a professional fight.' There were two brothers promoted fights in the Olympic A.C. on 21st Street and they put me on in a four-rounder so I became a fighter.

"In 1914 my father retired after 38 years as boxing instructor at the New York Athletic Club. He had some great and wonderful students like Teddy Roosevelt. In 1915 I succeeded him and I was instructor there 50 years to the day, to the hour, to the minute, to the second, to the time. I retired at 3 p.m., Sept. 1, 1965.

"I'll be 82 the 10th of this month. I've been trying to get with the Veterans Administration but I guess I don't have any influence. Hard to say how I spend my days now. Doing nothing is treacherous."

# MR. BOXING

IN the dark ages of 1956, a propeller-driven plane bound for Australia and the Olympic Games stopped to refuel in Fiji and passengers stepped down near a cluster of grass-roofed huts. So these were the fabled islands of Captain Cook, land of cannibals and head-hunters. It seemed unreal and unbelievably far from the Eighth Avenue subway.

Fiji's first Olympic team was waiting to get aboard: two boxers, one yachtsman and a huge discus thrower in a sulu, or wraparound skirt with a jagged hemline. All wore blazers of robin's egg blue bearing the Olympic emblem and so did their leader, an Englishman named Harry Charman.

"You should have been here yesterday," Charman said. "You'd have met a friend of yours—Nat Fleischer. He refereed some of our bouts."

On a wildly stormy night a week or so later, there was a fight card in Melbourne topped by lightweights of no special distinction. There was nothing much to recommend the show except that it was the last time professionals would be on display until after the Games, because Olympic boxers were taking over Melbourne Stadium.

The weather kept attendance down to a few hundred, but Nat Fleischer was there. He was introduced from the ring, made a little speech and sat down to boisterous applause. Then the main event started, with no more than half the customers watching. The others were queued up near ringside to get Nat Fleischer's autograph.

In London in another year, an American sportswriter had lunch with Harry Levene, the British fight promoter. They swapped lies over a cold roast, and Mr. Levene won.

Around closing time that evening, the sportswriter was having a nightcap in a Mayfair pub called the Duke of Albemarle, which he had never visited before. He was trying to retell one of Levene's tales to his companion, but the name of the central character eluded him.

"Excuse me a minute," he said, and walked across to the bar. He couldn't have said what a fight fan looked like, but he was pretty sure the ruddy man behind the bar would not disappoint him.

"What was the name of a heavyweight Harry Levene brought over from Canada?" he asked. "He came over on a cattle boat and knocked out national champions all over the continent and gave Primo Carnera the only whipping Primo ever took in London."

"Half a mo'," the innkeeper said, and from under the bar he brought a copy of Nat Fleischer's *Ring Boxing Encyclopedia and Record Book*. He ran his forefinger down Carnera's record. "Mmmmmm, let's see. Here we are, 'London, England—L 10.' Larry Gains, right?"

He handed the book over.

"Look at the flyleaf," he said.

"To my friend Alf Robertson," an inscription read, "with best wishes, Nat Fleischer."

That's how it always was. In Fiji or Melbourne or London, in Tokyo or Thailand or Tierra del Fuego, Nat Fleischer was there or had just departed. It won't be that way again, for Nat left us this week and will not return. He was 84, and one hopes he set off on the last journey with the same zest he had for all the others.

"A man who did more for boxing than any other man in the history of boxing," his friend Dan Daniel said in his eulogy. One had to be around with Nat or following on his heels to realize how true this was, what a genuinely international figure the little man with the bow tie was.

As a boxing historian, Nat began where Pierce Egan and Henry Downes Miles left off. For his three-volume *Pugilistica*, published in 1863, Miles borrowed freely from Egan's *Boxiana* (1818-24). Nat searched further and dug deeper than either, corrected their errors, fleshed out their facts, and in 1941 produced the most complete and accurate compilation of records assembled up to that time.

This was the first edition of the *All-Time Ring Record Book*. In the next 30 years he improved on his own work 30 times, expanding the record book into an encyclopedia that became in fact a bible.

It is a measure of the man's capacity that this monumental task was only a spare-time occupation. He was editor and publisher of *The Ring* magazine. He wrote 53 books on boxing and wrestling in addition to the record books. He was a collector and archivist who assembled the world's largest fistic library and museum of boxing memorabilia. As pugilism's roving ambassador to the world, he circled the globe on more missions than he could count to serve as referee or judge or consultant to boxing authorities.

Those jobs he worked at because he loved them. He didn't have to work at being the most friendly, helpful, patient and considerate little guy in his world. He just was.

# GOOD LUCK, FLOYD

THROUGH the day and into the early evening, guys asked other guys, "What do you think about the fight?" And four times out of five the answer was the same: "I hope Floyd doesn't get hurt."

Then it was 10:30 p.m. There were 17,378 in Madison Square Garden, 17,378 fight fans. Half a century ago, Irvin S. Cobb described the typical fight fan: "He is the soft-fleshed, hard-faced person who keeps his own pelt safe from bruises, but whose eyes glisten and whose hackles lift at the prospect of seeing somebody else whipped to a soufflé." These fans had paid $512,361 to see a strutting peacock named Muhammad Ali beat up a man about 30 pounds lighter, three inches shorter and seven long years older than he. When the fighters came into the ring it was the little old gentleman, Floyd Patterson, who got the warmer welcome, and in the voice of the crowd there was wordless entreaty:

"Good luck, Floyd. Take care of yourself."

There was one there of whom Floyd had asked a question years ago: "Do you consider boxing a sport?"

"Yes," the other had said. "And at its best, an art form."

"Good," Floyd had said, gratified, because to him boxing has been not only a sport but a way of life since boyhood.

This wasn't sport, though, and it wasn't art. For five rounds Ali swaggered and showed off, not because he particularly wanted to humiliate Patterson this time, but because he can no more refrain from showing off than abstain from breathing. Then, starting as the sixth round opened, he punched Floyd's left eye shut and broke the swelling open. When the doctor called it off after the seventh round, the only one in the house who hadn't had enough was Floyd Patterson.

He still hasn't had enough. When he returned to the Garden yesterday with an eyepatch covering a wound that had required seven stitches, he said again that he had no thought of retiring. He spoke wistfully of a rematch with Ali, saying he would be better next time, if there were a next time.

He might think otherwise if he had watched from outside the ropes. Never a big man, he looked shrunken alongside Ali's sleek 218 pounds. To be sure, more than one David has slain his Goliath since that main event in Gath. Jack Dempsey, for instance, weighed 187, Jess Willard 245 at Maumee Bay, but the Dempsey of 1919 was a jungle beast with a kamikaze complex. There was never an ounce of assassin in Floyd.

Schooled in caution, Patterson relied on fast hands and a pretty fair punch at the top of his game. The speed has left him, and much of the power. Fighting back in the sixth and seventh rounds, he was like a small boy teased into fury striking out blindly at his grown-up tormentor. Except that this boy was 37 going on 50.

He has been a professional for 20 years. He has had 64 fights, he won the heavyweight championship of the world twice, he lost it twice, he defended it successfully seven times and he failed three times to regain it. Advice is worth what you pay for it and unsolicited advice is an impertinence. But Dempsey was through at 32.

# FUN
# AND GAMES

When Stanley Woodward was sports editor of the
New York Herald Tribune, a man asked him to help
get a boy into Amherst College, where Stanley had
been a large, unruly tackle on the football team.
The kid was a football player, too, and the man proceeded to describe a creature embodying the best
qualities of Red Grange, Jim Thorpe, and Pudge
Heffelfinger—six-feet-four and 220 pounds, combining the speed of light and the violence of a crime of
passion.

"How's his Greek?" Stanley asked.

"Hell," the man said, "I'm not worried about his
Greek. He is a Greek. I'm worried about his English."

# DRINKING SONG

*Ring out the old! Ring in the new*
*With a hey, nonny-nonny and a view halloo!*
*The year that is gone was freighted with sorrows,*
*Perhaps we can hope for brighter tomorrows.*
*So step right up for a couple of snorts*
*To toast the guys and the dolls in sports;*
*Just name your poison, state your preference—*
*But first, let us hail with affectionate deference*
*Sage Frank Sullivan, upstate Kris Kringle,*
*Copyright-holder on this sort of jingle.*

*Then here's a tankard of foaming ale*
*To Lee and Larry and Bill MacPhail;*
*Ring out, wild bells, from Oakland to Venice*
*In joyous salute to Fury Gene Tenace,*
*Catfish Hunter, Blue Moon Odom,*
*And Manager Williams, the man who showed 'em*
*How to succeed without even trying—*
*Come now, Vida, enough of that crying,*
*Just turn a smile, no matter how thinly*
*In the general direction of Charles O. Finley,*
*The man, or the mule—oops! Heaven spare us!*
*Dagoberto Blanco Campaneris*
*Is taking dead aim with his Louisville Slugger!*
*Gentlemen, please, these huggermugger*
*Doings must cease! Let us whistle a tune,*
*A hymn, to His Majesty Bowie Kuhn,*
*Messiah, magistrate, baseball's saviour*
*From raffish, unmannerly, rude behavior.*

285

*Sing hey, sing ho for one and all,*
*For the boys of summer and the lads of fall—*
*For Lefty Gomez, Yogi Berra*
*And that lady umpire, Bernice Gera;*
*For Alex Webster, Upton Bell,*
*Harry Markson, Ray Arcel,*
*The Rooney family, Art Modell*
*And (blacked out locally) Pete Rozelle,*
*Marvin Miller, Earl Ubell,*
*Duke Stefano, Jean Ratelle*
*And Congressman Vinegar Bend Mizell;*
*Now give a strictly amateur yell*
*For Avery Brundage . . . what the hell.*

*Come on, let's hear it for Howard Cosell!*
*Kleindienst, Richard; Schoendienst, Red;*
*Ed Bennett Williams and Williams, Ted;*
*Boris Spassky, Bobby Fischer,*
*Franco Harris, Furman Bisher;*
*Howard Hughes, Clifford Irving—*
*If the last 12 months were a trifle unnerving*
*Cheer up! It wasn't the bitterest pill,*
*Suppose you were tackling Calvin Hill.*

*Fill the wassail bowl to overflowing*
*For stars on the rise and friends who are going—*
*For Lefty Jon Matlack, Johnny Unitas*
*(No longer permitted to charm or excite us),*
*Sparky Anderson, Frank Lucchesi,*
*Walter Alston, Buzzy Bavasi,*
*Teddy Brenner, Jerry Quarry,*
*And guys named Joe, like Namath and Torre.*
*A measure from Brahms or Shostakovich*
*To warm the cockles of Shirley Povich.*
*As sounds of revelry spiral higher*
*Beat the drum for Rocky Bleier!*
*A necktie by Yepremian (Garo)*
*As a holiday gift for Chris Cannizzaro;*
*Roll out the barrel, loosen the bung*
*And fill up a seidel for Buddy Young,*

*Henry Aaron, Warren Spahn,*
*Whitey Ford and Roger Kahn,*
*Larry Csonka, who breaks their bones,*
*Cleon, Reggie and Jimmy Jones,*
*Rosenthal, Harold; Rosenthal, Abe;*
*Melvin Durslag, Charley McCabe.*

*So lift a tall and tinkling glass*
*To Pittsburgh's Stephen Robert Blass,*
*To Major Houk, if Ralph ever drinks,*
*To Johnny Bench and Scipio Spinks,*
*Mercury Morris, Rod Carew,*
*Evonne Goolagong—here's to you!*
*Here's to all who struggled through*
*The year of nineteen seventy-two!*
*And pray this land of the brave and free*
*Can make it through nineteen seventy-three!*

# HEADY WINE OF VICTORY

THERE are these young guys, Bill Ballon and Don Kessler, friends and partners in various enterprises, who had a bet on the Super Bowl. Kessler had the Miami Dolphins. The stakes were a $1,000 dinner for four, the two guys and their wives. After the Dolphins stomped the Washington Redskins, Ballon would have taken potluck at McDonald's, but Kessler had other ideas. They consulted Craig Claiborne, who used to be the truffles critic for *The New York Times*, and he suggested the Four Seasons. Paul Kovi, director of the restaurant—joints that serve dinners at $250 a cover don't just have managers—said but certainly, he would create a menu suitable to the occasion.

The idea pleased Kovi, who says he used to be the Joe Namath of soccer in Hungary, the best player in Transylvania before Hungary had to give Transylvania back to Rumania. The comparison with Namath occurs to him readily because Broadway Joe's parents come from the same district where Kovi grew up, and when they are in New York Joe brings them to the Four Seasons.

The director also has ties with Pete Gogolak, the sidewheel place-kicker for the Giants. In Hungarian junior soccer they played the same position—center half—on the same team, wore the same number and used the same locker, 20 years apart. Marty Domres, quarterback on the Baltimore Colts, is a frequent luncheon customer and the Knicks' Dave DeBusschere and Bill Bradley have their own beer glasses at the bar with their names on them. In short, Paul Kovi digs sports.

The Kesslers and the Ballons sat down about 8:30 p.m. after the theater crowd had finished the $10.50 table d'hote and departed. The centerpiece was a floral football. Waiters wheeled in caviar on an ice sculpture of a dolphin standing on its tail.

Kovi poured a Moët et Chandon 1964 Dom Perignon—"named," he said, "for the man who invented champagne"—not into stemmed glasses, but into tall, slender cones of thin crystal. The caviar was served with buckwheat blinis and blinis flavored with carrot, both traditional in Russia, the director said.

"This is a great bet," a man said, "because even the loser can enjoy it."

The loser made a face. "Boy, am I stuffed!" he said.

Kovi exhibited a Chateau Lafite-Rothschild, 1952—the best year, he said. "I opened it about 40 minutes ago," he said. "Now we will decant it and let it breathe." Gently, the red wine was poured into a decanter with a candle lighting the neck so the first specks of sediment could be seen and left in the bottle.

"Miami should have won by at least 21 points," Kessler said.

"I like Kansas City," Ballon said. "The Chiefs have all the ingredients of greatness. I don't know what happened to them."

Waiters were serving a clear, mahogany soup with a rose petal floating in it. "Essence of roses," Kovi said. "I have created it for a woman I used to be in love with." With it came Bual Madeira, 1860. "There are only 600 bottles in existence and this is one. Now there are 599."

"Before the season opened," Kessler said, "I wanted to parlay Miami through the 14 regular games, the two playoffs and the Super Bowl. I wanted to bet $1,000 and send it all back through 17 games, that's how confident I was. I know when you bet the points with a bookie you have to lay 6-to-5 but I thought on a 17-game parlay I might get even money on a straight win bet, no points. At even money I would have won $62-million. I wanted to give each of the 40 Dolphins a million. That would leave me $22-million."

Don Kessler has original ideas but his arithmetic totters. A bet of $1,000 doubled 17 times comes to $131,720,000. "I spoke to a couple of people but couldn't get a bet," Kessler said. "I'd make the same bet for 1973. The Dolphins are building a dynasty."

The fish course was mahi-mahi, the Hawaiian version of dolphin, baked in a delicate crust with a sauce compounded from ambrosia. With it came a noble Montrachet, Domaine du Baron Thenard, 1969. "I love dolphin," Ballon said, polishing his plate.

There was a pause for meditation and prayer cooled by a dab of cold duck sherbet. Then came the Lafite-Rothschild accompanied by filet

mignon topped with fresh Hungarian goose liver, with stuffed arti-
choke hearts and broiled tomatoes.

"There was some thought of having you eat crow," Kovi told Ballon,
"but instead I have created this: tiny quail stuffed with truffles and a
sweet and encased in a young pheasant." With the birds were white
grapes in a crispy covering of crumbs. A Saint Emilion washed it
down, Chateau Cheval Blanc, 1934.

From there it was a breeze—crêpe Suzette with a Chateau d'Yquem
1959, an ice cream sherbet football on a field of green cotton candy
as ragged as the artificial turf in Miami, with a second champagne,
Taittinger Blanc de Blanc, 1964. Tiny football-shaped chocolate cakes
went unchallenged so they were packed to be taken home for the
children.

With espresso came brandy or Grand Marnier, and euphoria. It was
1 a.m. And Garo Yepremian was forgiven.

# I REMEMBER PAPA

ERNEST HEMINGWAY was sitting with the proprietor at one of the front tables in Toots Shor's when Lawrence Peter Berra finished his lunch at another table and started for the door.

"Hey, Yoge," the proprietor bawled, beckoning, and when Yogi answered the summons Toots made introductions. Yogi stood chatting for a few minutes and took his leave. At the bar he said hello to Tom Meany, the sportswriter.

"Well," Tom said, "I see you've now met Papa Hemingway. What did you think of him?"

"Quite a fella," Yogi said. "What does he do?"

"He's a writer," Tom said.

"Yeah?" Yogi said. "Which paper?"

It was an anniversary that recalled the incident, for it was just 10 years ago that Ernest Miller Hemingway blew his brains out in Ketchum, Idaho.

News of that tragedy had just reached the East when Rod Serling, the dramatist, drove into a small town in upstate New York where he had been a frequent visitor. As he parked in front of the general store, the storekeeper emerged and recognized him.

"Hey," the man said, "that fellow out West, that writer fellow, terrible, wasn't it? That Hemingway?"

"It's dreadful," Serling said. "What a loss!"

"It's that, all right," the storekeeper said, "but tell me something, just between us. Makes things a little easier for you, don't it?"

What curious twists and turns we all must take on this journey, what a strange freight of friendships and prejudices, affections and crotchets we pick up en route. If Ernest Hemingway were alive today he would be approaching his 72nd birthday, and if he happened to be in New York he would almost certainly want to celebrate it at Shor's.

Only there doesn't happen to be a Shor's right now. At least, though, we still have Toots. Still very much with us is the outrageous and wonderful and, praise be, inimitable personality that made the brick house on 51st Street the most famous saloon in America and possibly in the world.

So now it is ten years later. It has been a decade of growth for Hemingway, but nothing compared to the growth he will have in decades to come when the myths and misconceptions fade and he is measured only by the power and purity of his crisply economical prose, by the enormous influence he had on the writing of English.

Today the myth and misconceptions still get in the way. We still read about his swagger and bombast, his pettiness and feuds, his hairy-chested posing, his glorification of violence. Maybe I didn't know him well enough, but the man I knew showed none of these traits.

He was warm and companionable, quick of wit and laughter, with a strange but genuine shyness. "Here we can talk," he said in his home outside of Havana. "When we meet in New York it's always somewhere like Toot's or 21, and those crowds make me nervous. I get so nervous I find myself being polite to Arthur Brown!"

The talk could be wonderful, like the analogy he drew between a headlong fighter of the day and a writer we both knew: "It's like when so and so sets out to write a piece to end writing; he's going to leave writing dead on the floor."

A few years before he died, we were all together as guests of Toney Vaughn, then manager of the Hotel Nacional in Havana. It was the time Juan Fangio, the champion driver, was kidnapped by Fidel Castro's men when he arrived for an auto race on the Malecon, the avenue along the seawall. The race started without Fangio and we were ostensibly watching from the terrace of Toney's apartment over the course, though actually we were talking about bullfighting.

No aficionado like Hemingway, I had nevertheless been captivated some years earlier by Armallita, who was good enough to be chosen with Manolete himself to open the new bullring in Mexico City. Hemingway remembered him well: "Skinny guy, high-waisted like Alvin Dark with the crotch clear up here."

Just then a car plunged through the crowd. The race ended in gory disorder. In Hemingway's face, anger struggled with concern as he viewed the scene.

"A cruddy sport," he said. "In bullfighting, the matador can take as much risk as he chooses, but these creeps always take somebody else with them."

# CZARS AGAINST SIN

IT was billed as a symposium on gambling jointly sponsored by the National District Attorneys Association and the celestial hierarchy of professional baseball, football, basketball and hockey, which translates simply as Czars Against Sin. Lined up in a forbidding phalanx of rectitude were: William Cahn, the Nassau County D.A. who is past president of the NDAA and chairman of its gambling committee; Bob Carlson, commissioner of the American Basketball Association; Pete Rozelle, pontiff of the National Football League; Carol S. Vance, current president of the NDAA from Houston; Bowie Kuhn, the Dalai Lama of baseball; J. Walter Kennedy, archdeacon of the National Basketball Association; and Don Ruck, vicar of Clarence Campbell, the high priest of hockey.

They sat shoulder to shoulder at a long table and the shoulders were faultlessly tailored. There was a slightly abandoned splash of scarlet in Walter Kennedy's necktie, but rags are royal raiment when worn for virtue's sake, and nowhere this side of the College of Cardinals could you encounter more solid righteousness yesterday than in the gathering in the Plaza.

"I want to thank each and every one of you for being present at what I consider a very unique and historic meeting," said Carol Vance, the lawman from Texas. He went on to say that the NDAA convention in Puerto Rico had adopted a resolution opposing the "extension and legalization" of gambling on sports events. Since then steps have been taken to mobilize the forces of good, as represented in the united front now marshaled in Manhattan, the stronghold of Howard J. Samuels and his Off-Track Betting Corp.

Literature handed out at the door included a page captioned "From the Commissioners." Following were statements by Kuhn, Rozelle,

Kennedy, Carlson and Campbell, in that order, agreeing that legal gambling would multiply the occasions of sin, stimulating attempts to fix games, subjecting athletes to greater temptation, creating a climate of suspicion and weakening the public faith in the integrity of sports.

"The something-for-nothing syndrome is not what the American dream is all about," Vance said, sounding the keynote of sanctimony.

Rozelle said the sports hierarchy had been called naive, because "everybody gambles and we put our heads in the sand." Was it naive, he asked, to employ special security forces and spend "over $200,000 just to try to eliminate some of the suspicion about the sport created by losing bettors"?

He said he didn't want to see Joe Namath sitting on a three-point lead with "the vast majority" of spectators in Shea Stadium booing because the point spread favored the Jets by six points.

He said he was pleased to find that there was one area (this one) where owners, commissioners and the players' associations could be in agreement. "If we are naive," he said, "there are 5,000 district attorneys naive with us." He mentioned that "naive" was a favorite word of Howard J. Samuels.

A summit of eloquence was scaled by William Cahn. "The effect of legalized gambling upon the mores of a society," said the Nassau prosecutor, "is beyond the competence of rhetoric to describe." After that the show tended to drag, in spite of efforts by the audience to prod the panel with questions.

Walter Kennedy stood by his statement in the handout that "so far as we can determine there are not more than a few people attending basketball games who patronize bookmakers to bet on the outcome of the games." Sometimes when the score fluctuates around the level of the point spread, basketball crowds in Madison Square Garden grow highly vocal, but it may be that Walter doesn't hear them. He has a lot to distract him—$25,000 fines against the Atlanta Hawks, $2-million antitrust suits filed by the Hawks, etc.

Bowie Kuhn said increased gambling would increase the "quantum of suspicion," meaning the amount of suspicion.

Commissioners and lawmen said legalization of gambling would invite betting and losing by people who couldn't afford to lose. There is, of course, only one group that can afford it. Alfred Vanderbilt pointed this out one day at the old Jamaica track, where horseplayers were standing four deep peering into the shadow paddock.

"I look at them," Alfred said, "and I ask myself, 'How can they do it? Where do they get the money to come out here every day and bet?' I think maybe I've found the answer. It's the money they save on neckties and razor blades."

# GENTLE GIANT

*Bethlehem, Pa.*

**T**HE last honest wrestling match seen through these bifocals pitted Jock Sutherland, then coach of the Pittsburgh Steelers against Stanley Woodward, then sports editor of the *New York Herald Tribune,* in the Pittsburgh home of Frank Souchak, a star end on Sutherland's 1937 University of Pittsburgh team. "Stonley," Jock said, "I don't suppose you would care to wrostle." Stanley was fresh from a bout with pneumonia, but he never could resist a challenge. He removed his glasses, which left him sightless, and they stripped to the waist. They assumed the position—right hands clasped, left behind the other's neck. Stanley lunged for a headlock and missed. Jock was on top when a quarter-ton of gristle hit the tiles with a horrid "splat!" Everybody had one more drink.

Now, 25 years later, here were 20 honest wrestlers in assorted shapes and sizes from 118 pounds to 455, all in one small auditorium called Grace Hall on the Lehigh University campus. The crowd of 3,000 would have been larger in a bigger hall, partly because Lehigh has been a stronghold of college wrestling for 60 years but mostly because the program—the National Collegiate Athletic Association's annual East-West All-Star meet—was topped by Joel Kislin, a shy, earnest, 300-pound sociology student at Hofstra, and the scenic Chris Taylor of Iowa State. Taylor rivals Disneyland as a tourist attraction, and the Iowa State team breaks attendance records wherever it goes.

Taylor is a king-size kewpie with red hair, blue eyes and a smile that is just plain sweet. He seldom knows exactly what he weighs because most platform scales don't register above 250 or 300. Now and then he chins himself on the meathook of a big scale Iowa State uses for weighing sides of beef. The last reading they got that way was 455.

As a 380-pound high school student in Dowagiac, Mich., Chris played defensive tackle and offensive center on the football team. He swims, plays pool, roller skates forward and backward, bowls, and can lift prodigious weights. His quickness surprises everybody. He is an athlete, almost surely the best athlete of his size—or the biggest good athlete—in recorded history. (Goliath stood 9-foot-6, about three feet taller than Chris, but his won-lost record was 0-1.)

As America's super-heavyweight in Munich, Taylor was the victim of one of the countless controversies that fouled up the 1972 Olympic Games. In the first-round of free-style competition he hooked the Soviet Union's Aleksandr Medved, 6-7, 280 pounds, eight times world champion and now owner of three Olympic gold medals. The referee imposed two penalty points on Chris for stalling, giving Medved the match, 3 points to 2. The referee got fired but the result stood and Chris finished third.

"I didn't take a step back," he said yesterday. "I heard the referee said he had to help my opponent because I weighed 400 pounds. He was back to referee my Greco-Roman match with Wilfried Dietrich. When the German threw me, his shoulders touched the mat first and that should have been a fall. Then I was pinned and the referee called it. I don't think he liked me."

In collegiate competition, Chris won 39 matches last year, pinning 26 opponents. He lost none and had one draw. So far this season he is 35-0, with 33 falls. He worries, though. In high school he was Michigan state champion as a junior but not as a senior. At Muskegon Junior College he was state champion his first year but not his second. Now he is the defending national champion but the season isn't over.

"I could get too cocky and lose," he said. "Everything's been going so well that sometimes I get too full of myself."

That Olympic referee is in the minority if it is true that he doesn't like this gentle giant. Everybody else does, including Lynne Hart of Muskegon and Iowa State, who plans to marry him in September.

Bethlehem crawls with wrestling fans, none more devoted than Chuck Bednarik, the rugged alumnus of the Philadelphia Eagles, center on the National Football League's all-time team and a deity enshrined in both the college and pro Halls of Fame. "Only Jim Thorpe, Don Hutson and I made all three," said Bednarik

"I still make a lot of dinners and sports affairs," he said. "I was telling one audience: 'When I finished Penn I got a $5,000 bonus and a $10,000 contract, making me the highest paid Eagle next to Steve

Van Buren. A few years ago Atlanta signed Tommy Nobis out of Texas for $300,000 and he's a linebacker like me. What's the difference?' Somebody in the audience called, 'Two hundred eighty-five thousand dollars.' "

During the matches, Chuck kept up a running comment in a low tone tense with excitement: "Oh-oh, that kid's going to get pinned . . . no, he escaped. One point for him. . . . Ooh, beautiful! He reversed the other guy, broke the hold and took control. That's two points . . . Took him to the mat, that's two points . . . strong, strong . . ."

They started with the swift little guys and worked up through the weight divisions. Two matches from the end, the West team took the lead, 15 points to 14, but then the East's Russ Johnson of Ohio University started with a rush for a 9-1 lead over favored Greg Strobel of Oregon State. All of a sudden Strobel stopped wrestling and began stroking the mat. In a moment six or eight guys were creeping about, searching for a contact lens. They found it, Strobel came on implacably, and won his match, 13-11.

Now Taylor and Kislin locked horns like rutting moose. The West was in front, 18-14, a safe margin unless Kislin could pin his man in the upset of the year. They tugged and heaved through two scoreless minutes. Then slowly, resisting the irresistible with all his 300 pounds, Kislin was forced to the mat, where he lay face down in pain, his right knee useless.

Taylor stood over him, his great face puckered with concern. After a few moments they got the loser up on one leg with an arm across the winner's shoulders. Ever so gently, Chris helped him hobble off.

# THE MOTHER LODGE

T HE tall man at the bar was Dick Stuart, the batter they used to call "Stonefingers" or "Dr. Strangeglove" when he tried to play first base. The quiet man at a table for two was Mike Cowles of the publishing family and the pretty lady a few tables away was Fran Alison of "Kukla, Fran and Ollie." Frank Gifford, who for 12 years took everything people like Chuck Bednarik could dish out in the National Football League, limped in on the ankle he broke trying to slide downhill. Bowie Kuhn was there with his shadow, Joe Reichler, and the Yankees' Bob Fishel was accompanied by Marsh Samuels of Cleveland. Some of the Yankees' new owners probably were scattered around, since they seem to be scattered everywhere. It was lunch hour in Toots Shor's and somewhat less cluttered than usual, much like the day when a thoughtful poet returned to his office and wrote:

> "The joint is quieter
> Without the proprietor."

This time the proprietor was present but not shouting, sitting off in a corner chatting with friends. The sports scene in New York is a changing scene because it is alive. Baseball teams called Giants and Dodgers fade in a fog of legend and a team called the Mets springs up garnished with green legends of its own. Stillman's Gym gives way to high-rise apartments, and housing developments replace Ebbets Field, the Polo Grounds and dear old Footsore Downs, Jamaica racetrack.

Once Friday night was magic because it was fight night in the Garden; now it is the night after Thursday. Never again, probably, will the autumn air be electric with excitement because Notre Dame is playing Army in the Stadium.

In the midst of change, one landmark stands triumphant. Like old

Madison Square Garden, Toots's joint has crept uptown—from 51st Street to 52d to 54th—but it remains what it has been for more than 30 years, the mother lodge. This is where it's at, the tribal headquarters, the water hole where the herd assembles under the benign supervision of a lout.

In April, 1945, Bob Hannegan, Postmaster General and national chairman of the Democratic party, was on his way to Hyde Park, N.Y., for the funeral of Franklin D. Roosevelt. "I'll stop in on the way back," he told Toots over the telephone, but he didn't stop in. About 10 that night, the phone rang in the brick house on 51st Street.

"I'm in Washington, Toots," Hannegan said. "The train didn't stop in New York. But here, say hello to the President."

"Hello, Toots?" said Harry Truman, the best bourbon drinker of the seven Presidents for whom Toots has poured booze.

He has poured booze for seven and probably offered advice to seven, as he has offered advice to players and club owners and managers and commissioners and coaches over the years.

Someday someone must get on the record the Toots Shor definition of "class." It will have to be distilled from stories like the one about Jack Kearns coming to town when Toots was running The Tavern on West 48th Street. Doc Kearns had managed Jack Dempsey and Mickey Walker and had committed many other depredations, but on this particular visit he wasn't "holding." Meaning he was broke. Nevertheless, a party started and ran for a couple of days.

"Finally he called me over," Toots relates. " 'Tootsie,' he says, 'lend me a hundred.' I went to the cash register and got him a C-note. He handed it to the head waiter, signed the check and blew. Now, there was a guy with class!"

Before people traveled by plane, Toots took a train to California and got off in Pasadena where Mark Hellinger, Bob Hope and Gene Fowler met him. The limousine taking them to Los Angeles passed a crummy little restaurant with a big sign reading: "The Original Toots Shor."

"Stop the car!" said the original Toots Shor.

Striding in, they were brought up short behind a hulk who looked, from the rear, exactly like Toots himself. Toots clamped a paw on the big man's shoulder and spun him. The guy was an actor recruited from Central Casting by Hellinger, who had framed the entire scene. There was another guy had class, Mark Hellinger; knocked off a quart of brandy a day.

But now, talking with friends at lunch, Toots was getting exercised about a guy who had been bugging him. "He's a bachelor," Toots was saying. "Trouble with bachelors, they got nobody to think about except themselves. A bachelor is the most miserable creep—"

"Does that go for Jesus Christ?" Bob Considine asked.

Toots was shocked. "Was he a bachelor?" he said.

# SPORTSPEAK

ONE measure of the stature of sports in the American scene is the extent to which sporting terms are employed away from the playing fields. Politicians talk earnestly about carrying the ball and playing the game because they think this brings them down to the intellectual level of the voters and at the same time invests them with a healthy, outdoor quality of cleanliness and vigor.

It seems here that in recent days borrowing the language of the playground has become more popular than ever, possibly because the tenant now occupying the White House sets the example with his telephone calls to Roller Derby winners. At any rate, newspapers lately have fairly crawled with examples of "sportspeak," to use the word coined by Bob Lipsyte, whose talent used to illumine *The New York Times*. Trouble is, four times out of five the men who use sportspeak are not much better informed than the distinguished historian who compared a victorious general to "the pinch-hitter who steps up to the plate and hits the ball over the fence for three bases." For example:

"Mr. Cahn's got a very bad track record—long on publicity, short on performance," says Jesse Moss, attorney for the Standardbred Owners Association of New York, referring to the district attorney of Nassau County who was calling in harness race drivers to ask whether they had been fixing races. (They said no.)

It should not be necessary to point out that Mr. Cahn holds no track records. A track record is what it sounds like—the best time ever made on a particular racecourse at a particular distance. Mr. Moss was referring to Mr. Cahn's past performance sheet.

Mr. William Safire, the most recent addition to the cast performing on the Op-Ed page of *The Times,* appears to be addicted to sportspeak. This may be because of the company he has been keeping, for he is a refugee from the White House staff. In his first column he asked permission to "trot around the bases to get the feel of this place," forgetting that before you may trot around the bases you have to hit one out of the park.

In his second piece he laid down the dictum that "not every hardball is a beanball." In sports terminology there is no such thing as "*a* hardball." When the word is used, which is seldom, "hardball" means the game of baseball as distinct from softball. It does not mean a high, fast pitch. Probably Mr. Safire should be excused, for this was a column applauding Richard Nixon's forthright behavior in the Watergate case. It had an understandably agitated tone.

"That was not my ball park," said John N. Mitchell in reply to a reporter's question about secret funds employed in the campaign to re-elect Mr. Nixon. "That was their ball park," he said, passing the buck to other campaign leaders.

Like Jesse Moss, Mario Biaggi turned to the race track rather than the ball park to express his indignation over charges that he had taken the Fifth Amendment before a grand jury. The charges were published, said the Congressman who would prefer to be Mayor of New York, "just as this Democratic primary was heading into the homestretch."

President Nixon and George Meany, president of the A.F.L.-C.I.O., had an exchange regarding Peter J. Brennan, the Secretary of Labor, that made them sound like Billy Martin arguing with Earl Weaver. They were talking about the Administration's minimum wage legislation, and the President said Mr. Brennan had fought a losing battle on labor's side.

"Peter Brennan is a team player and he knows you can't win them all," Mr. Nixon said.

"If Pete is a team player," Mr. Meany responded, "he will have to admit he can't be on two competing teams."

Mr. Nixon said the Labor Secretary had lost an argument on minimum wages, but won one with Secretary of Agriculture Earl L. Butz on a ceiling for meat prices.

"In this Cabinet," the President said, "you win some and you lose some." Earl Weaver would have completed the cliché: "And some days you get rained out."

As to Phase 3 of the economic program, Mr. Meany said labor was "still in there pitching."

It appears that somebody in John W. Dean's circle, not now identified, is conversant with the prize ring. In a story about Watergate, *The Washington Post* quoted an associate of the Presidential counsel: "[H. R.] Halderman and [John] Ehrlichman have been trying to get John Dean to take a dive."

Finally we have William J. Ruckelshaus, whom the President called out of the bull pen to relieve L. Patrick Gray 3d as acting director of the Federal Bureau of Investigation. As Ruckelshaus entered the game, his office released a biographical sketch that credited him with a "disputed title" as the "best smallmouth bass fisherman in America."

Considering the present state of affairs in Washington, one is reluctant to challenge Mr. Ruckelshaus's credibility, but the truth is he does not hold that title, disputed or otherwise. I do.

# SOUND OF MUSIC

*Monticello, N.Y.*

W HEN the crowd at Kutsher's left the dining room for the annual Maurice Stokes benefit basketball game, Joe Frazier remained behind to rehearse with the Knockouts and Odessa and Pearl Chapman, the Frazierettes.

The heavyweight champion of the world is part gladiator, part troubadour. He has made recordings and he has worked with the Knockouts in a few small clubs in Washington, Atlantic City, and East Orange, mostly topless joints. This would be their debut in a big club. It was like going into Madison Square Garden after boxing windups in Ridgewood Grove and the Eastern Parkway Arena.

Half an hour after leaving the table, Frazier telephoned down for a bottle of scotch—"not for me, for the boys in the band."

A little later he called to say that Bob, the bass guitar, had a fever and needed a doctor. Joe had said at dinner that he got more nervous before a performance than before a fight.

"In a fight," he said, " I only got myself to worry about."

The performance was scheduled for 11:30 p.m. in the hall the Kutshers call the Palestra, but it was midnight before the basketball crowd started showing up, and 12:40 when a hairy master of ceremonies named Harvey Norman introduced the Knockouts. The combo, in sky-blue dinner jackets, included an organ, the bass guitar, a lead guitar, a saxophone, and traps. They sounded like kitchenware falling downstairs.

The Frazierettes appeared in yellow gowns with midiskirts slit to the knee. Their lips shaped the lyrics. "For Once in My Life I've Found Someone Who Needs Me," but the words couldn't be heard over the combo. Then the star entered to friendly applause.

His dinner jacket was a dark blue. He wore patent leather pumps of burgundy red and a cerise shirt with ruffled bosom and cuffs. A thin mustache and a fringe of whiskers from ear to ear framed a gleaming smile.

He and the girls sang with the band. Mrs. Frazier, at a ringside table, said the number was "Knock On Wood."

Then Joe sang a song he has recorded, "Truly Lovin' You." He put a lot into it, going almost to the floor in a crouch and then bringing it up hard, the microphone clutched in his left fist, his right hand gripping the slack of the microphone cord.

"Now everybody's searrrching for the real thing. . . ."

"He sings the way he fights," a man said. "All out."

"Works hard at anything he does," said Yank Durham, his manager.

"You got to love," Joe sang, and when he finished he was sweating. He walked to the edge of the stage and his wife, who was drinking ginger ale, handed up her glass. Joe tasted.

"I don't guess she'd fool me," he told the audience. "If she would now, she been foolin' me all these years."

He walked around smiling. "Y' know, I enjoy this," he said. "Anytime you folks get tired and wanta go to bed let me know, 'cause I can do this all night. I just wanta make people happy. I don't care what color you look like, I just like people."

There was applause. Joe's smile was warm and winning.

Alternately crouching and straightening up to jiggle on shifting red shoes, he sang "Come and Get Me, Love."

"Something is wrong with my bayby . . . something is wrong with me . . . we been throughooh so much together. . . ."

It was 1:35 when he bowed off. The Knockouts unplugged their instruments.

"Well," a music critic said, "it keeps him occupied between fights."

"Better than booze and broads," another said.

"Well," the first said, "yes. For him."

# AMERICAN LETTERS

$\mathbb{T}$HE greatest book I ever read up to the age of ten was *Jack Harkaway, Afloat and Ashore,* and the second best was *Pitching in the Pinch* by Christy Mathewson. Mr. Mathewson was an intellectual type. He had attended college and he played an acceptable game of chess, so it is conceivable that he wrote his own stuff, though not likely.

If he had a ghostwriter, the spectre got no credit line in the book. In those artless days, readers were expected to believe that the man whose name appeared on the title page had indeed spelled out every word, emerging from the heat of athletic combat only to plunge into the throes of literary composition.

Indeed, it wasn't only the readers who believed this. The late Bozeman Bulger ghosted the autobiography of Battling Nelson, who won the lightweight championship of the world from Joe Gans in 17 rounds and lost it to Ad Wolgast in 40. Bulger was pleased to receive one of the first copies off the press. On the flyleaf was an inscription: "To my good friend, Boze Bulger," signed, "The Author."

"Writing," Mr. Bacon assures us, "maketh an exact man." But sometimes a guy wonders.

The locker rooms of sport have always been a source of literature, but what used to be a trickle has become a Niagara. There has been in recent times such a spate of belles-lettres tinctured with liniment and sweat that one is forced to conclude that the creative urge among athletes is as strong as the procreative instinct.

Moreover, in the opinion of some critics like Bowie Kuhn, it can cause at least as much trouble. Yet in spite of an unfavorable review from Bowie, or perhaps because of it, Jim Bouton's magnum opus, *Ball Four,* is on the best-seller list. It hasn't achieved the popularity of *Everything You Always Wanted To Know About Sex* or *The Sensuous*

*Woman,* but it outsells *Body Language, Human Sexual Inadequacy,* and the Bible.

Like most other works of sinewy authors, *Ball Four* was ghosted. This is an age of specialization, when precious few can master both the knuckleball and the simple declarative sentence. In fact, only one comes to mind whose work on the typewriter matched his performance on the field.

This was Jim Brosnan, who pitched well enough to earn a living in the major leagues for nine years, and wrote better than he pitched. His first book, *The Long Season,* is an original and as such a bona fide classic in its field. First of the unbuttoned diaries, it set a style that has been slavishly copied by the muscular masters who followed. Brosnan was "telling it like it is" years before Bouton started taking bows for inventing candor.

Other ballplayers disapproved when Brosnan celebrated the martini in print. (Other martini lovers were aghast that he was a shaker, not a stirrer.) Managers and coaches smarted because Brosnan raised doubts that they were divinely inspired.

Brosnan is provocative, blunt, and highly entertaining. He is equipped with two qualities most of his imitators lack—instinctive taste and ability to spell.

He writes well enough so he doesn't have to rely on obscenity and scatology as a substitute for an ear for dialogue. When he writes about drinking, it is his drinking. He doesn't say, "There is a good deal of dog in Yastrzemski." Instead he tells of Fred Hutchinson coming out in disgust and anger to change pitchers and saying, "That was the most miserable performance I ever saw"—to Jim Brosnan.

Nobody can lay down rules to define good taste, but Dave Hill, the golfer, came pretty close. An outspoken guy himself who has ruffled the stuffed shirts of golf more than once, Hill was talking about the Peeping Tom approach to locker room literature.

"If I see a guy chasing a girl around the swimming pool," he said, "I'm going to root for him, I'm not going to write a book about him."

# CHRISSIE

C HRIS EVERT, who regards grass with less enthusiasm than some other 18-year-olds, is practicing on the clipped lawns of the Longwood Cricket Club here for the United States Open tennis championships in Forest Hills. Revisiting Forest Hills is a little like recapturing love's young dream, for it was on the turf of the West Side Tennis Club that her romance with the galleries burst into flower. Playing in her first National Open two years ago as a pigtailed pixie of 16 with her neat features set in an expression of sweetly childish intensity, Chrissie captivated the fans completely as she won, and won, and won again before Billie Jean King defeated her in the semifinals.

What emotions are uppermost now as she returns to the scene of that popular triumph as an internationalist and professional with a chance to lift her prize money for the year over $100,000? Eagerness? Apprehension? Confidence? Anxiety? "Eagerness, I think," she said. "I'm grateful that I had a good Wimbledon. It convinced me I could play well on grass, after all."

Lissome and trig and fastidiously turned out in a green and white cardigan with matching green pants, she sat sipping a ginger ale. One gets the impression that Ms. Christine Marie Evert would sooner commit a double foot-fault at match point than neglect eye shadow or nail polish. The eyes are brown and direct; the long hair framing the oval face is the color of Vermont maple syrup in the sun. "Thoughtful" and "undissembling" are the adjectives that occur first to describe her manner. Ask a question, she takes as long as she needs to turn it over and around. Then: "Yeh," she'll say in unaccented American, and elaborate as the topic merits.

She was asked about the European tour leading up to Wimbledon, when she blew a lead of 7-6, 5-3 in the final round of the French Open and lost to Margaret Court, lost to Evonne Goolagong in the finals of the Italian Open, got creamed by Virginia Wade, 6-1, 6-2, on the grass at Nottingham, England, and finally was beaten by Julie Heldman in the London grass court championships.

"It was pretty bad," she said. "France was the worst because I thought I'd been doing well."

"Yet there was no outward sign that you were discouraged."

"I guess I kept it pretty much inside."

"Considering that you had beaten all the girls who beat you, doesn't it seem now that your trouble must have been mental?"

"Each match has to be considered separately," she said, and left it there. In other words, you couldn't lump all the defeats under a single easy explanation, and who wanted a detailed stroke analysis now?

"Winning from Margaret was a big help," she said. "That was a good match." She meant her smashing upset of the top-seeded Margaret Court at Wimbledon. In the final, however, she caught Mrs. King at her supreme best and was knocked out, 6-0, 7-5.

"I wasn't ready for that match," she said. "Billie Jean and I waited six hours the day before, and it was rained out. I dreamt about the match that night. I dreamt of winning Wimbledon. Then when the match started I was flat, I couldn't get interested. And Billie Jean was great."

"Did you panic after the first set?"

"I made up my mind it wouldn't be love-love."

Chris has been swinging a racquet for 13 of her 18 years, but tennis is still fun for her. "I love the game, I really do, although I wouldn't say an hour and a half of concentrating in a hard match is all fun. At first I'm nervous. Then if I win a few games I feel more confident. Everybody asks how long I want to keep playing and I tell them two or three years more, but you can't put a limit on it. I'm enjoying it now, traveling and going out nights and having fun. Forest Hills now—I love New York.

"I keep thinking stars like Billie Jean and Margaret can't go on forever and then maybe—but I don't know. Rosie Casals and others are young and there are so many new ones coming up. I may not be cut out to be Number One.

"The most important thing right now?" There was a long pause. "My family is important. I'm away a lot, but I still want to be close to my family."

Turning pro hasn't made much difference. "I was keyed up for my first pro tournament, I liked the idea of playing for money. I won that for $10,000, and it was fun. But the money isn't all that important. I never see it, it just goes to the bank."

So far about $76,000 has gone to the bank this year, income from endorsements probably will match that figure, and first prize at Forest Hills is $25,000, thanks to the "Ban equalizer." This is a $55,000 grant the manufacturers of Ban deodorants have made so women players will not only smell nice, but also stand as straight as men in the Chase Manhattan. Chris is pleased that for the first time, women will compete for the same money as men.

"I don't think I would have fought for it as hard as Billie Jean did," she said, "but it's right. We can't play the men's game, but we put out just as much in competition and we draw as many people."

"How do you feel about Bobby Riggs versus the girls?"

"I think it's good for tennis, but I don't like him putting down women's tennis."

"He's only out to make a buck, Chris. He isn't serious about that chauvinist pig act. He's just found a new gimmick—"

But Chrissie was wrinkling her nose.

# BOAT RACE

IN many American newspapers, the most absurdly overplayed event in sports is the "competition" for the America's Cup. This is a boat race in the horseplayer's sense of the term. Under the terms dictated by the New York Yacht Club, it is almost totally devoid of competition. It is frequently deficient in sportsmanship. A dentist filling a tooth offers livelier entertainment for spectators. It commands substantially less reader interest than the Treasury's statement of gold balances.

Still, there are papers that assign one or more staff men to the story for an entire summer, publish lengthy daily accounts of the trials leading up to selection of a challenger and a defender, and devote six or eight columns of space to the predictable results while the races are underway.

Perhaps the gazettes are motivated by a mistaken notion that national pride and prestige are somehow involved in the fortunes of *Intrepid* or *Gretel II*, or maybe publishers are impressed by the staggering cost of these sleek and comfortless craft. At any rate, the trivial adventures of a few millionaires getting their bottoms wet at play are reported with a respectful solemnity that borders on servility.

The first race of the current challenge series was sailed in rain and cold and controversy and frustration. When it was over, only the race committee knew who won, and the committee wasn't telling. After preliminary jockeying for position, both yachts went over the starting line with protest flags flying, but the nature of the objections was not disclosed and the skippers were instructed not to talk.

Fans and readers, if any, owners of the boats and their crews had to wait until the next day to learn that *Gretel*'s protest had been rejected and the Australian challenger had, indeed, been walloped by almost six minutes. The authorities were right there on the committee boat when the protest flags were broken out. If the evidence of their own eyes wasn't sufficient, the committeemen could have talked with the skippers and issued a ruling immediately after the finish. But the New York Yacht Club doesn't work that way.

Not that anybody expected the committee to uphold a foreign protest. For 119 years, the New York Yacht Club has applied the rules with the single aim of keeping the America's Cup right where it is, bolted to a heavy oak table in the trophy room on West 44th Street. You'd think the old ewer was the Kohinoor diamond instead of a singularly ugly pitcher with a hole in its bottom, not fit to hold a pint of beer. The tiger mother protecting her young is a gentle old tabby compared to the New York Yacht Club in defense of its hardware.

After the rakish schooner *America* won the mug by whipping 15 British boats in a race around the Isle of Wight on Aug. 22, 1851, the custodians of the trophy took steps. The first challengers were required to sail against a whole fleet of defenders, and for years the races were conducted over the "inside" course in New York harbor, where familiarity with local conditions was an overwhelming advantage. "A penny show in a puddle," was how the late William P. Stevens, yachting editor of *Forest and Stream,* described those competitions.

Little by little the unfair conditions written in New York gave way to moral pressures over the years, but they have never given way altogether. No longer need the challenger submit a complete description of the challenging yacht ten months in advance with the defender not even identified until just before the start. No longer need the challenger be sturdy and seaworthy—and slow—enough to travel to the scene of the match on her own bottom.

She still must be designed and built in the country of the challenging club, however, and this condition has been stiffened since the first Australian challenge. Back in 1962 *Gretel I* was permitted to use some American-made sails and rigging—which Australia didn't have the facilities to duplicate—and her designer was given free use of the towing tanks at Stevens Institute of Technology in Hoboken.

*Gretel* won one race and made the other four so close that plaster fell from the ceiling of the New York Yacht Club. Never again the sporting gesture.


The story goes that when Phar Lap, the great racehorse from down under, was campaigning in America, a Melbourne newspaper kept two headlines standing in type. One read: "Australian Wonder Horse Wins." The other: "New Zealand Champion Beaten."

Poor old Phar Lap has been dead almost 40 years, and more than half a century has passed since Les Darcy, the middleweight from New South Wales, departed this life. Yet both were exhumed editorially when the race committee of the New York Yacht Club snatched victory away from the Sydney sloop *Gretel II* in the second race of the America's Cup series.

"It's enough to make Les Darcy, our wonder boxer, and Phar Lap, our wonder horse, turn in their graves," cried the *Sydney Daily Mirror*.

That's literary license. Gifted though he was—and he won the two-mile Melbourne Cup in 1930 carrying 138 pounds, more than any other winner in this century—Phar Lap would play hell turning in his grave because he hasn't any. He rests, or at least his hide does, in a display case in the Melbourne Exhibition Building known to horseplaying Aussies as Phar Lap's Stable.

In Australian legend, Phar Lap and Les Darcy are symbols of injustice, victims of Yankee perfidy. Phar Lap's American visit in the early 1930s was tragically short but he left an indelible impression on American horsemen; the astute Marshall Cassidy, for one, regarded him as the greatest he ever saw.

Though he appeared in superb health, Phar Lap died suddenly of an acute internal disorder not long after reaching these shores. Probably it was colic or something like that, but in Australian folklore he was poisoned by villainous Americans.

If the poison story is fiction, the infamous tale of Les Darcy is true. If he wasn't as brilliant in his field as Phar Lap in his, Darcy was still the most talented boxer Australia ever produced, and the most popular. His treatment in America was shameful.

Darcy started boxing in the amateurs at 15, and before he was 20 he had cleaned up every welter and middleweight of note on his continent along with a gaggle of top Americans including George Chip, the former middleweight champion of the world, and Jimmy Clabby and Eddie McGoorty, who claimed the world championship.

Darcy's first bout with McGoorty was recognized in Australia as a world title match, and the 19-year-old won on a knockout in the 15th round. On Christmas that same year he cooled McGoorty again in eight.

At 21, Darcy came to the United States. It was 1917. Australia was in World War I and we were soon to enter. Passions were inflamed, and the patrioteers ran strictly true to form. Gov. Charles S. Whitman of New York publicly branded Darcy a slacker who had fled his country to avoid military service—though Australia had no draft.

To this day, they will tell you in Melbourne or Maitland, in Coolgardie or Wagga Wagga, that the Yanks broke Les Darcy's heart. It is difficult to get medical evidence to support this, but the fact is the kid wasn't allowed to box one round here and in Memphis he "took a fever" and died. It could, of course, have been an early case of the flu epidemic that took 20 million lives in the next two years.

Now the prospects are that *Gretel* will go into legend as the third Australian martyr to scheming Yankee parochialism. When *Intrepid* won the first race, *Gretel* claimed foul and the claim was rejected. When *Gretel* won the second, *Intrepid*'s protest was sustained.

No doubt the race committee called 'em as it saw 'em. Probably the judges felt they could make no other decision, though their view was not shared by the challengers. It must seem to many outsiders that if there was room for argument, a reasonable doubt had to exist, but the America's Cup committee hasn't given house room to a reasonable doubt in 119 years.

"Nobody should be God in this country or any other," said Martin Visser, *Gretel*'s helmsman. "There should be an international committee to rule on protests and another international committee to handle appeals."

Sometimes being an American can be embarrassing. We got Spiro Agnew, we got George Wallace, we got Lester Maddox, we got the New York Yacht Club. Could we ask for anything more?

# THE COWBOY FROM WOUNDED KNEE

GIVE 10 little Indians the choice and nine would rather be cowboys. It isn't merely the wish to be on the winning side for once. "A bronc rider," explains Dawn Little Sky from the Standing Rock Reservation in South Dakota, "a good one, is our idea of the greatest athlete. Horses have always been important to us. They were a form of wealth. And Indians respect bravery."

"To the kids on the Pine Ridge Reservation what is the most famous name in athletics?" a man asked Richard Redbow of the Oglala Sioux.

"Casey Tibbs," Redbow said. Fearless, flamboyant and master of the meanest rogue that any three men could get a saddle on, Casey Tibbs is so distinguished that a sign at the city limits of Fort Pierre, S.D., advises motorists that this is the "site of the world's largest earthen dam and birthplace of Casey Tibbs." Yet even Casey may have to step aside one of these days and let a scrawny little Indian named Howard Hunter take the bows.

In the rowdy world of rodeo this week, attention is focused on Oklahoma City, where all the best riders, ropers and bulldoggers are winding up the sport's richest season in the National Finals. Around Sioux council fires, however, this is only a preliminary to Howard Hunter's debut as a card-carrying member of the Rodeo Cowboys' Association, and if the R.C.A. directors don't vote him Rookie of the Year they may wish they could have it good like Custer.

Hunter is 21 years old, stands 5 feet 5 inches, weighs 130 pounds with boots and spurs, and wears scraggly chin whiskers that make him look like a vest-pocket D'Artagnan. He was one of eight children in a family that ran cattle on the Pine Ridge Reservation, and as far back as he can remember he was trying to ride calves, colts or anything else he could catch.

At Oglala Community High he was a one-man rodeo team. In the South Dakota high school finals, he won bareback and bull riding and was second on saddle broncs. The tribe scratched up $240 to send him to the national high school finals, but the cosmopolitan splendors of San Antonio, Tex., were too much for him. He fell off everything except one bareback mount.

Nevertheless, Charlie Colombe was sold on the kid. Colombe is an Indian who rode broncs, a member of the Tribal Council of the Rosebud Sioux (their reservation is adjacent to Pine Ridge), and deeply concerned about the problems of youth in "the fresh-air ghettos." Believing it would be good for the young to have their own sports heroes, he put on a show called Indian Athletic Recognition Day. Shawn Davis, winner of three national saddle bronc championships, and Billy Mills, the Pine Ridge Sioux who won the 10,000-meter race at the 1964 Olympics, showed up.

Davis, a Mormon from Whitehall, Mont., was there as Three Eagle, an honorary member of the Blackfoot tribe. He has taken a lively interest in Indian affairs since 1969 when, unable to ride because of a broken back, he helped recruit Indians for a rodeo tour of Italy. During that trip he decided to run some rodeo schools just for Indians, and when Indian Athletic Recognition Day came around last May, he had his first school almost ready to open in Blunt, S.D. He heard so much about Howard Hunter's talent that he told Colombe to make sure the young man attended.

"Everything they said about him was true," Davis says. "Watching him on his first bronc, I knew he was a natural."

Shawn decided to "haul" Hunter for the rest of 1972—that is, pay his travel expenses and put up his entry fees in exchange for a share of his winnings. Howard was on a permit from the R.C.A., which allows a green hand to ride in amateur and professional rodeos until he has won $1,000. He boomed along so fast that by the time the Denver office of the R.C.A. could add the figures, he had won $2,168.

Now he has his membership card and Davis plans to haul him again in his first official year. Shawn says the kid has the right attitude for a rookie: "I was in a rush leaving Sidney, Iowa, and asked him to send my laundry out. When I got back I found he had done it himself in a Laundromat."

Howard's home town of Kyle (pop. 70) is just 20 miles from the riverbend below Porcupine Butte, where the Battle of Wounded Knee took place Dec. 29, 1890. It was the last bloody engagement of the Indian Wars and it was a massacre, not a battle. Using Gatling guns on an Indian encampment occupied mostly by women and children, the Seventh Cavalry under Col. George A. Forsythe slaughtered about 300.

That night a terrible blizzard swept in. Next day Indian searchers under guard found an infant alive in a snowdrift. The baby grew up to be Howard Hunter's grandfather. If Colonel Forsythe's command had been a little more efficient or a little more murderous, there would be no cowboy from Wounded Knee going for Rookie of the Year.

# MONEY WRANGLER

LARRY MAHAN, a cowboy who can extract money from a rogue bronco or misanthropic bull almost as efficiently as Herbert W. Kalmbach can squeeze it out of an airline executive, is up to his old tricks. After two years when his hospital bills ran a bang-up second to his earnings, Mahan is back at the top of his form and raking in loot at a rate no wrangler ever attained before, himself included. At last count, the winner of five consecutive All-Around championships had pocketed $30,315 in prizes in 1973, the juiciest sum anybody ever reached by this date, and he was hellbent for an unprecedented sixth All-Around title.

In rodeo's half-century of recorded history, only Mahan and the peerless Jim Shoulders managed five All-Around championships—the title goes to the cowboy with the highest total of prize money won in two or more events—and only Mahan got his five in a row.

During his title run from 1966 through 1970, rodeo's laughing boy won $240,702. In 1967 he became the first to break the $50,000 barrier and in 1969 he set an all-time record of $57,726. This might not represent much more than caddie fees to Jack Nicklaus, for it is one of the ironies of athletics that a man can earn four times as much beating an inoffensive little ball with a stick as he could in hand-to-horn combat with a ton of infuriated sirloin. However, when Mahan reads his bank balance, he does so through the eyes of a kid who worked after school sacking groceries in a Salem, Ore., supermarket.

In 1971 and 1972, two things happened to Larry Mahan. He suffered a succession of disabling injuries, and an extraordinary young man named Phil Lyne grew up as a rodeo hand. In 1971 Lyne won the All-Around with earnings of $49,245. In 1972 he collected a record $60,852 in the arena and got $20,000 of the bonus money the Winston cigarette people tossed into the game. Another $3,600 in special awards brought his boodle to an implausible $84,452.

Naturally, when Bob Ragsdale took an early lead this year and then was overtaken by Mahan, rodeo buffs asked, "Hey, what's happened to Phil Lyne?" The answer is that at the age of 26, after making the sport pay him as it never had paid anybody else, Lyne just turned his back on the bitch goddess and walked away. He is down on the home ranch at George West, Texas, and there he stays except for limited participation in rodeos nearby. It is like Steve Carlton quitting the Phillies to pitch softball, like Nicklaus going back to Columbus to play dollar Nassaus with the members at Scioto.

Sitting in Ferguson's Restaurant in George West not long ago, Lyne groped for words to explain his decision. "I've been on the road since high school," he said. "I've got some cattle now with my brother and I'm in business building trailers, and rodeo—" he hesitated, cautious lest he sound critical of rodeo—"no matter how it looks, rodeo isn't all just play."

Rodeo, as a matter of fact, is the harshest form of athletic competition this side of the Roman Colosseum, and Lyne never ducked punishment. A comparatively little guy at 5 feet 8 inches and 165 pounds, he competed in all five standard events—saddle bronc, bareback and bull riding, calf roping and steer wrestling—plus team roping. Logging tens of thousands of miles, he worked as many as 125 rodeos in 48 weeks and it wasn't just the pounding on the highways and the battering in the arena that wore him down.

An unwritten rule demands that no matter how many cowboys show up unannounced, you never turn one away from your motel room. Sometimes there will be half a dozen sleeping on the floor. "You can go two weeks," Mahan says, "and never get first run on a towel."

Some, like Mahan, thrive on such confusion, but it is something else for a guy gaited to life in George West. The most exciting thing in George West is Geronimo, an obsolete longhorn steer with a 6-foot wingspread who belonged to George West, the man who founded the town. Geronimo's stuffed cadaver stands in a glass case in front of the courthouse and sharing his see-through tomb are a coyote, a bobcat, a skunk, a javelina or wild hog, and a "chicken hawk." The implacable sun has faded everything to the same dusty beige.

Inside the courthouse are other exhibits—a stone axhead, an 8-foot rattlesnake skin, and ornamental glass buttons on a pink satin ribbon with a card reading: "These buttons came off of Grandma Conn's dress. They are 150 years old and belong to her granddaughter, Mrs. Tiny Gilmore Mahoney."

The Lyne ranch is west of town, out past the sign at the city limits that gives the population as 2,022 and reads: "George West, Texas, home of Phil Lyne, Worlds Champion Cowboy." Phil grew up here with his parents and an elder brother, Leonard Joe, called Poochie. His daddy, Joe Rufus, a calf roper before rodeo had an organized circuit, was the kid's only coach. As a sophomore, Phil won just about everything in the state finals of high school rodeo. As a junior, he won the national high school calf-roping title and was second in the all-around.

"When I harnessed him up for that trip," Joe Rufus said, "I sure made him bear down practicing. I never had pushed him, but the one thing I was strict about was him being ready to use all the ability he had whenever he nodded for a calf. I wasn't all that keen about him riding bulls, but he could do a good job so I never throwed a hissy about it."

Phil raced through college rodeo, was Rookie of the Year in his first season on the professional circuit, and was a world champion two years later. What could he do for an encore? Just defend his title and win all the money there was. Then he turned and walked away.

# HOW TO TIE A CALF AND CATCH A THIEF

THE thermometer registered 100 degrees when the calf roping started, and spectators were clustered in the shade of live oaks on the slopes that form three sides of a natural amphitheater in Woodlake, Calif. The first calf came tearing out of the chute with Bib Wiley riding hard at his heels, lariat whistling overhead. In a single unbroken flow of movement, Wiley threw his loop and pitched the slack, came out of the saddle on a dead run, flipped the calf, tied three legs and flung both hands aloft for the timer. From chute to finish, the operation consumed 10.6 seconds.

Bob Wiley is a lawman, sheriff of Tulare County, and crowds these days aren't much disposed to cheer for the fuzz, but this crowd roared. The flat farmlands of the San Joaquin Valley are sports country—when there's a big high school football game or a major track meet, shopkeepers lock up at noon—and Tulare County's buffs have known Wiley virtually all his 35 years, as the comrade and teammate of Rafer Johnson from the fourth grade through high school, then as a rodeo hand who once ran second to the incomparable Dean Oliver for the world roping championship and since 1965 as a dedicated officer whose efforts to combat juvenile delinquency have been applauded in the *Congressional Record*.

Wiley is an athlete by nature, a roper by avocation and a cop by popular demand. Hard campaigning got him his job the first time but when he ran for reelection he swept 78.5 percent of the vote.

When he and Rafe Johnson were on the football and track teams at Kingsburg High, Bob carried 210 pounds on a figure measuring 6 feet 1 inch from top to bottom and a trifle less across the shoulders. Now there's an additional 25 pounds under the belt buckle. He walks with the purposeful lurch of a boar grizzly in the mating season and his habitual expression is just this side of a scowl, though on the rare occasions when he smiles it is sudden sunrise. If you drew a seine through Central Casting you couldn't match more exactly the stereotype of a Western sheriff.

Wiley was born in Kingsburg, down Highway 99 a piece from Fresno. Rafer Johnson was 9 when his family moved in from Hillsboro, Tex., and games soon brought the boys together. In football Rafer was the outside runner and pass receiver. Bob was the other halfback, a straight-ahead smasher and a sensational blocker. Exceptionally fast for his size—he ran 100 yards in 9.9 as a freshman—Bob was leadoff runner and Rafer the anchorman on a relay team that was the talk of the state.

Rafer went to the University of California, Los Angeles, took the silver medal in the decathlon in the 1956 Olympics and four years later won that punishing event in Rome. Bob stayed in San Joaquin Valley and attended Porterville Junior College. He had one of his better days against Reedley Junior College when he gained 279 yards. This got him mention for Little All-America but by that time roping had become an addiction.

The rodeo bug had sunk its fangs in him when he watched a roping in Tulare during his senior year in high school. He paid $50 for an old nag that he hauled in a 17-year-old Chevvy pickup that could make 35 miles an hour downhill when the wind was right. He couldn't travel far, but any weekend when there was a rodeo within driving distance of the campus, he made it.

In 1956 he met Dean Oliver, who had won the world championship once and would win it six times more. Struck by Wiley's speed, strength and reflexes, Oliver coached the young man, hauled him and mounted him on his own horse. At a few rodeos he even paid Wiley's entrance fees in exchange for one-quarter of his winnings, and The Rope doesn't bet long shots.

From 1960 through 1965 Wiley's average winnings were slightly more than $12,000 a year with a top of $18,180 in 1963, the year he ran second to Oliver. Meanwhile he was working three to five days a week as a deputy in Tulare County. When friends talked him into running for sheriff, his campaign fund was a rope.

In one respect he is a political freak even for California, where oddballs abound: He keeps campaign promises. As a deputy it had bugged him that he seldom got to meet kids unless they were in trouble, so he made the main plank in his platform a pledge to work with the young. Once elected, he heckled his Board of Supervisors for funds to launch the programs.

Now Tulare County deputies seek out youth. Two deputies on special assignment travel from school yard to campus to gathering place in a van showing movies and slides or just rapping with the kids. Wiley himself made 97 appearances last year. Figures show a decline in "juvenile related incidents."

Wiley's operation is not exactly like Matt Dillon's. He sits in an up-to-date office in Visalia receiving teletype reports from all over the county's 4,970 square miles. To run a check on a stolen car, he presses a button on a computer. He has a force of 183 in Visalia and three substations. As it was in his college days, rodeo is strictly a weekend proposition now but as he demonstrated recently in Woodlake he can still go to a calf like an irate mongoose homing in on a cobra.

His friend Rafer Johnson is still in the area. Since the Olympics, Rafer has been a movie actor and a sportscaster; he stumped for Robert F. Kennedy and was present the night of the assassination; now he is with Continental Telephone Corporation as vice-president for personnel. This guy was president of the student body in grammar school, high school and college, and for the opening of the 1960 Olympics the American team chose him as the leader to carry the flag.

"Sometimes," Wiley says, "I feel I've always been in the shadow of a great guy, Rafer or Dean. Then I think, well, if I'm second, I picked two winners to run behind."

# BUT IT WAS THE VERY BEST SOAP

NINETEEN hundred years ago the Emperor Nero won championships in the Olympic Games by bribery and intimidation, and when Roman kids of his day raced their toy chariots down the Capitoline Hill, some of them cheated. It was their example, most qualified students of history and human behavior agree, that led to the Soapbox Scandal of 1973 in which it was discovered that the winning car in the All American Soapbox Derby in Akron, Ohio, was illegally souped up.

"Winning isn't the most important thing," Nero said, tilting his laurel crown at a rakish angle, "it's the only thing."

"When it's listed under 'W,'" said his disciple Leo Durocher, referring to the won-and-lost columns in the league standings, "nobody asks how it got there."

"He had a different definition of being a good loser," Richard M. Nixon has said of his coach at Whittier College. "He said: 'You know what a good loser is? It's somebody who hates to lose. . . .'"

Two days after a 14-year-old boy from Boulder, Colo., finished first in the Soapbox Derby, authorities took back the big shiny trophy, lifted the young man's title and stripped him of the $7,500 college scholarship which is the winner's purse. Hidden under fiberglass in the kid's streamlined car was an electromagnetic dornick that officials said enabled him to beat the field away from the start. A sad, small, mean business this seems to be, and unhappily the disclosures made so far may be only the beginning, like the discovery of garage doors taped open in the Watergate Office Building.

When Jimmy Gronen's victory was declared inoperative, people remembered that his cousin Robert Lange Jr. had won the 1972 Derby in a car of similar design. Jimmy Gronen has been living with the Lange family. Considering that kids from all over the country gather in Akron to coast down a 953-foot hill, it seemed remarkable that two boys from the same household should win in consecutive years.

It was the only time in 36 years that anything like that had happened. Some students with long memories were reminded of the time Blinky Palermo offended boxing epicures by bringing a jungle beast named Blackjack Billy Fox out of Philadelphia with a record of something like 43 knockouts in 43 bouts. The fact that Fox couldn't fight didn't bother the fastidious. What affronted them was that Blinky lacked the nicety of taste to give his man a record of 42 knockouts and one decision or maybe even 41-1-1.

Anyhow, though there had been no complaint when young Lange won the race, the car he had used turned up missing just about the time flak started flying about young Gronen's racer.

On top of this came rumors that neither machine would qualify under the rule limiting construction costs to about $75. In fact, there were reports that young Lange's car was a $22,000 job tested in the wind tunnel at the University of California, Los Angeles. Soapboxes like that are used for only the very best soap.

There's hell to pay in Boulder, but this shouldn't surprise anyone. Leaders of livery stable society like to consider themselves more sophisticated than the soapbox set, yet no single group has a monopoly on envy. Let somebody in horsey circles come up with a better animal than the next fellow and there will be somebody to put the knock on (a) the horse, (b) the owner, (c) the trainer, (d) the jockey, (e) the groom, (f) the exercise boy and (g) the stable agent if the stable has an agent.

So it is only to be expected that the neighbors in Boulder should talk, district attorneys investigate, parents of losers threaten to file suit and practically everybody ask about the possible involvement of higher-ups. In the parlance of the day, some highly motivated individuals are suspected of engaging in specific activities.

There is little enthusiasm in this corner for moralizing, yet it is hard to shake off a suspicion that our national preoccupation with winning leads to many excesses. The victory fetish is commonly associated with Vince Lombardi—unfairly, it says here, because the late coach of the Green Bay Packers denied saying that winning was everything. According to him, what he really said was that making the effort to win was everything.

We have had painful reminders of the tragic effects of a victory-at-any-cost attitude in an election campaign. Now we see what it can do to children.

# Index

RED SMITH started as a local reporter on *The Milwaukee Sentinel* in the summer of 1927, just after graduating from Notre Dame with an A.B., moved on to newspapers in St. Louis and Philadelphia and then joined *The New York Herald Tribune* as World War II was ending. His columns have been syndicated since then even though *The Herald Tribune* and its short-lived successor, the *World Journal Tribune,* have disappeared. In November, 1971, Smith joined *The New York Times,* where he continues to write his column. He has won literally scores of awards, has contributed to, in his words, "all magazines, alive and dead," and has written five previous books. Smith and his wife Phyllis split their time between homes in New Canaan, Conn., and Martha's Vineyard. He has one son, one daughter, five stepchildren, and four grandchildren.